MW01010323

Mirror of Light

A Commentary on Yuthok's Ati Yoga

VOLUME ONE

Nida Chenagtsang

Translation by Ben Joffe (Jigmé Dorje)

SKY
PRESS

Interior images:

SKY PRESS
2926 NE Flanders St - #1A
Portland, OR 97232
www.skypressbooks.com

Printed in the United States of America on acid-free paper.

Library of Congress Control Number: 2016955801

ISBN
978-0-9977319-1-0

Cover Art by Anna Artemyeva
(www.a-artemyeva.ru)

Design and Typesetting by Pearse Gaffney

Contents

May I achieve wisdom in all medicine sciences,
And benefit all sentient beings like the sun and the moon.
May all that is spoken be omniscient.
May all compounded formulas be medicine.
May all that is given be beneficial.
Grant me the common and uncommon siddhis.

Yuthok Nyingthig Aspiration Prayer

I

PREFACES

Ati Yoga is one of the simplest and most sophisticated meditation techniques in the Tibetan Vajrayana tradition. 'Ati Yoga' is a Sanskrit term. Ati means 'extreme' or 'very' and Yoga, as can be seen in the Tibetan term naljor (rnal sbyor) means achieving or uniting with the original or ultimate state. Thus, Ati Yoga is the 'utmost yoga,' the practice for directly realizing the ultimate state of mind or reality. As Leonardo da Vinci is reported to have said in the fifteenth century, "simplicity is the ultimate sophistication." This is a very Western exposition of the view of Ati Yoga — the most sophisticated thing about Ati Yoga is its simplicity. However, there is a Tibetan proverb that says, "the eyes can see everything except themselves." In line with this proverb, many people end up complicating the sophisticated simplicity of this teaching. Today Ati Yoga is often mis-transmitted. Sometimes it is not properly distinguished from shamatha and vipassana training. Because Ati Yoga is so simple, it is easy to misunderstand and to misuse. For this reason, in order to truly understand Ati Yoga, we need a very precise and authentic teaching. It is essential that we receive clear guidance and clear understanding.

The great Yuthok, through his kindness, gave us this very simple and direct Ati Yoga teaching which is in line with Garab Dorje's Ati Yoga style. Garab Dorje's approach is transmission through three steps: the introduction or 'pointing out', the decision, and the confidence. Yuthok gives his introduction to the ultimate nature of mind in a medical way by using the five elements, five colors, five mental poisons and so on as a means to see the nature of self-awareness. The decision on what is introduced comes from an understanding of the five wisdoms, five Buddhas, and five pure lands that are within our inner dimension — from the realization that nothing is separate from ourselves. The confidence in this realization is then gained through the self-liberation that comes from being present with the experiences of our five senses and from the self-liberation of our mental afflictions. Yuthok described nine

different levels of ability and gave Ati Yoga instruction according to different people's mentalities and capacities. This is a very unique presentation of Ati Yoga, one which is tremendously clear and helpful for each of these different practitioners.

I truly thank all my Vajrayana masters, and especially the ones who taught and guided me in the Ati Yoga tradition: Ani Ngawang Gyaltsen — the great yogini who transmitted the Dzogchen tradition of Shabkarpa to me in her simple studio apartment in Lhasa, Tibet; Chonyi Rinpoche, the great yogi who transmitted to me the complete teaching of Ati Yoga according to the Rinchen Terzod and Dudjom Terzod in Lama Ling in Kongpo, Central Tibet, and in his family shrine in Lhasa; Khenpo Troru Tsenam who taught me Mahamudra and Ati Yoga in Lhasa; Amdo ngakpa, Kargyit Tulku who gave me direct introduction to rigpa; and my great nomad teacher, Aku Lhamokyab who kindly appeared in a dream and introduced to me the fresh awareness in a direct and experiential way before he passed away. It is my wish that the unbroken lineage of Ati Yoga will shine as a great and universal light that eliminates the darkness of suffering. The greater the darkness, the more this light will shine. Today there are so many meditation techniques, so many explanations and practices, and so many people are confused and don't know what or how to practice. Because our worldly life is so busy and miserable, this is the time when we really need direct Ati Yoga instruction. I pray that this simple and direct meditation will be awakened within many practitioners and that they will spontaneously benefit many others until samsara ends.

Dr Nida Chenagtsang,
July 2016 in San Francisco, USA

It has been an incredible privilege to work on this project. I am not a professional translator, and prior to meeting Dr Nida I was only vaguely aware of the existence of the Yuthok Nyingthig, let alone the unique and profound teachings it contained. My training is in socio-cultural anthropology, and at the time of writing this preface I am in the middle of doctoral dissertation fieldwork for a PhD in Cultural Anthropology from the University of Colorado, Boulder. My interests centre on the anthropology of Tibet and the Tibetan diaspora, and in 2010 I relocated from my natal country of South Africa to the USA in order to receive specialized instruction in these areas. My PhD dissertation deals primarily with Ngakpa and Ngakma (male and female Tibetan Buddhist non-celibate tantric ritual specialists) who live outside Tibet. Since the beginning of 2015 I have been living and conducting research in Tibetan exile communities in India and Nepal. I am interested in how Tibetan cultural and religious traditions are being circulated, mediated, appropriated and contested, both as part of the increasing globalization of Tibetan Buddhism and in light of Tibetans' efforts to make a Tibetan nation and Tibetan identities legible in exile and to preserve and reform Tibetan culture in different contexts, for different audiences.

It was due in part to these research interests that I was lucky enough to cross paths with Dr Nida. Prior to meeting him, I had stumbled upon some of his earlier Tibetan language writings on the Ngakpa tradition in Eastern Tibet. Reading them, I was immediately struck by the clarity and erudition with which he wrote about complicated, esoteric and frequently misunderstood subjects. I had not come across anyone else writing for general audiences in Tibetan like this, anyone who was discussing these aspects of Tibetan culture and history quite so lucidly and accessibly. Rather than just writing for fellow initiates or specialists, what Dr Nida was producing was more introductory and educational in quality - an overview of histories, theories and practices aimed at providing a broader readership of Tibetans with the context

Translator's Preface

and resources they needed to understand what esoteric tantric Buddhism was really about and what it actually entailed as part of current, everyday practice. The product of both a scholar and practitioner of Tibetan medicine and Tibetan tantric yoga, Dr Nida's work had a uniquely anthropological flavour, and yet Dr Nida was clearly interested in reaching wider audiences than those typical of the average professional academic social scientist. The secrecy and complexities surrounding Dr Nida's topic made his efforts all the more significant as well. Far from representing some sort of disregard for traditional injunctions about secrecy and initiation, it was clear that his candid discussion of Vajrayana practices was propelled by a deep reverence for these Buddhist traditions, and by his hope that they would be practiced more widely, with right motivation and genuine understanding and dedication. Dr Nida explained how regrettable it was that accurate information about non-celibate tantric practices was in such short supply, and stressed how important it was that the general public should be able to have their questions and misperceptions about tantric practice clarified. Rather than deteriorating or debasing the tradition, circulating information about esoteric practices could contribute to better understanding and appreciation of these teachings, and curtail abuses of power and distortions of practice fuelled by secrecy and misinformation.

I had no doubt that others would greatly benefit from having access to Dr Nida's work, and so I made some rough English translations of excerpts of his writings and shared these on social media. Dr Nida read and appreciated these. We got into contact, and I came to learn more about his extensive research and teaching activities all around the world. I discovered that Dr Nida's efforts to preserve and develop Tibetan traditions of medical and religious knowledge were pitched at both Tibetans and non-Tibetans, which was of particular interest to me given the focus of my research. More specifically, I learned that Dr Nida was an active promoter of the Yuthok Nyingthig, the cycle of revealed tantric Buddhist teachings which form the core of this book. Dr Nida and I were subsequently able to meet in person during his first ever visit to India early in 2016 and it was there that he discussed with me the possibility of translating Tibetan language commentaries which he had written on Yuthok's unique Ati Yoga teachings. Being far from the most qualified or experienced translator for the job, I agreed to produce an initial translation of such profound material solely at Dr Nida's insistence. Without his blessing and encouragement, I would never have dared to undertake such a task. Thankfully, Dr Nida and I found that our interests were happily aligned. I was impressed and inspired by Dr Nida's broad knowledge and devotion to the teachings, his sincerity and warmth, and his remarkably flexible, frequently hilarious teaching style. We began working together closely on the project, and what was initially meant to serve as just a rough draft translation for supplementing oral teachings on Ati Yoga in Portland, Oregon ended up becoming the book you are now reading.

Although it is maybe not as well-known as some other Buddhist meditative traditions like Japanese Zazen and contemporary forms of Vipassana training coming out of Burma, with the invasion of Tibet by China in 1950, the exodus of Tibetan teachers worldwide, and the dramatic transformation of Tibetan socio-economic, political, and cultural structures and institutions over the last few decades, information about Dzogchen and translations of Dzogchen teachings have become increasingly accessible worldwide. As such, readers may be surprised to discover how sparingly the word 'Dzogchen' appears in this book. As Dr Nida points to in his preface, this spread of information about the Great Perfection has sometimes lead to distortions and misperceptions. Today, Dzogchen has become something of a buzz-word in certain contexts, one which has demonstrated well its capacity to lead to all sorts of self-aggrandizement and commodification. Insofar as the term Dzogchen has had the unfortunate side-effect of promoting elitist thinking, and now sometimes invokes fantasies of special honours, privileged access and grandiose attainments among students in the West, it has migrated quite far indeed from the signature humility and uncontrived simplicity of the great Dzogchen adepts of the past. Accordingly, Dr Nida has opted for 'Ati Yoga' over Dzogchen in this book, with the hope that this less familiar term will not play into readers' possible pre- and misconceptions, and that it will point them instead to the spirit of unaffected modesty, light-heartedness, non-fixation and openness which is the Great Perfection's hallmark.

As a term, 'Ati Yoga' has the additional benefit of emphasizing Dzogchen's moorings within Tibetan Buddhist esotericism more generally. Ati Yoga is the name given to the third and highest of the Inner Yogas in the 'Nine Vehicles' presentation of the Path to complete liberation found in the Nyingma or Ancient Translation school of Tibetan Buddhism. Ati Yoga's uniqueness and its call to move beyond the fetishizing of religious and ethical concepts and trappings has sometimes been used to justify the claim that it is in fact something entirely distinct from Mahayana or Vajrayana Buddhism as a whole. Yet, while scholarly debate about the Great Perfection's precise origins and influences is ongoing, it remains that the greatest Tibetan teachers of Ati Yoga have hardly presented it as something that makes all other forms of Buddhist practice or morality redundant. To the extent that it revolves around the basic nature or essence of mind, Ati Yoga can be said to transcend all cultural or historical contrivances or particulars. Nonetheless, exaggerating Ati Yoga's departure from the larger milieu of Tibetan Buddhism has led to problems and confusions. Readers of this volume will hear directly again and again from great masters about the feasibility, and moreover, necessity of integrating the Ati Yoga view with Mahayana motivations and compassionate conduct. The Yuthok Nyingthig clearly presents Ati Yoga as an essential part of the total Buddhist path, and as Dr Nida lays out so beautifully in his 'Spontaneous Ati Yoga' song in this book's appendix, Ati Yoga constitutes a kind of 'ultimate vantage point' which fits seamlessly with all and any other activities, 'spiritual' or otherwise. It stands as a quintessential orientation from which to approach everything, from the very first, faltering steps on the Path turning one away from the fixations of Samsara, all the way to the ultimate attainment of the rainbow body itself.

Some words on translation. In this book I have committed what some translators may well think of as a grave sin: in several places I have opted to be inconsistent with my translation of key, technical terms. Attentive readers will note for example, that I have sometimes translated the Tibetan term ngo sprod (pronounced something like 'ngo trö') as 'pointing out' and sometimes as 'introducing' or 'introduction'. Pivotal Ati Yoga terminology like gnas lugs ('nay loog') has been rendered variously as 'ultimate reality', 'basic nature' and so on. Gnas lugs is a tricky term to bring across into English – it is perhaps best literally translated as 'the abiding condition, state or system of a thing', the existing dispensation. In religious contexts it can carry the sense of 'ultimate reality', 'the state of things just as they are', 'the truth'. In a more 'secular' sense it can mean the facts of the matter or basic situation. In one place I translate the thabs lam of Karmamudra as 'a method', yet elsewhere I gloss thabs lam as 'technology' to get closer to the connotations of the term, only to render it immediately after in an overly literal way as 'path of skilful means'. Moreover, I have translated terms like Karmamudra ('the Action Seal') and Mahamudra ('The Great Seal') but have also retained the original Sanskrit terms sans diacritics in the English text. I have translated the single term gti mug, which is often rendered as simply 'ignorance', as 'the fog of ignorance' in one place and 'confusion and ignorance' in another, in order to convey the sense of hazy incomprehension suggested by mug and to distinguish gti mug (which connotes the kind of dull sluggish cognition and brutish stupidity that is associated with being reborn as an animal in Buddhist cosmology) from ma rig which can also be translated as ignorance but by contrast implies 'non-awareness', 'not knowing', a failure to realize.

So why this inconsistency? There is currently no unanimously agreed upon standardization of terms for Tibetan to English translation of Buddhist material. English translations of Dharma texts are frequently idiosyncratic to the extreme – when students read two different English versions of the same source text side by side it is often difficult to believe that they derive from the same source. The current circumstances of English translation efforts look pretty different from ninth century Tibet when imperial decree helped establish standardized glossaries for the translation of Indian Buddhist texts, an exercise which was often conducted by whole committees rather than individuals. While the spread of Tibetan Buddhism into Anglophone contexts more recently has seen the development of translation committees modelled on these earlier examples, it is nonetheless remains that there is nothing like the centralized authority or standardization of terms of earlier Tibet, and even when these newer committees and counsels exist they have established their own conventions separately. Part of my decision to render technical terms in different ways was simply because I knew that readers may very well have encountered alternative translations already, and I wanted to provide multiple options to help their understanding. In line with this didactic aim, we have chosen to include the Tibetan text of Dr Nida's commentaries here as well, for the benefit of readers who may be learning to read Tibetan or who may already have this skill. I have also from time to time resisted the urge to rewrite sentences in more elegant-sounding English when this might have made the transition from Tibetan to English less transparent. At the same time, the English text of this first edition includes parentheses which indicate where 'extra' English words have been added for the sake of at least moderately natural sounding English sentences. Overall, one could say we have chosen to prioritize readers' learning-in-progress over readability.

The chief danger of translating key terms inconsistently or of using similar English words to translate different Tibetan terms is the loss of crucial, technical precision. Yet the problem of precision goes beyond merely technical or institutional factors and cuts to the heart of the material itself. Ati Yoga literature is specialist, esoteric literature. But it is also experiential literature. The terms found here are part of vocabularies that have been developed and refined by expert scholar-practitioners over the centuries, based on their direct experience of the nature of things. Ati Yoga's jargon consists of labels for specific movements of mind, for precise flavours of awareness and subtle gradations of consciousness. These words are like the specialist vocabulary and allusions of a master sommelier, of a bird watcher, who sitting quietly in their bird-hide, has learned through intimate and careful observation to delineate the features and behaviours of wild birds whirring to and fro. On another then, somewhat contradictorily, my recourse to alternative translations of key terms also came from wanting to remind readers that when it comes to Buddhist practice and Ati Yoga in particular, words alone are not enough, cannot teach you everything. Root texts are pithy and frequently opaque by nature, and commentary and oral instruction by qualified teachers are essential. Yet, having said that, as Dr Nida announces in his Ati Yoga song:

"The essential, ineffable meaning is hidden by spoken words, transcendent mind is lost through thoughts of good and bad and moral prescriptions.

Request from the realized guru then, o ngakpas, that single awareness, which being realized, liberates all things in and of itself!"

And a few lines later:
"If you haven't perceived the unobstructed (*or transparent, pellucid, all pervading) naked awareness, what's the point of a whole lot of big words?" (See what I did there?)

When it comes to these teachings, coupling commentary with personal practice and experience is everything. We need to use whatever opportunities we can (so, all of them!) to investigate and recognize the nature of mind, to perceive the true face of whatever appearances may arise. For this words can point the way but they can also be a distraction, ever-expanding conceptualizing digressions that lead us away from the wordless suchness of things .

Ati Yoga is about 'naked' awareness. Rjen pa ('jenba') the Tibetan word Dr Nida uses in the line above, means 'naked' – laid bare, exposed, unclothed, but also 'raw' – unprocessed and untreated. The unadorned truth, like nudity, can make people uncomfortable. The temptation is always there to dress it up, to embellish or conceal it with fancy clothing, jewellery, and make-up. This choice of words is no accident.

One of the most remarkable features of Yuthok's Ati Yoga is that it manages to convey the nature of naked awareness incisively in only a few words. As Dr Nida explains in his opening essay, this clarity and conciseness can be seen throughout the Yuthok Nyingthig. Yuthok's brevity, his no-nonsense teaching style, the unprecedented extent to which he offers instructions on esoteric spiritual practice to individuals of every capacity, all of these can be linked to his medical orientation, to his compassionate commitment to making the greatest blessings as accessible as possible to as many beings as possible, whatever their level of practice. The King of Doctors, Yuthok has medicine for everyone, and measures out his doses judiciously in accordance with each of his patient's needs.

I have no doubt failed to adequately capture the freshness and brevity of both Yuthok and Dr Nida's words in this initial translation. Despite this, I hope that this work may still be of benefit to readers, and I pray that those errors and obfuscations which undoubtedly exist in this first edition will cause no obstacles to them, will ultimately give way to that wholly pure, insuppressible, unblockable awareness which is beyond all words and referents. My deepest thanks to Bob Thurman who was kind enough to read and comment on a full draft of my translations, and to Dr Nida, for being so generous in offering his own precious time and assistance to collaborate with me on this project. Dr Nida's unflagging devotion to Yuthok, his belief in the value of Yuthok's teachings for the world today, and the sheer power and beauty of Yuthok's own words have continually moved me and buoyed me in my efforts. It is a joy to be able to connect with Yuthok and the special practices of his lineage. I have no doubt that these will bless and transform many others as they have me. It is an honour to have been involved in the first ever publication of Yuthok's Ati Yoga teachings in English and I am deeply grateful to both Christiana and Pearse for their tireless work in putting together such a beautiful volume. A better duo of co-editors I could not have wished for.
Homage to Yuthok!

May whatever small merit I have accrued from helping with this book allow all beings everywhere to find the healing and peace they need. May they recognize their own nature and rest in the boundless joy and freedom this recognition brings.

Ben Joffe (Jigme Dorje)
27 September 2016
Kathmandu, Nepal

Foreword by Professor Robert Thurman

My respected teacher and dear friend, Dr. Nida Chenagtsang, is a force of nature—of the nature of the kindness and goodness that is the inclination of human beings. That nature is both the cause and the result of how we lucky beings who occupy that form of life have evolved from lower, and also higher, less interconnected with others, incarnations. I have only known Dr. Nida for a few years, and he is so busy dancing his dervish healing dance around the entire globe I don't see him that often, but every time I see his face it is a delight. More importantly, I always learn a lot from him, both when he teaches and when we work together teaching students. Though I deeply respect and have studied Traditional Tibetan Medicine, I have no practical healing knowledge as he does with such expert and committed wisdom. But he still always kindly requests me to give the students some preliminary background in the Buddha's "inner science," Nangi Rigpa, the science of mind and spirit known as the Buddha Dharma, to put in a clear light his skillful teaching of Buddha's healing science, Sowa Rigpa, the most important of the "outer sciences." All Buddha's sciences and arts derived from them help sentient beings thrive in harmony among themselves and with their environment in space and time.

When I first met Dr. Nida, at His Holiness the Dalai Lama's Menla Mountain Retreat in the hidden Shangrila Valley in the Catskills, he was brimming with excitement; he had been walking around the valley checking out its geomantic positioning. He made an expressive little sketch, which I have carefully preserved. "This place is so auspicious! You have a white tiger guarding the road of approach and entry from the east. There is a friendly dragon in the stream and pond to the south. A flying garuda bird keeps watch from the Panther Mountain in the west. And the mountain ridge to the north is a protective tortoise!"

Though I long had felt the magic of that valley, I had never felt so comfortably protected and inspired. As Dr. Nida visited Menla again and again, I learned more and more from him, especially the teachings and technologies of thriving and healing created by his beloved Yuthok Yonten Gonpo the younger, 11th century Tibetan saint, doctor, and magical adept (Tibetan Ngagpa, counterpart of the Indian Mahasiddha). I even have come to see Dr. Nida himself as a man who master Yuthok himself would be today if he were to emanate for the sake of suffering beings in our modern world, so full of beauty for those with eyes, but also all too beset with sicknesses and agonies from the delusions and frustrations of those without.

Dr. Nida is a well-trained, impeccably credentialed, traditional Tibetan Buddhist doctor, with the required knowledge of the spiritual roots of health and sickness, the scientific nature of the mindbody complex and its functions and malfunctions, the contextual influences of beings' ethical lifestyle, their food and drink, the changing climate and the seasons, and the blessings and dangers of the environment, the herbs and plants and waters and animals great and small, and even the ghosts and demons and angels that can inflict and bless. Also as an adept Ngagpa, Dr. Nida serves primarily his Tibetan community in the Northeast Amdo province of Tibet within Northwest China. He further serves the Tibetan Buddhist diaspora and Tibetan Buddhist communities in Mongolia, Chinese Inner Mongolia, the three Russian Federation Mongolian Republics, and in Nepal and India. As if that is not enough, he travels constantly to serve Chinese, Japanese, Koreans, Europeans, Australians, Americans—everyone. The vow of the Tibetan doctor is to serve any human or nonhuman animal to heal their illnesses and develop their positive existence and evolution, so that each of them can feel the joy of realistic living and be of more and better help and comfort to others.

I have also been delighted to discover that Dr. Nida has attracted and well instructed quite a number of fine students, who are already very knowledgeable, as well as jolly and cheerful, ethical, diligent, and kind. They exhibit the great sign of the excellence of a teacher—great respect toward the teacher but also sound self-confidence and independence of mind (the best mentor does not encourage over-dependence of students on her or him).

One can appreciate his impact on his near community in Amdo by savoring his song to the Ngagpas and Ngagmos, written exuberantly and spontaneously in the atmosphere of the yearly Drupchen Festival held there every summer. He encourages and chides, appreciates and teases, instructs and challenges both male and female fellow practitioners and their students, ministering so effectively to the people, we feel included in his song when we read it.

In the height of this work, meant mainly for his most advanced students, the good doctor really reaches the heights. I myself do not pretend to fully understand, experientially, his profound and beautiful teaching of Yuthok's Atiyoga practice and realization, but it opens my mind immeasurably and glows with authenticity and energy. It also seems to me to fit perfectly well with what I have learned over years in this life from the exoteric and esoteric inner science teachings of the Buddha and his great successors—the Pandit Adepts (khedrup) and Great Adept mahasiddhas (druptob) of India and Tibet, especially Vimalakīrti, Nāgārjuna, Chandrakīrti, and Shāntideva, Guru Rinpoche Padma Sambhava, Jowo Jey Atisha, and Jey Rinpoche Tsong Khapa—at least as I understand them from those few works of these great beings that I have read and tried to implement in my life. Not only does master Yuthok's and Dr, Nida's teachings of Atiyoga stand solidly on the reliable foundations established by these great ones, they reach so far, are so advanced, so intimate with the inconceivable goodness enlightened beings can reach, like all the teachings of Great Perfection, Great Seal, Great Path Fruition, and Great Communion Perfection Stage, that anyone who tries to practice and perform Atiyoga (ultimate yoga) can realistically feel confident—"this is the highest, the unexcelled, the unsurpassable!"

I will cherish this work and read it again and again, and hopefully some day, some future life perhaps, will actually realize its deep and astonishingly exquisite meaning. Thank you Yuthok Yonten Gonpo, Elder and Younger! Thank you Dr. Nida!

Robert A. F. Thurman
(Ari Genyen Tenzin Chotrak)
Ganden Dechen Ling, August 26, 2016

Publisher's Acknowledgments

SKY Press was born out of the inspiration to publish this book and to bring into the English language for the very first time the great physician and meditation adept Yuthok Yonten Gonpo's teachings on Ati Yoga (Tib: Dzogchen). Ati Yoga, literally meaning the 'utmost yoga,' is the pinnacle of Buddhist Vajrayana practice. It is the most simple, direct, and profound path to reveal the primordial wisdom which is one's own basic nature, the sky-like nature of our mind which is clear, vast, and unobtsructed by the clouds of afflictive emotions. This is the path to the rainbow body, the highest spiritual attainment and total transformation of body, speech/ energy, and mind.

2016 or 2143 in the Tibetan lunar calendar is the year of the fire Monkey, the birth year of Padmasambhava. It is a time when the spiritual energies of this great master are particularly potent and humans have the greatest opportunity to realize his teachings. This book has been published in commemoration of this auspicious year in order to assist beings on the path to liberation. Ati Yoga teachings have historically been some of the most secret of all Tibetan spiritual practices. However, as Yuthok was both a realized yogi and a highly accomplished doctor, he embodies the notion of the Buddha as physician and the dharma as supreme medicine. Because no one who suffers should be denied good medicine, he designed a unique spiritual system that presents even the highest teachings at a level that beings of any capacity can safely practice and understand. In keeping with Yuthok's compassionate intention and his commitment to accessibility and healing, Dr Nida has offered these teachings for publication (Volume One contains Chapters one and two of his four chapter commentary). Given Ati Yoga's emphasis on direct pointing out instruction, in order to derive the most benefit from the teachings presented in this text it is essential to receive proper transmission and guidance from a qualified teacher.

Many peoples' hard work have contributed to this text. Ben Joffe's beautiful translations have brought Dr. Nida's Tibetan commentaries on the Yuthok Nyingthig Ati Yoga root text alive in the English language for the very first time. His extensive anthrolopoligical research on Ngakpa communities in exile made him the perfect choice for this work. He worked directly with Dr. Nida on this project in order to clarify any doubts and questions and supplemented the main Ati Yoga commentary with additional translations of Dr. Nida's article on the 'Twelve Special Characteristics of the Yuthok Nyingthig,' his 'Spontaneous Song of Ati Yoga,' and a thorough glossary. We have included the Tibetan in this book for students of the language who wish to deepen their own understanding of these profound teachings. In order to help the reader to easily distinguish between Yuthok's own words and Dr. Nida's commentary and citations from other great masters, we have italicized all excerpts from the Yuthok Nyingthig root text.

The Prayer to Yuthok, Five Line Prayer to Yuthok, Yuthok's Song, Yuthok Nyingthig Outer Guru Yoga, and Short Practice of Medicine Protector Shanglon practices presented in this text were translated by Dr. Nida personally and edited under his guidance by Tam Nguyen, MD. These practices have been included here in their entirety so that this book may serve as a retreat manual for practitioners in this lineage.

All of the credit for the design and layout work involved in creating SKY Press's unique look and organizing these teachings into this final book form belongs to Pearse Gaffney. Anna Artemyeva kindly offered her beaufiful thangka paintings for use both on the cover and within the pages this book. I have no doubt that these images will provide an excellent support for meditation for practitioners on this path.

We are honored that as prestigious a scholar as Professor Robert Thurman has contributed the foreword to this book and that he offered his precious time in reviewing the Tibetan and English texts included here. His work to help promote Sowa Rigpa (Traditional Tibetan Medicine) is an invaluable contribution to the preservation of this unique element of Tibetan culture in modern times and we are very grateful for his continued support of Dr. Nida's activities.

This book is the direct result of Dr Nida Chenagtsang's great wisdom, generosity, and tireless efforts to preserve and transmit the teachings of Sowa Rigpa and the Yuthok Nyingthig spiritual lineage all over the world. His kindness knows no bounds.

May this book bring benefit to many beings!

Christiana Polites
SKY Press
Portland, OR, June 2016
info@skypressbooks.com

Mirror of Light: A Commentary on Yuthok's Ati Yoga, Volume One is the first in a special series of texts on the Yuthok Nyingthig spiritual tradition published by SKY Press (**www.skypressbooks.com**), a branch of Sorig Khang International, Foundation for Traditional Tibetan Medicine. (**www.sorigkhang.org**).

II

INTRODUCTION
12 SPECIAL CHARACTERISTICS OF THE YUTHOK NYINGTHIG

The Importance of the Yuthok Nyingthig: Its Twelve Uncommon and Special Characteristics by Nida Chenagtsang

I prostrate, give offerings, and go for refuge to the King of Medicine, Yuthok! The Yuthok Nyingthig (The Heart-Essence of Yuthok) was transmitted to Yuthok Yönten Gonpo in the twelfth century by the Queen of (Wisdom) Dakini Palden Treng ('Glorious Garland/Rosary'). It was then taught to Yuthok's heart-son Sumtön Yeshe, who made notes based on Yuthok's direct oral instruction. After this, Yuthok edited these himself and (it came to) comprise a complete dharma-cycle. It is called in full 'The Heart Essence of Yuthok, the Sunlight of Compassion, the Dharma-cycle of the Blessings of the Practice of the Guru that dissolves all Suffering and Darkness'. These days, the Yuthok Guru sadhana cycle is widely known for its inclusion in the 'Nectar of Good Qualities' from the Mahayoga cycle of teachings in the Rinchen Terzod [the 'Treasury of Precious Termas', the collection of revealed scriptures assembled by Jamgon Kongtrul Rinpoche in the late 19th century]. The entire Dharma-cycle of all of the assorted ritual procedures, medicine empowerment rites, Creation and Completion stage and Great Perfection practices is also included as part of the original block-prints from Chagpori ('Iron Mountain'), Drophen Ling . In accordance with the wishes of the great medical professor Gojo Wangdu, and after obtaining authorization from the great and esteemed scholar Troru Tsenam, the Ngakmang Shipjook Khang or Tantric Community Research Institute typed up copies of the Chagpori set for the first time and everyone was able to see it.

In Yuthok's heart-son Sumton Yeshe's hymn or words of offering we read:

"This guru sadhana of the definitive meaning of the Highest (Yoga) Tantras is the blessed oral lineage that is not known to all. It is the swift path that bestows Buddhahood in one lifetime, it is unadulterated by the admixture of individual fabrications or mental assumptions."

The uncommon significance or twelve special characteristics of this oral lineage, of what Sumton Yeshe describes as 'the guru sadhana which is the definitive meaning of the Highest Yoga Tantras' will be explained as follows:

1) (It brings) blessings quickly
2) It's easy to accomplish
3) It's simple and convenient
4) It's comprehensive (i.e. it includes all the essential points)
5) It's connected with medicine
6) Its sequence of practice is clear
7) It's non-sectarian in its doctrine
8) It's of an appropriate or convenient length
9) It's timely
10) It's (capable of) 'taming' anyone
11) It's a set of instructions without equal
12) It condenses the ultimate meaning and all of the essential points of the Buddha's teachings

The points will be explained a little below.

Characteristic One – Speedy Blessings:

The guru-sadhana confers blessings in even just seven days. As is clearly stated in the King of Medicine Yuthok's song of realization:

"If you are able to have confidence in yourself, if you can pray one-fixedly, if you are able to cast off doubts and second thoughts, if you have hope for a place of refuge in one lifetime, then the two obscurations (i.e. of afflictive emotions and cognition) will immediately be kept in check. Having met me in actuality, in meditative visions or in dreams, I will reveal the supreme path of temporary and ultimate attainment."

As Kongtrul Yonten Gyatso lays out in his commentary and in his notes for readers on the practice of the outer, inner, and secret aspects of 'The Sunlight of Compassion, the Blessings of the Guru Sadhana that Dissolves All Suffering and Darkness' (called the) 'Well-spring of All Good Qualities':

"As Yuthok taught:"

"There's greater merit in praying to me for one year than in praying to other gurus for a whole lifetime; there's more merit in praying to me for a month than in praying to others for a whole year. Rather than praying to others for a whole month, by praying to me for just a day, one minute, or a mere instant, blessings will come quickly. If this isn't true, for having deceived sentient beings, may all the Buddhas and their spiritual offspring of the ten directions smash my skull into pieces like shattered plaster."

Thus, by virtue of the power of his prayers of aspiration in general the special compassion and blessings of this venerable being are especially exalted for us beings that need to be tamed in these degenerate times, and the blessing-powers of his guru sadhana in particular are extremely fast-acting.

"As is explained in Yuthok's own authentic teaching which resounds unfailingly like the great roar of a lion":

"For beings in this degenerate age who don't have the blessing that accomplishes simultaneously even as one practices, who are impatient and have little follow-through, and who can't draw out their practice – if individuals with faith practice this sadhana which is my own life-force without distraction for seven days, I promise that I will hold to these instructions and will reveal myself thoroughly: to the greater practitioner in actual life, to the average one through meditative visions, and to the lesser one through dreams."

"Yuthok clearly explains this extremely quick accomplishment of blessings:"

"If with belief that is free of doubts, greater practitioners commit themselves to the practice of the Creation and Completion stage, average practitioners commit themselves to the approaching-accomplishing recitation-meditation practices, and the lesser practitioners commit themselves to the daily yoga(s) which establish a connection with the guru and lineage, they will spontaneously accomplish the two kinds of benefit (i.e. the benefit for others and for themselves), without any effort at all."

In the history called the 'Iron Hook of Virtue' it says that after he had finished writing the Four Medical Tantras of the Tibetan healing system (the Gyushi) and had been graced with a direct vision, had 'seen the face of' the lords of the three families (i.e. the Sugata, Vajra and Lotus family beings) The three lords told Yuthok:

"For any beings who see, hear, remember, touch, have faith, or hate you, they will go from (ordinary) bliss to (ultimate) bliss. Because you are inheritors of the lineages of all the Sugatas, regardless of whether they imagine you above the crown of their head or in the center of their heart, the very instant they do, the blessing-current of all the Buddhas of the ten directions will surely enter (into their being)"

Thus, from these extensive prophecies, we can see truly the swiftness of Venerable Yuthok's blessings.

Characteristic Two: Ease of Accomplishment

Both the preliminaries and the main practices of the Yuthok Nyingthig are described as easy to accomplish. The method for accomplishing the preliminaries that is taught in the root-text has two aspects: the approaching-recitations of time and the approaching-recitations of signs. Of these, the approaching-recitation of time is the accomplishing of the uncommon preliminaries as well as all of the guru-sadhana within seven whole days or a week. Yuthok himself states that *"(you will) attain at the same time as practicing"*, and Kongtrul Yonten Gyatso says, regarding establishing a connection and entering into a relationship with the guru and lineage, that one is even allowed to just do the preliminaries over four days and the guru-sadhana over three.

Regarding the guru-sadhana as well, Kongtrul says:

"This is in fact made up of (four parts) - the system of guru yoga of the outer sadhana, the complete Medicine Buddha Creation and Completion stage practices of the inner sadhana, the Assembled Mandala of the Three Roots of the secret sadhana, and the daily practices of the concise sadhana – each of which is a stand-alone practice."

From this, we can see how the sadhana is easy to accomplish both in its (complete) four-fold form and as individual stand-alone practices.

Characteristic Three: Convenience and Simplicity

As Venerable Yuthok says: *"If one's compassion is great, whatever one does will be Dharma."* If one makes loving-kindness one's primary foundation, any medical undertakings and altruistic actions one might accomplish will also become Dharma. For this reason, the daily preliminaries of the Yuthok Nyingthig are those things that are done compassionately to preserve and benefit others. These can be seen as convenient applications (of the teachings) in the midst of our daily lives. No matter what sadhana one's doing, they all only have a few chants and prayers and so on, and all and any of the sadhana cycles are convenient (to perform).

This wonderful convenience can be seen with Yuthok's teachings on Phowa, or the Yoga of Transference. The preliminary Phowa recitations, the main yogic practices, and the different ritual applications of Phowa for others, are laid out in their entirety on a single page. The seven physical 'magic wheel' exercises that are part of the channel and wind practices of Tummo, or Inner Heat Yoga – the first two of which purify stale wind in the channels, and the remaining five of which are for unblocking or untying the five channel-wheels or chakras – are also laid out simply and with great precision. (The various aspects of) the Great Seal or Mahamudra – mental stability, mental agitation, resting in the natural state, and the basic essence – are also extremely condensed and are explained in a practical way.

Characteristic Four: Comprehensiveness

All of the essential points of the path of Vajrayana are contained within the thirty-five sections of teachings within the single volume of the Yuthok Nyingthig. Its practices include the preliminaries (Ngöndro) that are the root of Mahayana; Guru yoga; Creation Stage practices; Creation Stages practices combined with Completion stage ones; the Approaching-Accomplishing sadhana practices of the Three Roots as well as the practices for resolving obstacles; Completion stage practices; Channel-Wind and Magic Wheel practices (trulkor); the 'Path of skillful Means' Karmamudra or physical consort practices; and Mahamudra and Dzogchen practices. Its collected ritual procedures include medicine 'accomplishment' rites or empowerments, protection-circles/charms, fire offering ceremonies, sadhanas for the Dharma-protectors, the root goddesses, sages and so on, practices for calling down tra or special spirits for mirror-divination, the 'signs on the path' practices for the resolving of mental obstacles, and the medical traditions on the resolving of physical obstacles, and so on. In short, it teaches all of the most important elements of Vajrayana in their entirety.

Characteristic Five: Connection with Medicine

Pretty much all of the fifteen cases of symptoms and treatments of the three humours of rlung, tripa, and beken are taught in the context of the gegs sel or 'obstacle resolving' practices of the Yuthok Nyingthig, which in their secret aspect involve the resolving of demonic obstacles, in their inner aspect involve the resolving of obstacles of the mind, and in their outer aspect deal with the resolving obstacles of the body. As such, even someone who hasn't studied Tibetan medicine will benefit greatly from this section of the text. Also, in later times, Zurkhar Nyamnyi Dorje's volume of extended commentary on these and the Yuthok Nyingthig, which is known as 'The Pith Instructions of the Ten Million (Pearl) Relics' or just 'The Pearl Relic' for short, became a pre-eminent part of medical tradition.

Characteristic Six: Clear Sequence

The stages of practice have been taught clearly and without confusion: first there are the preliminary practices, which purify one's mind-stream. Then there are the Mahayoga practices which generate the antidote for anger, or the Creation Stage traditions. (Then comes) Lung Anuyoga which is the antidote for desire, or the Completion Stage teachings, after which comes the Great Perfection Ati Yoga which is the antidote for ignorance.

At the start, there's the guru-sadhana, 'The Assembly of the Three Roots', which has four aspects, the outer, inner, secret, and concise sadhanas. All the main bodies of the teachings on the Six Dharmas of the great saint Naropa are taught in order:

The Inner-Heat channels practice, which includes transmuting one's body into that of a deity in the Bardo, the purifying/training of the channels, the intermediate vital-breath practices, and the seven 'magic wheel' exercises of the channels, the daytime yogas of the fierce breath Tummo, which involve refining one's speech into mantra through the basis of the vajra-recitation and of the Illusory Body; the night-time yogas are those of Dream and Clear Light; the instructions on the Six Bardos, or interim states – the Phowa or 'Transference' practice that allows one to practice at the moment of death, along with the 'Buddhahood without meditation' Phowa practices of inserting one's consciousness into another body after death, and Self-Liberation into the Dharmata, the ultimate nature of reality, in the Bardo.

Then, the Path of Great Bliss of the Lower Gates, the Yoga of the 'Action Seal' or Karmamudra which is part of the methods for refining the thiglé or blissful energy-drops of the mind and the Path of the Complete Liberation of the Upper Gates is taught based on the Great Seal of Mahamudra. Then, finally, the Pointing out Great Perfection practices of the Self-Liberation of Samsara-Nirvana are taught fully and extensively. The ripening empowerments and liberating instructions, methods of cultivation, signs of accomplishment on the path, and the resolving of obstacles and hindrances are taught in their entirety and in clear succession with great precision.

Characteristic Seven: Non-Sectarian Philosophy

The 'body-offering' or Kusali practice that is taught in the Yuthok Nyingthig preliminaries epitomizes the (teachings of the) Pacification and Severance (traditions). The Six Dharmas of Naropa are taught fully and in sequence. Likewise, the Path of the Great Bliss of the Lower Gates method of relying on a physical consort, (which is found in) the Kalachakra, Chakrasamvara, and Guhyasamaja systems of Highest Yoga Tantra, is taught in its entirety. Condensed Mahamudra and Dzogchen are also taught. Given this, whatever tradition or philosophical system one happens to study, the Yuthok Nyingthig (remains) authentic.

Characteristic Eight: Appropriate Length

The empowerments, sadhanas, ritual procedures, guru-practice and so on are all taught skilfully in an unembellished way. As it states in the (prophetic) introduction of the Yuthok Nyingthig:

"The Vast and All-pervading Expanse of Great Bliss' that ripens those who are fortunate condenses the essential empowerment and contains its whole meaning for those of limited capacity."

For complex beings, the Yuthok Nyingthig includes the extensive empowerment of the Vast and All-Pervading Expanse of Great Bliss, and in its 'unelaborated' system there is the condensed empowerment of the essential meaning. It includes the two-stage torma empowerment, the four empowerments of the Highest Yoga Tantras, the authorizations of the sages and goddesses, and the life-entrustment rituals of the medical protector Shanglon. All of these are represented in their entirety. All of the guru-sadhanas are also distinguished according to their level of elaboration, and are taught as either outer or secret pith instructions in perfect accordance with each practitioner's capacity.

In the outer sadhana, 'The Wish-Fulfilling Jewel', the way in which one meditates on the outer mandala encircled by the four classes of Yuthok goddesses is fairly extensive. If one can't manage that though, one has the much simpler option of meditating on the guru in one's heart-center and reciting/visualizing the short mantra there. The inner sadhana, 'The Oral Advice, or Pool of Siddhis (Spiritual Attainments)' is a combination of Creation and Completion stage practices of the Medicine Buddha. It summarizes all of the essential points, and through it, one meditates on the five guru-families in the five chakras and realizes the meaning of the four glorious (medical) tantras. Even though the visualizations of (the tantric meditational deities) Hayagriva and Vajravarahi found in the secret sadhana, 'The Swift Guide for Fortunate Individuals' are somewhat extensive, and although it's taught that one should do 100,000 approaching-recitations, in the 'Esteemed Oral Advice of the Path of Bliss' the meditational deities, chakras, and mantra-letters are all taught in a really condensed way. As such, one can see that the sadhanas of the Yuthok Nyingthig are extremely moderate in length.

Characteristic Nine: Timeliness

By virtue of his clairvoyant perception of the future, Yuthok stated the following, which is his vajra-oath:

"For beings in this degenerate age who don't have the blessing that accomplishes simultaneously even as one practices, who are impatient and have little follow-through, and who can't draw out their practice – if individuals with faith practice this sadhana which is my own life-force with without distraction for seven days, I promise that I will hold to these instructions and will reveal myself thoroughly: to the greater practitioner in actual life, to the average one through meditative visions, and to the lesser one through dreams."

Given that most of the Six Dharma/Yoga practices are also done during seven day-long retreats, the Yuthok Nyingthig's practices are in accordance with the psychology of today's super-stressed and busy individual, and even those doctors that are mostly focused on somewhat more superficial activities can put its teachings into practice.

Characteristic Ten: Works for (or 'Tames') Anyone

The Yuthok Nyingthig contains the medical teachings, accomplishing medicine empowerments, and medicine/medical elixir offerings required by doctors; it contains the ritual procedures, the deity propitiation rites, and the protective charms needed by ngakpas; it contains the sadhana practices for acquiring divinatory powers (i.e. calling down pra) needed by astrologers and diviners; it contains the 'magic wheel' exercises (for manipulating) the channels and winds needed by yogis; it includes the technologies of desire and Great Bliss needed by people who are filled with, and are working skillfully with lust; it has the Great Seal of the path of complete liberation needed by the disciplined; it contains the pointing out instructions of the Great Perfection that are absolutely indispensable to Dzogchen practitioners; it possesses the life-enhancing sadhanas needed by the sick; it contains the three rites of pressing down, burning, and casting out that are indispensable to great magicians; it has the wrathful mantras that guard the teachings that are truly needed by the protectors of the faith; and it contains the medicine empowerments and fire offerings of the four tantric activities that are needed by everybody. People with discernment can thus grasp that, this guru-sadhana that establishes a connection with the lineage, is a supreme and most precious path for practitioners of whatever doctrine of the Secret Mantra, one that can point out the way for anybody.

Characteristic Eleven: Unparalleled Instruction

The procedures found in the texts of the Yuthok Nyingthig for acquiring divinatory powers or Tra spirits that are sought out by doctors of the faith and astrologer-diviners are virtually impossible to find anywhere else. The instructions given in the inner guru-sadhana, or 'The Oral Advice, the Pool of Siddhis' that allow one to realize the meaning of the Gyushi or Four Medical Tantras through the power of meditation, are also clearly unique and wonderful. Furthermore, as the great Sumton put it:

"This blessed oral lineage that is not known to all, is the swift path that bestows Buddhahood in one lifetime."

If one examines the Yuthok Nyingthig corpus carefully, (one will realize) that one isn't likely to see the essential points of meditative cultivation taught so clearly anywhere else. For example, in the context of the subtle channel-refining practices of Tummo that transform one's body into the form of a deity, there is the teaching where, once one has had some meditative experiences from this practice, one does vajra-recitations/breathing for seven days as part of a darkness retreat, so as to transform the winds of speech into mantra. This teaching is an uncommon oral-lineage darkness-retreat practice.

The experiences of non-conceptuality and of bliss-and-clarity that emerge during meditation as signs of achievement on the path of the guru-sadhana and Completion stage practices, the ten signs of attainment of the Completion stage, the special, direct perception of Samsara as the thigle or light-spheres, are taught in an extremely clear way and are unlike any other teaching. In the context of the technology or 'path of skilful means' of the Great Bliss of the Lower Gates (i.e. the Karmamudra teachings), the Yuthok Nyingthig describes two categories of yogi, 'those who are trained in and those who aren't trained in (rtsa) rlung or the subtle channels-and-winds practices'. The teachings that are given for the latter, for those people who haven't trained in the subtle-wind practices, are really unique instructions that aren't taught anywhere else. It's clear too that the teachings on achieving the rainbow-body by relying on the path of the Great Bliss of the Lower Gates and a physical consort are really unique as well.

Characteristic Twelve: The Importance of the Teachings

According to Yuthok's oral-lineage biography, the Yuthok Nyingthig was first taught in the pure-land of Tanaduk by the Medicine Buddha. In the interim, it was taught in Oddiyana by the Lotus-Born Master Padmasambhava, where it was requested by Yuthok the Elder, after which it was finally taught to Yuthok Yonten Gonpo the Younger by the wisdom-dakini Palden Trengwa, through which it became known as the profound, pure-vision Dharma-cycle (it is today).

This is how the primary teaching of Sowa Rigpa appeared in history, through Yuthok the Younger's great compassion:

"Resolving the 404 kinds of illness* that torment this precious human body, which is made up of the three poisons and five elements can be understood as the single most important dimension of the medical treatments of Sowa Rigpa. For this reason, Yuthok generated pure and authentic bodhichitta in every possible way and taught this as the single and foremost remedy. For him there was no other teaching more primary than this."

From this we can see that maintaining the welfare of sick beings as one's primary aim is the sign of extensive and authentic bodhichitta, and is the achievement of mastery as a Bodhisattva. From this profound path, Yuthok the Elder achieved in his lifetime the state of an Awareness-Holder or Vidyadhara - he lived until the age of 125, and then along with his consort and all of his holdings, achieved the Great Transference of the rainbow-body. And in the twelfth century, in front of many attendants, Yuthok the Younger passed into the rainbow-body of the Great Transference without any obstacles as well. So there can be no doubt at all of the great significance of the guru-lineage of the Yuthok Nyingthig.

---

*According to Sowa Rigpa, the 404 kinds of illnesses are:
101 karmic diseases
101 illusory diseases (similar to psychosomatic diseases)
101 diseases caused by spirit provocation
101 diseases of the three humors

(This commentary) was written in Winterthur, Switzerland on the 3rd of April 2015 by Dr Nida, who received the three-fold empowerment, reading transmission, and oral instruction for this Dharma-cycle and who has absolutely pure, unadulterated faith in it.

Dr Nida Chenagtsang 2001

III

SONGS AND PRAYERS

Prayer to Yuthok

གང་སྐུ་གསང་ཆེན་མ།

(gang ku sang chen ma)

The One of Secret Form

ན་མོ་གུ་རུ།

Na mo gu ru

Homage to the Guru

གང་གི་སྐུ་ཡི་གསང་ཆེན་མཆོག།

Gang gi ku yi sang chen chok

Whose supreme secret body

དངོས་པོ་ཀུན་ཁྱབ་བདེ་བ་ཆེ།།

Ngö po kün khyap dewa che

Is the nature of great bliss that pervades all existence,

རྣམ་ཀུན་མཆོག་ལྡན་རྡོ་རྗེའི་དབྱིངས།།

Nam kün chok den dor je ying

In all ways supremely endowed with the vajra realm;

མཚུངས་བྲལ་གྱུ་ནའི་སྐུར་ཕྱག་འཚལ།།

Tsung drel gu ne kur chak tsel

To Yuthok's incomparable form, we prostrate.

གང་གི་གསུང་གི་གསང་ཆེན་མཆོག།

Gang gi sung gi sang chen chok

He who's supreme secret speech

སྒྲ་གྲགས་ཀུན་ཁྱབ་གཞོམ་བྲལ་བ།།

Dra drak kün khyap zhom drelwa

Is the indestructible quality that pervades all sound,

བརྒྱད་ཁྲི་བཞི་སྟོང་ཆོས་སྒྲ་སྒྲོགས།།

Gye tri zhi tong chö dra drok

Roaring the sound of the 84,000 dharmas,

མཚུངས་བྲལ་གུ་ནའི་གསུངས་ཕྱག་འཚལ།།

Tsung drel gu ne sung chak tsel

To Yuthok's incomparable speech, we prostrate.

གང་གི་ཐུགས་ཀྱི་གསང་ཆེན་མཆོག།

Gang gi tuk kyi sang chen chok

He whose supreme secret mind

སྤྲོས་པ་ཀུན་བྲལ་བདེ་བ་ཆེ།།

Trö pa kün drel dewa che

Is unconditioned great bliss

ཤེས་རབ་ཕ་རོལ་ཕྱིན་ལ་གནས།།

She rap pa röl chin la ne

Dwelling in the perfection of wisdom,

མཚུངས་བྲལ་གུ་ནའི་ཐུགས་ཕྱག་འཚལ།།

Tsung drel gu ne tuk chak tsel

To Yuthok's incomparable mind we prostrate.

རྒྱལ་བ་ཀུན་ཀྱང་འདྲེན་པ་ཁྱེད།།

Gyelwa kün kyang dren pa khye

You who are even the leader of all the buddhas,

ཁྱེད་ལས་གཞན་པའི་སྐྱོབ་པ་ནི།།

Khye le zhen pe kyop pa ni

There is no refuge other than you

འགྲོ་བ་ཀུན་ལས་འགང་མ་མཆིས།།

Drowa kün le gang ma chi

For all sentient beings,

དེའི་ཕྱིར་ཁྱེད་ལ་སྐྱབས་སུ་མཆི།།

De chir khye la kyap su chi

Because of this, in you I take refuge.

བྱིས་པས་ཁྱེད་མཚན་མ་ཐོས་པར།།

Ji pe khye tsen ma tö par

Immature beings who haven't heard your name,

ཐོས་ཀྱང་གུས་པར་མི་བསྟེན་པར།།

Tö kyang gü par mi ten par

Or they are able to hear your name but cannot be taught,

དེ་ལས་སྙིང་རྗེ་གཞན་མེད་པས།།

De le nying je zhen me pe

For them, there is only compassion;

བརྩེ་བའི་ཁྱེད་ཀྱིས་རྗེས་སུ་བཟུང་།།

Tsewe khye kyi je su zung

Lead them with your loving kindness.

ཁྱེད་ཀྱི་མཚན་ཐོས་སྐྱབས་སོང་བས།།

Khye kyi tsen tö kyap songwe

Through hearing your name and taking refuge in you

དེ་ནི་ནམ་ཡང་སྲིད་མཚོར་མིན།།

De ni nam yang si tsor min

They will no longer be in the ocean of samsara,

དེ་ཕྱིར་མིག་ཆུ་གཡོ་བཞིན་དུ།།

De chir mik chu yo zhin du

Because of this, with eyes filled with tears,

སྙིང་ནས་དུས་ཀུན་གསོལ་བ་འདེབས།།

Nying ne dü kün sölwa dep

I pray to you at all times from my heart.

རབ་འབྱམས་རྒྱལ་བའི་དཀྱིལ་འཁོར་མཆོག།

Rap jam gyelwe kyinkhor chok

Infinite supreme mandalas of the buddhas

གསང་ཆེན་ཁྱེད་སྐུར་རོ་གཅིག་པས།།

Sang chen khye kur ro chik pe

Are one taste to your supreme body;

དེ་རིང་ཁོ་ནར་མངོན་སུམ་དུ།།

De ring kho nar ngön sum du

Today, right now and in actuality,

མཁའ་ཁྱབ་འགྲོ་བས་ཐོབ་པར་ཤོག།

Kha khyap drowe top par shok

May all sentient beings pervading space attain this.

Ati Sarwa mangalam.

May virtue spread.

Five Line Prayer to Yuthok

དུས་གསུམ་རྒྱལ་ཀུན་གསང་བ་གཅིག་བསྡུས་པ།།

Dü sum gyel kün sangwa chik dü pa

To the secret union of all buddhas of the three times,

བླ་མ་སྨན་པའི་རྒྱལ་པོ་གཡུ་ཐོག་པར།།

La ma men pe gyel po yu tok par

To the Guru Yuthok, the King of Medicine,

སྙིང་ཁོང་རུས་པའི་གཏིང་ནས་གསོལ་བ་འདེབས།།

Nying khong rü pe ting ne sölwa dep

I pray from the depths of my heart and bones:

སྐུ་གསུང་ཐུགས་ཀྱི་བྱིན་གྱིས་རློབ་པ་དང་།།

Ku sung tuk kyi jin gyi lop pa dang

Bless me through your body, speech and mind,

མཆོག་དང་ཐུན་མོང་དངོས་གྲུབ་སྩོལ་དུ་གསོལ།།

Chok dang tün mong ngö drup tsel du söl

Grant me the supreme and common siddhis.

Yuthok's Song

When Yuthok the Younger reached the age of seventy-six he summoned all his disciples to offer a teaching and presented them with many gifts. On that occasion, he briefly recounted his life story in the following song:

Hey! Listen fortunate ones!
Listen well, people of the world!
In particular, you who are gathered here,
Even though you have listened much before,
All those were meaningless illusory words.
Today you will listen to what is really meaningful.
Even though you have seen much before,
They were just designs of false and deceptive visions.
Today, that which you see will purify the two obscurations.

If you do not know who I am,
I am the emissary of all the Buddhas,
I am the refuge of all beings.
All the animate and inanimate world is pervaded by my body,
voice, and mind.

The illusory form of this body is of the nature of a host of sacred deities,
Its materiality is instrinsically pure.
Like a rainbow it cannot be grasped,
Yet like the moon's reflection on the water, it appears everywhere.

The empty sound of my voice is the song of the echo,
Reverberating with the sound of the eighty-four thousand dharmas.
It manifests as a rain of teaching for those who need to be guided,
And sets all beings on the path that ripens and liberates.

In the clarity and emptiness of my mind, the ineffable authentic state,
Bliss is omni-pervasive, arising unceasingly,
And emptiness and compassion are undifferentiated.
Hence, the phenomena created by mind are naturally liberated through the shortest instant of time.

In an instant I am a fully awakened Buddha;
In an instant I travel to hundreds of Buddha fields;
In an instant I encounter hundreds of Buddhas;
In an instant I manifest hundreds of emanations;
In an instant I guide hundreds of beings,
And I accomplish the totalities and masteries.

With a faith that does not know uncertainties,
Pray without having any doubt!
Even though the cataract of impure vision prevents you from seeing all these qualites of mine,
In the ordinary perception shared by everyone:

I am the doctor who, with the medicine of skillful compassion,
Cures the inner mental illness of the three emotions,
And the outer illnesses of the three humors, wind, bile, and phlegm.
The title 'doctor' applies to me.

I explain the Buddhist canon and its commentaries by heart.
With logic I overcome the challenges of fundamentalists,
I issue the banner of victory of the Buddhist doctrine.
The title 'scholar' applies to me.

I went to Sri Parvata and robbers created obstacles on my way,
But with a gaze I paralyzed them all.
The title 'siddha' applies to me.

On my way to Odiyana, flesh eating dakinis sent meteorites and lightning to strike me.

I made the threatening gesture and all the dakinis collapsed.
The title 'siddha' applies to me.

On my way to Ceylon the boat fell apart in the midst of the waves.
I flew like a bird and also saved my companions.
The title 'siddha' applies to me.

When I went to the Kali forest, a vapor of venomous snakes spread like dark fog.
I meditated on compassion and the fog quickly vanished.
The title 'siddha' applies to me.

When I went to Persia I encountered the army of the Mongols,
So I penetrated the rocky mountains back and forth.
The title 'siddha' applies to me.

When I visited Swayambhu I competed with the Bonpos in magic.
For half a day I remained sitting in space.
The title 'siddha' applies to me.

I went from Bodh Gaya to Tibet taking only a single day,
Carrying a fresh flower as a gift.
The title 'siddha' applies to me.

At the place of Tshongdu Kormoru in Western Tibet,
I prevented the sun from setting and caused a rain of Aruras, golden in color, to fall.
The title 'siddha' applies to me.

It would be endless to recount all the events of my life.
For one who has gained mind freedom,
There are no disturbances caused by earth, water, fire and wind, gods and demons, etc,
And by animate and inanimate enemies.

He flies in the sky swifter than birds,
He dives in the waters with nothing to stop him,
He penetrates mountains like a meteorite or lightning,
In the midst of fire he is the fire god.

The beings of the degenerate age are of little merit,
And few are those who meet and listen to me.
Those who see, listen, think, touch me, and have faith in me,
Create the sprout of the spirit of enlightenment,
Purify negativities accumulated throughout eons,
Overcome obstacles and adverse conditions of this life,
Liberate themselves, liberate others, liberate both, and liberate all their followers.

I will connect to happiness even those, who harboring negative views, harm me.
Hence, I will lead them from (ordinary) happiness to (ultimate) happiness.
There is no doubt about this.

If you give up your heart and mind to me, beseech me in a sincere way,
Overcome your lack of faith and hope in me as a refuge throughout your life,
Immediately your two obscurations will diminish.
Upon meeting me in reality, in vision, or in dream,
I will reveal the path to the temporal and ultimate goal.

All of you present now and the students to come,
My sons, and disciples, remember this!
For the time being, my work of training beings in this world is complete.
I will now go to the pure land of the Medicine Buddha.

After he had said this and had given a lot of advice to the doctors, he exhibited enlightened bodily activities that were perceived by beings in many diverse ways, surpassing what each of them could conceive of. The expanse of the sky was completely covered by a net of rainbow light, in the center of which, in the midst of hundreds and thousands of deity-princes bearing an array of flower-garlands and offering substances, were ten thousand wisdom-dakinis. From the tips of their fingers manifold rays of rainbow light emanated. This rainbow light touched the body of the great being Yuthok and he drifted off into the heavens. It is said that people saw many different things: some saw him ride off on a lion, some saw him fly away on a garuda, while yet others saw him ride off on a bull, and so on.

IV

YUTHOK NYINGTHIG
OUTER GURU YOGA

Refuge and Bodhichitta

སངས་རྒྱས་ཆོས་དང་ཚོགས་ཀྱི་མཆོག་རྣམས་ལ།།

Sang gye chö dang tsok kyi chok nam la

Buddha, Dharma and Sangha,

བྱང་ཆུབ་བར་དུ་བདག་ནི་སྐྱབས་སུ་མཆི།།

Jang chup bar du dak ni kyap su chi

Until enlightenment I take refuge in you;

བདག་གིས་སྦྱིན་སོགས་བགྱིས་པའི་བསོད་ནམས་ཀྱིས།།

Dak gi jin sok gyi pe sö nam kyi

Through my merit of generosity and so on,

འགྲོ་ལ་ཕན་ཕྱིར་སངས་རྒྱས་འགྲུབ་པར་ཤོག།

Dro la pen chir sang gye drup par shok

May I attain Buddhahood for the good of all sentient beings.

"If the supreme teaching of the Guru Sadhana Dharma Cycle of the Yuthok Nyingthig did not have the blessing of simultaneous practice and accomplishment, then the people of the degenerate age, entangled in worldly desire and weak in determination for long retreats, would not be able to practice. However, if this, the accomplishment of my life-force itself, is practiced without distraction by a faithful person for seven days, then I vow that I shall reveal well my face to him, and I shall grant them teachings and closely instruct them."

Yuthok Yonten Gonpo, 12th Century

Outer Mandala

1. Self Visualization

Visualize yourself as

Medicine Buddha (seed syllable HUNG), 

Four-Armed Chenrezig (HUNG),

or Tara (TAM).

2. Guru Visualization

On the crown of your head is a four-petalled lotus with a moon mandala in the center, on which is the guru [Yuthok], the embodiment of the body, speech and mind of all the buddhas of the three times. He is inseparable from all the buddhas, the King of Medicine, the Medicine Guru or any other form of Buddha.

Blazing with glorious splendor, he radiates supreme light. His body is pure white, and his face has a rosy complexion. He is beautifully dressed in various brocades, and sits in the lotus position. He has one face and two arms. His dark brown hair hangs loose and is crowned by a flower garland. His right hand displays the mudra of Supreme Generosity, and holds the stem of a blue Utpala flower. The flower is open at the level of his right ear; inside the open petals there is a perfect-wisdom text and a wisdom sword. His left hand displays the mudra of Dharma Speech, and holds a lotus flower which is open at the level of his left ear. Inside the lotus is a vase full of nectar-of-immortality. Fresh saffron flowers adorn the mouth of the vase. At the top of the vase there is a precious jewel; to the right of this is a golden vajra and to the left is a golden Arura flower [Terminalia chebula].

3. Dakini Visualization

Around Maha Guna [Yuthok], on four petals in the four cardinal directions, are the Four Dakinis:

- In front of him is the White Dakini playing a jeweled lute.
- To his right is the Yellow Dakini playing a flute made of a vulture's thigh bone.
- Behind him is the Red Dakini playing a flute made of a human thigh bone.
- To his left is the Green Dakini displaying a silver mirror.

Each of the dakinis face towards Yuthok. The Four Dakinis are in the form of beautiful sixteen-year-old maidens dancing: they have extremely beautiful smiles, they are dancing in flexible positions, their necks and waists are adorned by flower garlands. Their long hair is loose and adorned with red pearls; they wear bright and multi-colored skirts. All of them are playing melodiously and dancing, whilst endlessly offering illusory bliss to Yuthok the Great.

4. Radiating Light Visualization

Brilliant light radiates from Yuthok's head, throat and heart chakras. This light penetrates all primordial space, inviting the root masters, lineage masters, Medicine Buddha surrounded by the buddhas of the ten directions and the three times, the assembly of the medical protectors, the countless dakas, dakinis and deities, all of whom create an expansive mandala. All of the deities of this mandala are inseparable from the supreme nirmanakaya of Yuthok and the Four Dakinis. These deities arrive like massive clouds in the sky and then settle like snowflakes dissolving into Yuthok and the Four Dakinis.

5. Invocation

Make the following offerings to Yuthok:

- Outer Offering [the five sensory objects form, sound, smell, taste and touch
- Inner Offering [medicine, rakta and torma]
- Secret Offering [illusory bliss]

As you make these offerings, invoke simultaneously the presence of Yuthok with the utmost sincerity 'from the depths of your heart, from the inside of your bones and from the centre of your bone marrow.'

Ask him to grant all your deepest wishes and desires, whilst reciting the mantra of invocation:

སྨན་རྒྱལ་གཡུ་ཐོག་ཡོན་ཏན་མགོན་པོ་ལ་ཕྱག་འཚལ་ལོ།
མཆོད་དོ། སྐྱབས་སུ་མཆིའོ།།

MENGYAL YUTHOK YONTEN GONPO LA
CHAG TSEL LO CHOD DO KYABSU CHIO
(21x)

6. Receiving Siddhis

From the four points of Yuthok's body [the chakras of the head, throat, heart and navel], light radiates and touches the Four Dakinis, instantly commanding them to fulfill all of your wishes.

Again, from Yuthok's heart chakra light radiates to the ten directions, returning with the essence of the whole of universe and its sentient beings. The essence of the universe and buddhas' compassion combine and manifest as five-colored lights [blue, green, red, yellow and white]. These enter the vase, becoming the wisdom nectar of immortality. This vase fills and overflows; a stream of the wisdom nectar of immortality flows from the vase to the crown of your head, into the central channel and inside your body. As it flows into your body, speech and mind, all illness, provocations and sins are cleansed and purified. Your body becomes as crystal clear as a sparkling glass bowl.

7. Receiving the Empowerments

Gradually your entire body becomes filled with nectar, and you receive the Four Empowerments or Initiations [the Vase Initiation, purification of the body and attainment of the nirmanakaya; the Secret Initiation, purification of the speech and attainment of the sambhogakaya; the Primordial Wisdom Initiation, purification of the mind and attainment of the dharmakaya; the Word Initiation, purification of the three doors and attainment of the clear light state].

Focusing your mind on Yuthok as above, recite this mantra:

ཨོཾ་ཨཱཿཧཱུྃ་མ་ཧཱ་གུ་རུ་གུ་ཎ་སརྦ་སིདྡྷི་ཧཱུྃ་
ཛ་དེ་ཝ་ཌཱ་ཀི་ནི་ཧ་རི་ནི་ས་ཙིཏྟ་ཧྲིང་ཧྲིང་ས་མ་ཡ་ཛཿཧཱུྃ་བཾ་ཧོཿ

OM A HUNG MAHA GURU GUNA SARVA SIDDHI HUNG
DZA DEVA DAKINI HARINISA TSITA HRING HRING
SAMAYA DZA HUNG BAM HO

1. Self Visualization
Visualize yourself as Medicine Buddha, Four-Armed Chenrezig or Tara.

2. Mantra Visualization
In your heart chakra, visualize a five-petalled lotus. The guru, Maha Guna [Yuthok], is sitting in the centre of the lotus. In his heart chakra is a moon disc on which there is a silver syllable HUNG.
Surrounding the syllable, the mantra spins like a chain of blue fire:

OM A HUNG BAZAR GURU GUNA SIDDHI HUNG

3. Mantra Recitation
When you start reciting this mantra, visualize the mantra spinning fast like a chain of light, and as it spins it emerges from the guru's mouth, then comes out of your own mouth. This offering of light then radiates out to the entire universe [to all buddhas] eliminating and cleansing all provocations, all sins, and the negative energy of all beings. The mantra next enters your heart, returns to the guru's heart, and again comes out from the guru's mouth. Focus on the rotation of the mantra [as it rotates vertically, it spins horizontally at the same time].

At the end you dissolve into Yuthok, and Yuthok dissolves into space.

Torma Offering

1. Self Visualization

Visualize yourself as Medicine Buddha, Four-Armed Chenrezig or Tara.

2. Purification

From your heart chakra emerge the syllables:

རཾ་ཡཾ་ཁཾ

RAM YAM KHAM

(3x)

- Visualize fire coming from the RAM, burning away all faults and negative energies;
- wind comes from the YAM, blowing away all karmic traces;
- water arises from the KHAM, washing away the dirt of dualistic vision.

3. Creating the Torma

All becomes complete emptiness as you recite the Mantra of Emptiness:

ཨོཾ་སྭ་བྷཱ་ཝ་ཤུདྡྷཿསརྦ་དྷརྨཿསྭ་བྷཱ་ཤུདྡྷོ་ཧཾ

OM SOBHAVA SHUDHA SARVA DHARMA

SOBHA SHUDHO HANG

(1x)

Out of complete emptiness, we create the perfect offering:

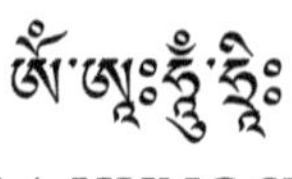

OM A HUNG SHRI

(3x)

- With OM the five nectars dissolve into light, transforming into a white energy drop;
- A transforms the entire cycle of existence into a red energy drop;
- HUNG transforms the torma into the five sense offerings, encapsulating all of creation and filling the entire span of space;
- with SHRI all substances are purified and become perfect.

4. Inviting the Guests

Light radiates from your heart, inviting all guests: the Three Roots [guru, deva, dakini], medicine buddhas, drangsong and rigzin. As you recite:

བཛྲ་ས་མ་ཡ་ཛཿ

BAZAR SAMAYA DZA

(3x)

The guests are invited.

ས་མ་ཡ་སྟྃ

SAMAYA TAM

(1x)

The guests settle in, present in space in front of you.

5. Torma Offering

Offer the torma, inviting the guests to enjoy the offerings:

ཨོཾ་ཨཱཿཧཱུྃ་བཛྲ་གུ་རུ་གུ་ཎ་དེ་ཝ་ཌཱ་ཀི་ནི་ས་པཱ་རི་ཝཱ་ར་མ་ཧཱ་སརྦ་པཉྩ་ཨ་མྲི་ཏ་མ་
ཧཱ་རཀྟ་མ་ཧཱ་བ་ལིཾ་ཏ་སརྦ་པཱུ་ཛ་ཁ་ཁ་ཁཱ་ཧི་ཁཱ་ཧི༔

OM A HUNG BAZAR GURU GUNA DEVA DAKINI
SA PARI WARA MAHA SARVA PAZA AMRITA MAHA RAKTA
MAHA BALINGTA SARVA PUZA KHA KHA KHA HI KHA HI

(7x)

6. Prayer

Pray to all medicine supreme beings: Yuthok and all medicine buddhas, devas, dakinis, drangsong, rigzin, nature dakinis, etc. reciting Yuthok's special prayer ['The One of Secret Form'].
Make your special requests at this time.

7. Purification of Speech

To correct any mistakes in your mantras or your practice, recite:

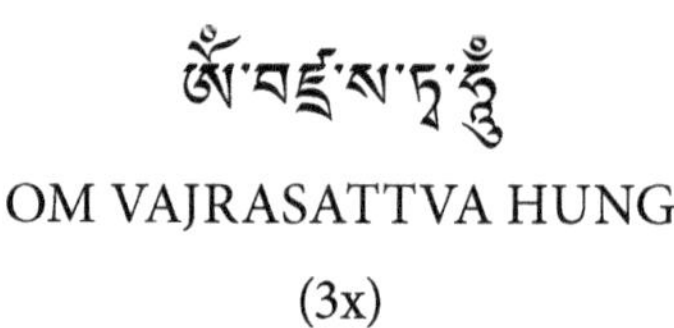

OM VAJRASATTVA HUNG

(3x)

8. Dissolution

The Three Roots vanish; the Four Dakinis dissolve into Yuthok; then the guru, with great bliss, dissolves into light and into your body. The guru's vajra body, vajra speech and vajra mind are inseparable with your own three doors.

བཛྲ་མུ་སཿ

BAZAR MUSA

(1x)

9. The guests leave. Dedication

Recite:

དགེ་བ་འདི་ཡིས་མྱུར་དུ་བདག

Gewa di yi nyur du dak

By the merit, may we quickly

སྨན་རྒྱལ་གཡུ་ཐོག་འགྲུབ་གྱུར་ནས།

Men gyel yu tok drup gyur ne

Achieve the state of Yuthok, the King of Medicine,

འགྲོ་བ་གཅིག་ཀྱང་མ་ལུས་པ།

Drowa chik kyang ma lü pa

And through this, may all beings,

དེ་ཡི་ས་ལ་འགོད་པར་ཤོག

De yi sa la gö par shok

Be placed on this level.

From the original Yuthok Nyingthig Ladrub text (woodblock print)
Published by the Chagpori Medical College, Lhasa, Tibet;
Final edition by Chokyi Sangye, 19th century

1

YUTHOK'S ATI YOGA INTRODUCTION AND PRELIMINARIES

གཡུ་ཐོག་རྫོགས་ཆེན་འཁོར་འདས་རང་གྲོལ་ཆེན་མོ།

གཡུ་ཐོག་སྙིང་ཐིག་གི་རྫོགས་ཆེན་ངོ་སྤྲོད་འཁོར་འདས་རང་གྲོལ་ཆེན་མོའི་
འགྲེལ་བ་དང་ལྷན་ཐབས་
འོད་ཀྱི་མེ་ལོང་མ་
ཞེས་བྱ་བ་
བཞུགས་
སོ།།

བཅོམ་ལྡན་འདས་དེ་བཞིན་གཤེགས་པ་དགྲ་བཅོམ་པ་ཡང་དག་པར་རྫོགས་པའི་སངས་རྒྱས་
སྨན་གྱི་བླ་གཡུ་ཐོག་ཡོན་ཏན་མགོན་པོ་ལ་ཕྱག་འཚལ་ལོ། མཆོད་དོ། སྐྱབས་སུ་མཆིའོ། །

The Great Self-Liberation of Samsara-Nirvana of the Great Perfection of Yuthok

Here follows the commentary and supplementary instructions on the Great Self-Liberation of Samsara-Nirvana, the Great Perfection pointing out teachings of the Yuthok Nyingthig, known as the 'Mirror of Light'.

I prostrate to the Conqueror-Gone Beyond, the Tathagatha Arhant, the authentic and perfect Medicine Buddha Yuthok Yonten Gonpo - to you I give offerings, to you I go for refuge!

ངོ་བོ་སྟོང་བ་གདོད་མའི་མགོན་པོ་ཀུན་བཟང་སྨན་གྱི་རྒྱལ།།
རང་བཞིན་གསལ་བ་ལོངས་སྤྱོད་རྫོགས་སྐུ་རྡོ་རྗེ་སེམས་དཔའ་ཆེ།།
ཐུགས་རྗེ་ཀུན་ཁྱབ་སྨན་གྱི་བླ་མ་གཡུ་ཐོག་ཡོན་ཏན་མགོན།།
སྐུ་གསུམ་བདག་ཉིད་རྩ་བའི་བླ་མས་དུས་ཀུན་བྱིན་གྱིས་རློབས།།
བྱང་ཆུབ་སེམས་མཆོག་ཡང་དག་རྟེན་འབྲེལ་ལྟ་བ་མཆོག།
བསྒོམ་པའི་མཆོག་གྱུར་འོད་གསལ་ཨ་ཏིའི་གནས་ལུགས་མཆོག།།
མཆོག་གི་སྤྱོད་ལམ་འཇའ་ལུས་འོད་སྐུ་འབྲས་བུ་མཆོག།
བླ་མའི་ཡང་མཆོག་གཡུ་ཐོག་རང་གྲོལ་རྫོགས་ཆེན་མཆོག།
རྟ་ཕག་ཡབ་ཡུམ་མཆོག་ཐུན་དངོས་གྲུབ་ཆར་དུ་ཕོབས།།
ཡེ་ཤེས་མཁའ་འགྲོས་སྲོག་སྙིང་འབྲི་བར་གནང་བ་སྩོལ།།
སྐལ་ལྡན་ཚེ་གཅིག་འཇའ་ལུས་འཕོ་ཆེན་ཐོབ་པར་ཤོག།
དམ་ཅན་སྡེ་དགུས་བསྟན་དང་བསྟན་འཛིན་གཡེལ་མེད་སྐྱོང་།།
སྒོ་གསུམ་མཐར་ཕྱིན་དྲི་མེད་སྦྱང་བའི་སྔོན་འགྲོ་དང་།།
ལྟ་བའི་མཐར་ཐུག་ཀ་དག་ཁྲེགས་ཆོད་གཉུག་མའི་སེམས།།
སྐུ་ཡི་ལྷུན་གྲུབ་འོད་དང་ཐུན་པའི་ངེས་དོན་བསྒོམ།། འདི་རུ་འགོད་པར་འཇའ་ལུས་བླ་མས་
གནང་བ་སྩོལ།།

King of Medicine, Essence of Primordial Emptiness, Lord Samantabhadra!

Perfect Enjoyment Body of Natural Luminosity, Great Vajrasattva!

Guru of the Medicine of All-Pervading Compassion Yuthok Yonten Gonpo! Root-guru who personifies the very essence of the three kayas, bless me at all times!

Supreme Bodhisattva, supreme and authentic view of inter-dependence, the supreme natural state of the pre-eminent Clear Light Ati meditation! The supreme result of the Rainbow Body of the Body of Light of the highest conduct! The supreme Great Perfection of Self-Liberation of the supreme guru Yuthok!

Father and Mother Hayagriva and Vajravarahi rain down in your ecstatic union the supreme and common attainments!

O Wisdom Dakini grant me permission to write down the vital-heart mantras!

May I obtain the Great Transference of the Rainbow Body in this single human life that I am so fortunate to have!

May the teachings and those who hold them be protected unwaveringly by the nine-fold Oath Bound Protectors!

I will cultivate the preliminary practices that purify the three gates and bring them into stainless perfection! I will meditate on the consummation of the view, the primordial purity that cuts through hardness that is the mind of the natural and original state! I will acquaint myself with the spontaneous perfection of body and wisdom, the definitive meaning of light and darkness! Oh Rainbow-body Guru, grant me permission to put down (these commentaries) here!

དེ་ཡང་འཛའ་ལུས་འཕོ་བ་ཆེན་པོའི་སྐུར་བཞེངས་པའི་སྨན་རྒྱལ་གཡུ་ཐོག་ཡོན་ཏན་མགོན་པོས་ཐུན་མོང་གདུལ་བྱར་གཞན་ཕན་གཙོར་བྱས་གསོ་རིག་རྒྱུད་བཞི་གསུངས་པ་དང་། ཐུན་མིན་གདུལ་བར་ཚེ་གཅིག་ལུས་གཅིག་ལ་གྲོལ་བྱེད་ཀྱི་རྡོ་རྗེ་ཐེག་པའི་གདམས་པ་གཡུ་ཐོག་སྙིང་ཐིག་བསྟན་ལ། གཡུ་ཐོག་སྙིང་ཐིག་བྱིན་རླབས་བླ་སྒྲུབ་ཀྱི་ཁ་བྱང་དུ།

“རྫོགས་རིམ་ཡང་ཟབ་མཁའ་འགྲོའི་སྙིང་ཐིག་ནི།། སྐལ་ལྡན་ཚེ་གཅིག་མངོན་སངས་རྒྱས་འདོད་སྒྲུབ།། ངོ་སྤྲོད་འཁོར་འདས་རང་སར་གྲོལ་ཉམས་ལོངས།།” ཞེས་གསུངས་པ་བཞིན།

གཡུ་ཐོག་སྙིང་ཐིག་ནི། འོད་གསལ་སྒྱུ་འཕྲུལ་གྱི་ལུགས་བཞིན།
སྐྱེ་བའི་དྲི་མ་བྱང་བྱེད་དམ་ཐ་མལ་སྣང་ཞེན་དག་སྣང་དུ་བསྒྱུར་བྱེད་བསྐྱེད་པའི་རིམ་པའམ།
ཁོང་ཁྲོའི་གཉེན་པོ་བསྐྱེད་པ་མ་ཧ་ཡོ་ག་དང་།
འཆི་བའི་འཁྲུལ་སྣང་སྦྱོང་བྱེད་དམ་རྩ་རླུང་ཐིག་ལེ་རྡོ་རྗེ་གསུམ་དུ་བསྒྱུར་བྱེད་རྫོགས་རིམ་མམ། འདོད་ཆགས་གཉེན་པོ་ལུང་ཨ་ནུ་ཡོ་ག
དག་བྱ་དང་དག་བྱེད་ལས་འདས་པའི་སྤྲོས་མེད་རྫོགས་རིམ་མམ་གཏི་མུག་རང་སངས་འཁོར་འདས་ཀ་དག་ལྷུན་འགྲུབ་འོད་གསལ་རྫོགས་པ་ཆེན་པོ་གསུམ་གྱི་གནད་ཡོངས་སུ་ཚང་བའི་ཟབ་མོ་དག་སྣང་གི་ཆོས་སྐོར་ཞིག་ཡིན་པ་དང་།

The King of Medicine, Yuthok Yonten Gonpo, who upon his death manifested the rainbow body of the Great Transference, taught the four, principle root-tantras of Sowa Rigpa as a common teaching for taming beings and benefitting others and the Yuthok Nyingthig, 'The Heart Essence of Yuthok' as an uncommon, direct Vajrayana instruction for achieving liberation in one (human) lifetime and one body. Accordingly, in the prophetic introduction of the Yuthok Nyingthig Guru Sadhana of Blessings it says:

"Regarding the most profound completion stage, the Dakini's Vital Heart Essence, if you wish to truly actualize Buddhahood in a single fortunate human life, then practice the pointing out (instructions) that liberate (the phenomena of) Samsara-Nirvana in their own ground."

In accordance with the Clear Light Early Translation (Nyingma) system, the Yuthok Nyingthig is a profound, pure-vision dharma-cycle, which is in accordance with the Clear Light Early Translation (Nyingma) system, and which covers all of the vital-points of the three (Inner Tantras) completely:

The Mahayoga that generates the antidote of anger, namely, the Creation Stage that cleanses the defilement of birth or transforms clinging to ordinary appearances into pure perception; the Lung Anu Yoga that is the antidote for desire, a.k.a. the Completion Stage that purifies the illusory appearances of death or that transforms the channels, winds, and drops into the three vajras*; and the unelaborated (non-conceptual) Completion Stage that goes beyond either a subject who purifies or an object to be purified, a.k.a the primordial purity that dissolves ignorance (and the phenomena of) Samsara-Nirvana of its own accord, the Spontaneously-realized Clear Light Great Perfection.

*Vajra Body, Vajra Speech, Vajra Mind

དེ་ལས་བསྐྱེད་པའི་རིམ་པ་ནི་བླ་མ་ཡི་དམ་མཁའ་འགྲོའི་རྩ་བ་གསུམ་ལས།

ཡི་དམ་ལ་ཞི་ཁྲོ་གཉིས་སྟེ།

ཞི་བ་སྨན་རྒྱལ་ཀུན་ཏུ་བཟང་པོ་དང་རྒྱལ་བ་རིགས་ལྔ་དང་།

ཁྲོ་བོ་ནི་ཁྲོ་རྒྱལ་རྟ་མགྲིན་དང་རྡོ་རྗེ་ཕག་མོ་ཡབ་ཡུམ་དང་།

མཁའ་འགྲོ་ནི་ཁྲོས་མ་ནག་མོ་སྟེ་ལྔ་རྣམས་རྩ་གསུམ་ཀུན་འདུས་ཀྱི་བླ་སྒྲུབ་སྟེ།

བླ་མ་གཡུ་ཐོག་ཡོན་ཏན་མགོན་པོའི་སྒྲུབ་ཐབས་སམ། ཕྱི་སྒྲུབ་ཡིད་བཞིན་ནོར་བུ། ནང་སྒྲུབ་དགོས་འདོད་ཀུན་འབྱུང་། གསང་སྒྲུབ་སྐལ་ལྡན་སྨྱུར་འདྲེན།

དྲིལ་བའི་བླ་སྒྲུབ་ཡེ་ཤེས་འཁོར་ལོ་བཅས་རིགས་བཞིས་བསྟན་པ་དང་།

རྫོགས་རིམ་སྐོར་ལ་གཞི་ལུས་ངག་ཡིད་གསུམ་རྩ་རླུང་ཐིག་ལེར་སྦྱངས་ནས།

ལུས་ལྷ་སྐུར་འཆར་བ་རྩ་ཡི་ཁྲིད། ངག་སྔགས་སུ་འཆར་བ་རླུང་གི་ཁྲིད།

སེམས་ཆོས་སྐུར་འཆར་བ་ཐིག་ལེའི་ཁྲིད་བཅས་ཆོས་དྲུག་གོ་བདེ་ཞིང་ཞལ་གསལ་བའི་སྒོ་ནས་བསྟན་པ་སྟེ།

ཉིན་མོའི་རྣལ་འབྱོར་གཏུམ་མོ་དང་སྒྱུ་ལུས། མཚན་མོའི་རྣལ་འབྱོར་འོད་གསལ་དང་རྨི་ལམ།

འཆི་ཀའི་རྣལ་འབྱོར་འཕོ་བ་དང་།

བར་དོའི་རྣལ་འབྱོར་གྲོང་འཇུག་དང་བཅས་གསུངས་པ་དང་།

དེ་ནས་རྫོགས་རིམ་མཐར་ཐུག་ལ་འོག་སྒོ་བདེ་ཆེན་ལམ་མམ་ཐབས་ལམ་དང་།

སྤྲོས་མེད་རྫོགས་རིམ་ལ་སྙིང་སྒོ་གྲོལ་བྱེད་ཀྱི་ཕྱག་རྒྱ་ཆེན་པོའམ་ཀ་དག་ཁྲེགས་ཆོད་གནས་ལུགས་ཀྱི་ཁྲིད་གནད་དང་ལྡན་པར་གསུངས་སོ།།

In the Creation Stage we find the three roots of Lama, Yidam and Khandro (Guru, Deva, and Dakini). Of these, there are the two (classes of) yidam, peaceful and wrathful. The peaceful ones are Mengyal Kuntu Zangpo, the Medicine King All-Beneficient (Samantabhadra) and the five victorious Buddha families. The wrathful ones are the Wrathful King Hayagriva and Vajravarahi (united as) Father-Mother. With the khandros, there are the five classes of Troma Nagmos, the Black Wrathful Goddesses. These comprise the Guru Sadhana of the Assemblage of the Three Roots.

Yuthok Yonten Gonpo's sadhana is taught according to four aspects: the outer sadhana, which is 'The Wish-Fulfilling Jewel', the inner sadhana which is 'The Source of (the Fulfilment) of All Wishes', the secret sadhana which is 'The Swift Delivery for the Fortunate' and the condensed guru sadhana which is the 'Wisdom-Chakra'.

When it comes to the Completion Stage, we find easy to understand and clearly explained teachings on the Six Dharmas or Yogas: once the triad of the Basic Body, Speech, and Mind have been purified through the channels, winds and drops, there are the instructions on the channels (where) one's body manifests as the form of the deity; instructions on the winds where one's speech appears as mantras, and instructions on the drops where one's mind is experienced as the dharma or ultimate-reality body. The daytime yogas of inner-heat and the illusory body, the night-time yogas of clear light (sleeping) and dreaming, the yoga of the moment of death (known as) Transference (phowa), and the yoga of the intermediate state (bardo), of 'Entering into one who has died' are all set forth. Next, instructions on the consummation of the Completion Stage, the path or method of the Great Bliss of the Lower gates, and the Liberating Great Seal of the Upper gates of the un-elaborated Completion Stage, or the natural state of the primordially pure 'Cutting Through Hardness' practices, are laid out with great significance*.

*The path of the lower gates refers to Karmamudra; the path of the upper gates refers to Mahamudra.

སྤྱིར་རྫོགས་ཆེན་སྐོར་ལ་སྔ་འགྱུར་སྙིང་མའི་བཀའ་མ་དང་གཏེར་མ་གཉིས་ཀར་རྫོགས་ཆེན་སྟོན་པ་མཆོག་རྣམ་པ་དང་གཏེར་ཆེན་རྣམ་པས་གསལ་པོར་གསུངས་ན་ཡང་།
རྩ་བ་དང་འགྲེལ་བ་ཁ་ཤས་རྒྱས་དྲག་ནས་རྟོགས་དཀའ་ཞིང་།
རྟོགས་ལྡན་གྱི་བླ་མ་ཞིག་མེད་ན་ཉམས་ལེན་གྱི་གོ་རིམ་མང་པ་དང་མན་ངག་གི་གནད་ཤེས་དཀའ་ལ།
སྔོན་འགྲོ་དངོས་གཞི་སོགས་ཀྱི་གོ་རིམ་སྐོར་གསུངས་མི་འདྲ་བ་འདུག་པས།
མ་བསྒོམ་སངས་རྒྱས་འོད་གསལ་རྫོགས་པ་ཆེན་པོའི་རང་ཞལ་འདི་མཇལ་དཀའ་བ་དང་།
གཡུ་ཐོག་ལུགས་ཀྱི་རྫོགས་ཆེན་སྐོར་ལ་རྫོགས་ཆེན་ངོ་སྤྲོད་ཁྲིགས་ཐོད་ཟུང་འཇུག་གི་གདམས་པ་འཁོར་འདས་རང་གྲོལ་ཆེན་མོ་གསུངས་པ་ཞལ་ཤིན་ཏུ་གསལ་ན་ཡང་།

བློ་སྦྱོངས་བདག་དང་འདྲ་བའི་ཐོས་བསམ་བསྒོམ་གྱི་རྩལ་མ་རྫོགས་པའི་ལས་དང་པོ་པ་རྣམས་ལ་ཕན་ན་བསམ་ནས་རྫོགས་ཆེན་སྔོན་འགྲོའི་ཁ་བསྐང་དང་།
རྗེ་གཡུ་ཐོག་རང་ལུགས་ཀྱི་ཀ་དག་ཁྲིགས་ཆོད་ཀྱི་ཁྲིད་ཆ་ཚང་དང་།
མཐར་ཤུགས་བསྟན་གྱི་ཐོད་རྒལ་དང་སྨུན་ཁྲིད་ཀྱི་ཁ་གསབ་བསྡུས་པ་བཅས་ལེའུ་བཞིར་བཀར་ནས་ཚིག་ཚོགས་མང་པོ་མེད་པར་གནད་བསྡུས་ཙམ་འགོད་པར་བྱ་བ་ལ། མ་རྟོག་པ་དང་ལོག་རྟོག་དང་། མ་དག་པ་དང་། འགལ་འཁྲུལ་དང་མ་ཚང་ཅི་ཡོད་ལྷ་མེད་ཀློང་དུ་གཤེགས་སོ།།

Even though the highest masters and treasure-revealers teach the Great Perfection clearly in a general way in both the Kama (the canonical utterances of the Buddha) and Terma (revealed visionary scriptures) of the Ancient Translation or Nyingma school, some of the root-texts and commentaries are excessively detailed and are therefore difficult to understand. Without a realized guru, it's difficult to make sense of the many stages of practice and to understand the essential points of the pith instructions. Since so many different things have been taught about the sequence of the preliminary and main practices, it's difficult to see the true face or essential nature of the Great Perfection of the Clear Light of the Buddhahood of Non-meditation. The Great Perfection in Yuthok's system - i.e. the Great Perfection pointing out instructions on the union of 'Cutting through Hardness' (trekchö) and 'Direct Crossing' (tögal), the 'Great Self-Liberation of Samsara-Nirvana' – is taught extremely clearly.

Nevertheless, wondering how I might benefit beginners who, still somewhat uninformed, had not fully mastered the capacities of hearing, reflecting, and meditating, I decided I would compile a small summary of the essential points. This would be published in four chapters and without too many sections*. It would include additional commentary on the preliminary practices of the Great Perfection, as well as a supplementary digest with complete instructions on Yuthok's own system of the Primordial Purity Cutting Through Hardness teachings and on the ultimate 'indirect' (esoteric) instructions of Direct Crossing and darkness retreat. May all and any misconceptions, impurities, confusions and incompletions in this text, dissolve into the invisible vast expanse (of the basic nature)!

*Volume One of Mirror of Light contains the first two chapters.

ལེའི་དང་པོ། སྔོན་འགྲོ།

སྔོན་འགྲོ་ནི་ནང་པའི་ཐེག་ཆེན་དང་རྡོ་རྗེ་ཐེག་པའི་རྩ་བའམ་རྨང་གཞི་ཡིན་པས། རྣལ་འབྱོར་པོ་མོ་ལས་དང་པོ་པ་རྣམས་ཀྱིས་སྔོན་འགྲོའི་དོན་ཡང་དག་པར་ཤེས་པ་དང་ཉམས་ལེན་མཐར་ཕྱིན་པ་ཞིག་གནང་རྒྱུ་ð་ཅང་གལ་ཆེ། དེ་ལ་རང་རྒྱུད་སྦྱངས་བྱེད་རྡོ་རྗེ་ཐེག་པའི་ཐུན་མོང་དང་ཐུན་མིན་སྔོན་འགྲོ་དང་ཁྱད་པར་གྱི་རྫོགས་ཆེན་གྱི་སྔོན་འགྲོ་བཅས་གཉིས་ཡོད་པ་ཡིན།།

དང་པོ། རྡོ་རྗེ་ཐེག་པ་སྤྱིའི་སྔོན་འགྲོ།

སྤྱིར་གསང་སྔགས་རྡོ་རྗེ་ཐེག་པའི་སྔོན་འགྲོ་ལ་ཐུན་མོང་དང་ཐུན་མིན་སྔོན་འགྲོ་གཉིས་བསྟན་པ་བཞིན། གཡུ་ཐོག་སྙིང་ཐིག་གི་སྔོན་འགྲོ་ལ་ཐུན་མོང་། ཐུན་མིན་དང་རྒྱུན་སྤྱོད་གསུམ་ལས།

ཐུན་མོང་སྔོན་འགྲོ་ལྔ་སྟེ། དལ་འབྱོར་རྙེད་དཀའ། ། ལོ་ལོའི་གཉེན་པོ་འཆི་བ་མི་རྟག་པ། ལས་རྒྱུ་འབྲས་དང་འཁོར་བའི་ཉེས་དམིགས་བཅས་བློ་ལྡོག་བཞི་དང་། གནས་སྐབས་དང་མཐར་ཐུག་གི་ཐར་བའི་ཕན་ཡོན་བཅས་ཐོས་ཞིང་བསམ་ནས་བོགས་ཐོན་པར་བྱ་བའི་ཐུན་མོང་སྔོན་འགྲོ་དང་།

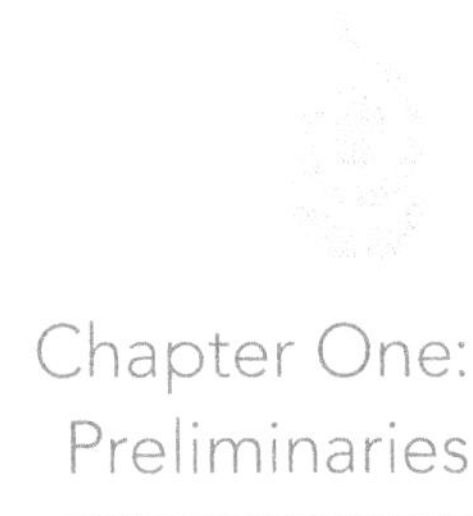

Chapter One: Preliminaries

Since the preliminary practices of Ngöndro are the root or foundation of Mahayana and Vajrayana Buddhism, it's very important that beginner yogis and yoginis understand the meaning of these preliminaries and practice them to perfection. With Ngöndro then, we have both the common and uncommon preliminaries of the Vajrayana, the Indestructible Vehicle that purifies one's own mind, and the special preliminary practices of the Great Perfection.

1) The General Vajrayana Preliminaries

In general, the preliminary practices of the Indestructible Vehicle of the Secret Mantra are presented as two-fold: the common and uncommon preliminaries. In the Yuthok Nyingthig system the preliminaries are three-fold: common, uncommon, and routine.

There are five common preliminaries:

- 'The Leisures and Resources that are Difficult to Find'
  (i.e. The benefits and freedoms of one's hard to come by human rebirth)
- 'Death and Impermanence that are the Remedy for Apathy'
  (the realization of death and impermanence that motivate one
  on the path)
- 'Action, Cause and Effect' (reflections on karma)
- 'The Disadvantages of Samsara' (the dis-satisfactoriness of conditioned
  existence)

These are the four contemplations that turn the mind (away from samsara and towards the Dharma). These, along with (the fifth) 'the benefits and advantages of temporary and ultimate release', are the common preliminaries which bring progress to one's practice when one hears about and reflects on them.

ཐུན་མིན་ཐེག་ཆེན་གྱི་སྔོན་འགྲོ་ལ། ས་དང་ལམ་ཐམས་ཅད་ཀྱི་རྨང་གཞི་སྐྱབས་འགྲོ། ཐེག་ཆེན་གྱི་སྨོན་འཇུག་གི་སེམས་བསྐྱེད་དང་ཚད་མེད་བཞི།
ཚོགས་བསགས་དང་སྡིག་སྒྲིབ་སྦྱོང་བྱེད་བསྟོད་ཕྱག རྒྱུད་ལ་ཡོན་ཏན་བསྐྱེད་བྱེད་མན་ངག།
ལུས་ཀྱི་སྒྲིབ་སྦྱོང་བསྐོར་བ།
ལུས་ངག་ཡིད་གསུམ་གྱི་སྡིག་སྒྲིབ་དང་བར་ཆད་འགལ་རྐྱེན་སྦྱོང་བྱེད་རྡོར་སེམས་དང་སྡུག་བསྔལ་ཞི་བྱེད་ཀུ་ས་ལི་བཅས་རྒྱུད་སྦྱོང་བའི་ཐབས་སམ་ཉམས་ལེན་བླ་ན་མེད་པ་རྣམས་ཞག་བདུན་ནམ་རྟགས་ཐོན་བར་དུ་བྱ་རྒྱུ་དང་།

རྒྱུན་སྤྱོད་སྔོན་འགྲོ་སྟེ། དགེ་འདུན་པ་དང་བཤེས་གཉེན་དང་རྒན་རིགས་ལ་བསྙེན་བཀུར།
དབུལ་པོ་རྣམས་ལ་ཟང་ཟིང་གི་སྦྱིན་པ་དང་། ནད་པ་རྣམས་ལ་སྨན་གྱི་སྦྱིན་གཏོང་།
ཆོས་མེད་རྣམས་ལ་ཆོས་ཀྱི་སྦྱིན་པ། ནད་ཅན་དང་དུད་འགྲོའི་འཆི་བ་བསླུ་བ།
ནང་པའི་ལྷ་ཁང་དང་དགོན་པ་སོགས་ཞིག་གསོ། ལམ་འཕྲང་བཅོས་པ།
རྒྱལ་བའི་བཀའ་སྒྲོག་པ་དང་ཚོགས་འཁོར་བསྐོར་བ་སོགས་མདོར་ན།
སེམས་པ་བཟང་ན་ས་དང་ལམ་ཡང་བཟང་ཞེས་པ་དང་།
རྗེ་གཡུ་ཐོག་པས་སྙིང་རྗེ་ཆེ་ན་གང་བྱས་ཆོས་སུ་འགྲོ། །
ཞེས་གསུངས་པ་བཞིན་དུས་རྟག་སྙིང་རྗེ་དང་སྙིང་རྗེ་ཆེན་པོས་གཞན་ཕན་འབའ་ཞིག་སྒྲུབ་རྒྱུ་ནི་རྒྱུན་འཁྱེར་གྱི་སྔོན་འགྲོ་ཡིན་པས།
དུས་ནམ་ཡང་བརྩོན་འགྲུས་ཀྱིས་བཏང་བར་མི་བྱ་བ་དང་།
གསོ་རིག་རྒྱུད་བཞིར་སྨན་པ་ཚོའི་ལྟ་བ་དབུ་མ་དང་བསྒོམ་པ་ཚད་མེད་བཞི་དང་སྤྱོད་པ་ཕར་ཕྱིན་དྲུག་གསུངས་པ་ནི་རྣལ་འབྱོར་པོ་མོ་ཚོའི་མི་ཚེའི་ཉམས་ལེན་ཁྱད་པར་དང་།
དེ་ལ་དྲན་པ་དང་ཤེས་བཞིན་བསྟེན་པར་བྱའོ།།

The uncommon preliminaries of the Mahayana, the Greater Vehicle, are:

Refuge that is the basis of every Ground and Path; the Four Immeasurables and the Arousing of Bodhichitta (the mind that aspires to enlightenment for the sake of all beings) which is the beginning and end of Mahayana; Praises and prostrations that support the accumulation of merit and protect against wrongdoings and obscurations; Mandala offerings which produce good qualities in one's mind-stream; Circumambulations that purify bodily obscurations; Vajrasattva practice, which purifies obstacles, impediments, and the wrongdoings and obscurations of body, speech, and mind; and the Pacification of Suffering Kusali (chod) practices - These are the means for purifying the mind-stream, or the unparalleled practices that ought to be done for seven days, or until signs (of accomplishment) appear.

The routine preliminaries are:

The veneration of the community of practitioners, the cherished spiritual guides and elders; the giving of material offerings to the poor; the dispensing of medicines to the sick; the giving of spiritual teachings to those who lack them; saving sick people and animals from death by means of ransom-offerings ('ritually seducing them away from death'); restoring Buddhist temples and monasteries and so on; improving dangerous roads and paths; expounding the teachings of the Buddha and organizing group practice celebrations and so on. In brief, as they say "If one's heart/mind is good, then the basis and path (of one's practice) will also be good." And as Venerable Yuthok said: *"If one's compassion is great, then whatever one does will be dharma"*. Since working with constant and great compassion to benefit others is what the daily preliminaries are all about, one should not give these up and should practice constantly with diligent effort. It states in the Four Medical Tantras of Sowa Rigpa that the doctor's View is that of Madhyamaka, their Meditation is that of the Four Immeasurables and their Conduct is that of Six Perfections. Yogis and yoginis ought to be mindul and understand this teaching and rely on it as their special life-practice.

དེང་དུས་འགའ་ཞིག་གིས་ཐུན་མོང་སྔོན་འགྲོ་ནི་གཞུང་ལུགས་ཙམ་ལས་བསྒོམ་རྒྱུ་མེད་པ་དང་། ཐུན་མིན་སྔོན་འགྲོ་འབུམ་ལྔ་སོགས་བསགས་ཚར་རྗེས། བསྐྱེད་རྫོགས་སོགས་ལ་སྔོན་འགྲོ་མི་དགོས་པ་དང་།

ཁྱད་པར་ཟབ་ཆོས་ཕྱག་ཆེན་དང་རྫོགས་ཆེན་ཉམས་ལེན་སྐབས་སུ་ཐུན་མིན་གྱི་སྔོན་འགྲོའི་རྒྱུན་བསྐྱང་མི་དགོས་པ་དང་།

ཡང་ན་ཕྱག་རྫོགས་ཉམས་ལེན་ལ་སྔོན་འགྲོས་རྒྱུད་སྦྱང་མི་དགོས་པར་འདོད་པ་ནི་ཉེན་ཁ་ཤིན་ཏུ་ཆེ་བས་ལོག་ལམ་ལ་ཞུགས་པར་མི་འཚལ་ཏེ།

འབྲི་གུང་འཇིག་རྟེན་གསུམ་མགོན་གྱིས་སྔོན་འགྲོ་དངོས་གཞི་ལས་ཀྱང་ཟབ་ཞེས་གསུངས་པ་ནི་རྟོགས་ལྡན་ཉམས་ལེན་པའི་དགོངས་པ་ཟབ་མོ་ཡིན་ནོ།།

གཉིས་པ། རྫོགས་ཆེན་སྔོན་འགྲོ།

དེ་ཡང་རྫོགས་ཆེན་སྔོན་འགྲོ་ལ་གཉིས་སྟེ། ཁྱད་པར་སྔོན་འགྲོ་དང་སྔོན་འགྲོ་དངོས་བཅས་གཉིས་ཡོད་ལ། ཁྱད་པར་སྔོན་འགྲོ་ནི་རུ་ཤན་ཏེ་ཕྱིའི་འཁོར་འདས་རུ་ཤན་དང་།

ནང་གི་རུ་ཤན་གནས་ཧུག་སྦྱང་བ་བཅས་གཉིས་དང་།

སྔོན་འགྲོ་དངོས་ལ་ལུས་ངག་ཡིད་གསུམ་གནད་དབབ།

ལྟ་སྟངས་གསུམ་སོར་བཞག་དང་སྒོ་གསུམ་སྦྱང་པ་བཅས་གསུམ་དུ་དབྱེ་བ་ཡིན།

དེ་ཡང་ཙུང་རྒྱས་ཙམ་གཤམ་དུ་བཤད་པར་བྱའོ།།

ཁྱད་པར་སྔོན་འགྲོ།

འོད་གསལ་རྫོགས་པ་ཆེན་པོ་ཉམས་སུ་ལེན་པ་ལ་ཁྱད་པར་གྱི་སྔོན་འགྲོ་གཉིས་སྟེ། ཕྱིའི་འཁོར་འདས་རུ་ཤན་དང་ནང་གི་རུ་ཤན་གནས་ཧུག་སྦྱང་བ་གཉིས་ལས།

These days, some people claim that the common preliminaries mean little more than meditating on mainstream scriptural traditions, and state that after one has accumulated five hundred thousand rounds of uncommon preliminary practices, one doesn't need preliminaries for the Creation and Completion stage practices. (They claim that) when it comes to the particularly profound teachings of Mahamudra, the Great Seal, and Dzogchen, the Great Perfection, one doesn't need to maintain the uncommon preliminaries. Or they say that for Mahamudra and Dzogchen one doesn't need to purify one's mind through Ngöndro. There is a very great danger that through these propositions people may be led unwittingly onto the wrong path. As Drigung Jigten Gonpo said, "the preliminaries are more profound than the main practices". This is the profound attitude (that informs) the practice of a realized person.

2) The Great Perfection Preliminaries

The preliminary practices of the Great Perfection are two-fold. There are both the special preliminaries and the 'actual' preliminaries. The special preliminaries involve the Rushen or 'Separating or Distinguising between' practices, of which there is both the outer 'Separating between Samsara and Nirvana' practice and the inner Rushen which purifies the six abodes. The actual preliminaries are differentiated into three categories: the striking of the essential points of body, speech, and mind; the three naturally-resting gazes; and the purifying of the three gates. These will be elaborated a little further below.

The Special Preliminaries:

There are two special preliminaries for the practice of the Great Perfection of Clear Light, the outer distinguishing between samsara and nirvana practice and the inner distinguishing which purifies the six abodes.

༧ ཕྱི་འཁོར་འདས་རུ་ཤན།

ཁྲིད་རྒྱས་པ་ཐོབ་པའི་རྣལ་འབྱོར་པོ་མོ་ཚོས་གནས་ཤིན་ཏུ་དབེན་པར་བླ་མའི་མན་ངག་ལྟར་འཁོར་འདས་རུ་ཤན་བྱ་སྟེ། ལུསཐལ་འགྱུར་ལས། འཁོར་འདས་རུ་ཤན་མ་དབྱེ་ན།། ཁམས་གསུམ་ལུས་ངག་ཡིད་ཀྱིས་ཀྱང་།། འབྲེལ་བ་ཆོད་པར་མི་འགྱུར་བས།། འཁོར་འདས་རུ་ཤན་དབྱེ་བར་བྱ།། ཞེས་གསུངས་པ་ལྟར།

ལུས་ཀྱིས་རིགས་དྲུག་གི་སྤྱོད་པ་འཁྲབ་པ་དང་། ངག་གིས་རིགས་དྲུག་གི་སྐད་སྒྲོག་པ།

ཡིད་ཀྱིས་རིགས་དྲུག་སོ་སོའི་ཚོར་བ་ཉོན་མོངས་བསམ་པ་སྟེ།

དམྱལ་བའི་དུག་ལྔ་སྡིག་སྒྲིབ་གྱི་འབྲས་བུ་ཚ་གྲང་སྡུག་བསྔལ། ཡི་དགས་ཀྱི་སེར་སྣ་བཀྲེས་སྐོམ་སྡུག་བསྔལ།

དུད་འགྲོའི་གཏི་མུག་མནར་གཅོད་ཀྱི་སྡུག་བསྔལ།

མིའི་མ་རིག་དུག་གསུམ་གྱིས་བསྐྱེད་པའི་སྐྱེ་རྒ་ན་འཆིའི་སྡུག་བསྔལ།

ལྷ་མ་ཡིན་གྱི་ཕྲག་དོག་དང་ཞེ་སྡང་དང་དམག་འཐབ་ཀྱི་སྡུག་བསྔལ།

ལྷ་ཡི་འདོད་ཆགས་འཆི་འཕོའི་སྡུག་བསྔལ་སོགས་མངོན་སུམ་ཡིན་སྙམ་དུ།

ལུས་ངག་ཡིད་གསུམ་གྱིས་སྦྱོང་ཞིང་གོམས་པར་བྱ་བ་སྟེ།

1) The outer distinguishing between samsara and nirvana practice:

In accordance with their gurus' direct instruction, yogis and yoginis who have obtained extensive instructions ought to perform the distinguishing between samsara and nirvana in a very secluded place as follows. As it states in the 'Body Consequence' (Lus Thal 'Gyur):

"One should distinguish between samsara and nirvana - if one doesn't one will not be able to sever the ties of the three realms of body, speech and mind."

With one's body, one acts out the behaviour of the (different kinds of beings) of the six realms; with one's speech, one shouts out the different kinds of calls or proclamations (they might make), and with one's mind, one reflects on the respective feelings and afflictive emotions of each of the six kinds of beings. Imagining that one directly perceives the sufferings of the six realms, one must use one's body, speech and mind to experience and familiarize oneself with each of these sufferings. Namely:

- Hell-beings' suffering of 'hot and cold', (the extremes of freezing and burning) which are the result of the wrongdoings and obscurations of the five poisons:
- Hungry ghosts' suffering of miserliness, hunger, and thirst
- Animals' suffering of mental dullness and brutal oppression
- Humans' suffering of birth, aging, sickness, and death, caused by the three poisons which are generated by un-awareness
- Demi-gods' suffering of jealousy, aggression and war-mongering
- Gods' suffering of sensual desire and (inevitable) death, transmigration and so on

མཁའ་འགྲོ་མ་མི་འགྱུར་དཔལ་སྒྲོན་གྱི་གསུངས་ཨ་ཏི་ཟབ་དོན་སྙིང་པོའི་ཁྲིད་དམིགས་ཟིན་བྲིས་ཀུན་བཟང་དགོངས་རྒྱན་ལས། "དེ་དག་ཆེ་ན་ཡང་རྩེད་འཇོའི་དབང་དུ་མ་སོང་བར་བྱས་ལ། དེ་དང་དེ་དངོས་ཡིན་སྙམ་པའི་གདུང་ཤུགས་དྲག་པོས་ལུས་ཀྱིས་སོ་སོའི་རྣམ་འགྱུར། ངག་གི་སྐད་བརྗོད། ཡིད་ཀྱིས་ཀྱང་དེ་དག་གི་སྡུག་བསྔལ་བློ་ལ་བླངས་ལ་ངེས་པར་རྒྱུད་ཐོག་ཏུ་ཉམས་སུ་མྱོང་བར་བསམ། དེ་ནས་སོ་སོའི་སྡུག་བསྔལ་བྱེད་ཤེས་ཀྱི་རང་ངོ་ལ་ཅེར་གྱིས་ལྟ། ཡང་རེས་འགའ་སངས་རྒྱས་ཞི་བ་དང་། ཁྲོ་བོའི་སྐུའི་རྣམ་འགྱུར་། ངག་གིས་ཆོས་ཀྱི་སྒྲ་དང་གསུང་དང་དབྱངས་དྲག་པོའི་གད་མོ་སྣ་ཚོགས་དང་། ཡིད་ཀྱིས་དེ་དག་གི་རྣམ་པ་ལམ་དུ་བྱས་ལ། ཡང་བྱེད་ཤེས་ཀྱི་རང་ངོ་ལ་ཚེར་གྱིས་བལྟ།

དེའང་རྩ་བར་ལུས་ངག་ཡིད་གསུམ་སོ་སོར་བྱ་བར་གསུངས་ཀྱང་།

བཤད་མ་ཐག་ཉིད་ཕྱག་ལེན་དུ་མཛད་པ་ཡིན་ཅིང་།

དེ་ལྟར་རུ་ཤན་དབྱེ་བར་དམིགས་ཀྱིས་འགྲོ་མ་ཁོམས་ན།

ཁྲིམ་དུ་དེ་ལྟ་བུའི་ཚུལ་ཡིད་ཡུལ་དུ་བསྒོམ་པས་ཀྱང་དོན་གྱི་གནད་ཚང་བ་ཡིན་ཅེས་ཞལ་རྒྱུན་དུ་གནང་ངོ་། དེ་སྦྱངས་པས་འབྱོངས་པའི་རྟགས་ནི་ལུས་ལ་ཆགས་ཞེན་དགག་སྒྲུབ་བཀྲེས་སྐོམ་མེད་པའི་ཉམས་འདུག་ན་ལུས་རུ་ཤན་ཕྱེད་པའོ།།

As explained in Dakini Mingyur Paldron's text, 'Samantabhadra's Mind-Ornament: Notes of Special Instruction on the Heart-Essence of the Profound Meaning of Ati':

"When (you practice) these, even if you haven't developed much capacity for theater or popular entertainments, being strongly overcome with the thought that this or that (suffering) is really happening, through each successive expression of body, each utterance of speech, and using your mind, imagine that these sufferings arise in your awareness and that you experience them definitively in your own mind-stream. Gaze directly then at the true and bare nature of what you have acted out and what you have come to know of each respective suffering. Moreover, having (acted out with one's body) the expressions of peaceful Buddhas in one moment and those of wrathful deity forms in the next, (having proclaimed) with your voice diverse forms of speech - dharma sounds, then mantric formulas (dharanis), and at other times fierce laughter melodies – and having brought all these manifested expressions onto the path with your mind, once more, successively behold the true face or nature of what it is that you feel and know (about these sufferings). As is taught in the root text, go through body, speech and mind successively, practice just as it's described there.

If you don't have the time or opportunity to 'distinguish the gap' by means of practices as described here, oral teachings affirm that even if one just visualizes everything as taught above at home, the basic significance or benefit of the practice will be entirely the same. The sign that one has purified oneself through practicing is if you experience meditative experiences devoid of desire and attachment, negation and affirmation, and hunger and thirst in your body - this is distinguishing the gap/difference (through) the body."

ཞེས་གསུངས་པ་བཞིན་དེང་དུས་ནི་མི་མེད་དབེན་གནས་ཁྱད་པར་ཅན་དུ་རུ་ཤན་སྦྱོང་དཀའ་བས་རང་ཁྱིམ་མམ་མཚམས་ཁང་དུ་དེ་ནི་བདུན་གཅིག་གམ་རྟགས་ཐོན་པར་བྱའོ།།

༢ ནང་གི་རུ་ཤན་ནམ་གནས་དྲུག་སྦྱོང་བ། འདས་རྗེས་ལས། ལུས་ནི་མ་རིག་རྒྱུས་བསྐྱེད་ཕྱིར།། རིགས་དྲུག་ས་བོན་ཉིད་དུ་གནས།། རིག་པ་སྐུ་གསུམ་དངོས་ཡིན་ཕྱིར།། སྐུ་གསུམ་ཡི་གེ་གསུམ་དུ་ཤར།། ཡི་གེ་རྩལ་སྦྱངས་རུ་ཤན་དབྱེ།། ཞེས་དང་།

ཀློང་གསལ་ལས་ཀྱང་། ནང་གི་འཁྲུལ་རྒྱུ་ཟད་བྱའི་ཕྱིར།། འཁོར་འདས་རུ་ཤན་ནང་ལྟར་དབྱེ།།” ཞེས་གསུངས་པ་བཞིན་དང་། ས་བོན་མ་སྦྱོགས་ན་སླར་ཡང་རིགས་དྲུག་གི་སྐྱེ་བའི་མྱུ་གུ་སྐྱེ་སྲིད་པས་ས་བོན་སྦྱོང་དགོས་པ་

Nowadays, seeing as it's difficult to go to an isolated place devoid of people specifically to train in rushen, one ought to do the practice in one's own home or in a retreat house for a full week. or until signs of accomplishment arise.

2) The inner distinguishing practice or 'the purifying of the six locations':

The Ati text 'After Passing Away' says:

"Concerning the body, in order to develop familiarity with non-recognition of rigpa (awareness, primordial nature), one must rest in the very nature of the seed syllables of the six realms; in order to (appreciate) the reality of the three kayas of awareness, the letters of the three kayas must shine forth threefold. Therefore, do the rushen practice that trains one to work with the creative energy of the syllables".

Also, as it says in the 'Clear Expanse':

"In order to exhaust the inner causes of illusory perception, distinguish the gap between samsara and nirvana internally," and "If the seed syllables are not burnt, then you will be reborn in samsara. Therefore you must burn the seed syllables of the six realms."

ཡིན་ཏེ། རིགས་དྲུག་གི་ས་བོན་གནས་ཚུལ་ནི། ཀློང་གསལ་ལས། སྤྱི་བོ་མགྲིན་པ་སྙིང་ག་དང་།། ལྟེ་བ་གསང་གནས་རྐང་མཐིལ་དུ།། ཨ་སུ་ནྲི་ཏྲི་པྲེ་དུ་གནས།། ཞེས་པས། སྦྱང་བྱ་ཡིག་དྲུག་ས་བོན་དྲུག རང་ལུས་ཀྱི་སྤྱི་བོར་ལྷ་ཡི་ས་བོན། ཨ་དཀར་པོའམ་སྐྱ་བོ། ལྷ་མ་ཡིན་གྱི་ས་བོན་མགྲིན་སུ་ལྗང་སེར། སྙིང་གར་མིའི་ས་བོན་ནྲི་སྔོ་སྐྱ། ལྟེ་བར་དུད་འགྲོའི་ས་བོན་ཏྲི་དམར་ནག། གསང་གནས་སུ་ཡི་དགས་ཀྱི་ས་བོན་པྲེ་ལྗང་ནག། རྐང་མཐིལ་གཉིས་ཀར་དམྱལ་བའི་ས་བོན་དུ་དུད་ཁ། སྦྱོང་བྱེད། འབྲུ་གསུམ་སྟེ། སྤྱི་བོ་བདེ་ཆེན་འཁོར་ལོར་རྒྱལ་བ་ཐམས་ཅད་ཀྱི་སྐུའི་བྱིན་རླབས་ཨོཾ་དཀར་པོ། མགྲིན་པར་རྒྱལ་བ་ཐམས་ཅད་ཀྱི་གསུངས་ཀྱི་བྱིན་རླབས་ཨ་དམར་པོ་དང་སྙིང་ཀ་ཆོས་ཀྱི་འཁོར་ལོ་རྒྱལ་ཀུན་གྱི་ཐུགས་ཀྱི་བྱིན་རླབས་ཧཱུཾ་སྔོན་པོ་བཀྲག་དང་ལྡན་པ་བསྒོམ་ཞིང་།

Concerning the location (in the body) of these seed-syllables of the six classes of beings, the 'Clear Expanse' says:

"Place the syllables AH (ཨ) SU (སུ) NRI (ནྲི) TRI (ཏྲི) DRE (དྲེ) and DU (དུ) at the crown, in the throat-center, in the heart-center, in the navel, at the secret-abode (i.e. genitals), and in the soles of the feet respectively."

One purifies oneself with the six purification syllables and seeds of the six (realms of beings as follows):

- At the crown of one's head, purify with the seed-syllable of the god-realm, a white or pale off-white AH (ཨ)
- In the throat-center, with the seed-syllable of the demi-god realm, a greenish-yellow SU (སུ)
- In the heart-center, with the seed-syllable of the human-realm, a pale, light blue NRI (ནྲི)
- In the navel, with the seed-syllable of the animal-realm, a dark red TRI (ཏྲི)
- At the genitals, with the seed-syllable of the hungry ghosts, a dark green DRE (དྲེ)
- In the soles of both feet, with the seed-syllable of the hell-being realms, a smoke-coloured DU (དུ)

Meditate on the three 'seed' syllables, radiating brilliantly, as follows:

- In the crown chakra of great bliss, meditate on the white OM (ༀ) of the blessing power of the Body of all the Buddhas
- In the throat-center, the red AH (ཨ) of the blessing-power of the Speech of all the Buddhas
- In the heart center in the absolute-reality chakra, the blue HUNG (ཧཱུྃ) of the blessing-power of the Mind of all the Buddhas

རྡོ་བཟླས་ཀྱི་དང་རིགས་དྲུག་ས་བོན་ཐམས་ཅད་རྩ་མེད་བསྲེག་ཅིང་བྱིན་བརླབས་བདུད་རྩིས་ལུས་ཡོངས་གང་བསྒོམ་པ་བསྙེན་པ་འབུམ་གཅིག་གམ་བདུན་ནམ། ཡང་ན་བདུན་གཅིག་དང་རྟགས་མ་ཐོན་བར་དུ་བྱའོ།། དགོས་པ་ནི་ལུས་ངག་ཡིད་གསུམ་གྱི་སྡིག་སྒྲིབ་དག་ཅིང་ཞེན་པ་ལྡོག་པ་དང་། མཐར་ཐུག་དགོས་པ་ནི་སྒོ་གསུམ་སྐུ་གསུམ་དུ་གྲོལ་བའི་རྟེན་འབྲེལ་ཡིན་ནོ།།

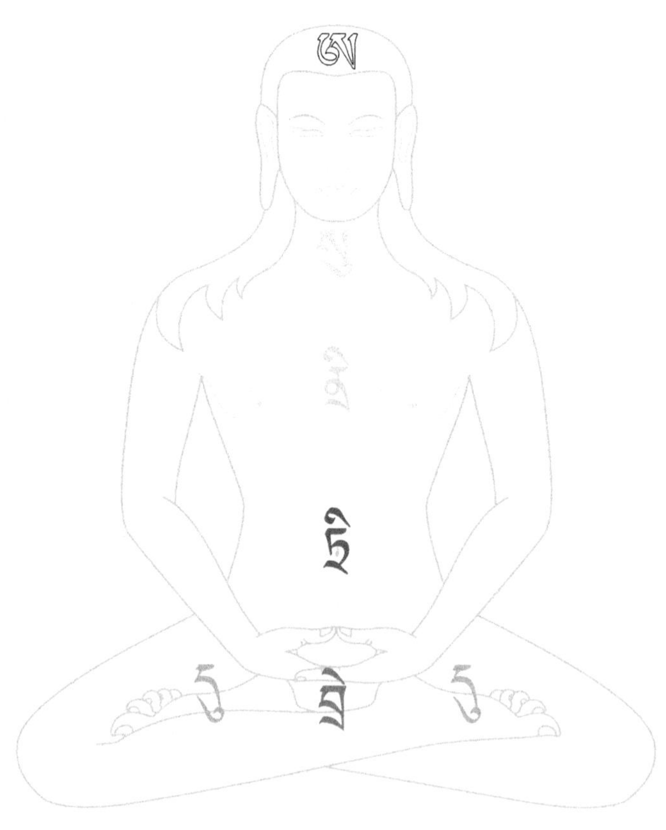

Inner Rushen to purify the six abodes

One ought to meditate and recite (OM AH HUNG) in the style of 'vajra recitation', imagining that the seed-syllables of the six realms are completely burned up and consumed from the root and that the body is filled with nectar and blessing-power. Do this 100,000 times, 700,000 times, for a week, or however long it takes until signs of accomplishment appear*.

The (temporary) purpose of these practices is to purify the wrongdoings and obscurations of the Body, Speech, and Mind, and to eliminate attachments. Their ultimate aim is to (produce) the auspicious connections that liberate the three gates and three bodies.

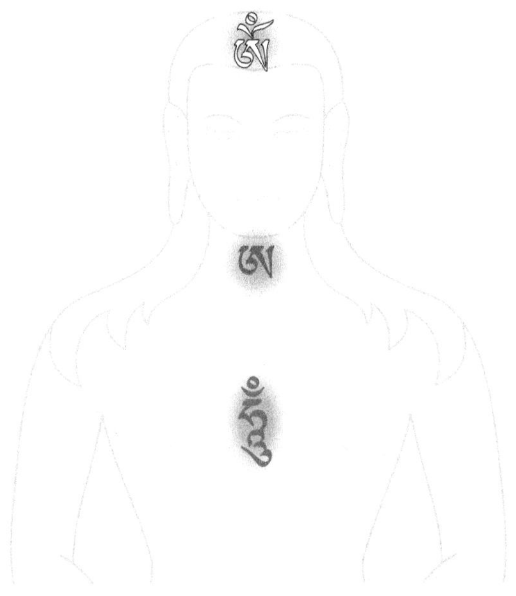

The three seed syllables representing the enlightened Body, Speech, and Mind of all the Buddhas

*The signs of accomplishment of the Inner Rushen practice are: dreaming of having a shower, cleaning dirt, burning negativities, finding crystals, the body becoming light and transparent, etc.

སྔོན་འགྲོ་དངོས།

འདི་ལ་སྒོ་གསུམ་ངལ་གསོའི་ངང་དུ་གནད་དབབ་པ་དང་།

མིག་གི་ལྟ་སྟངས་འོག་བར་གྱེན་དུ་སོར་བཞག་དང་། སྒོ་གསུམ་སྐེ་ལུས་རྡོ་རྗེ།

ངག་སྔགས་དང་སེམས་ངོ་བལྟས་ནས་སྦྱོང་བ་བཅས་སྒོ་གསུམ་སྔོན་འགྲོ་བཅས་གསུམ་རིམ་པ་ལྟར་སྦྱོང་དགོས་སོ།།

༡ གནད་དབབ།

ལུས་ངག་ཡིད་གསུམ་གྱི་ཕྱིའི་རྩ་ཤན་སྦྱོང་རྗེས་ལུས་ཐང་ཤ་ཆད་པ་དང་། ངག་འཛེར་ལ་འགག་པ་དང་། སེམས་འགྱུ་བ་སྤྱུན་ཐག་ཏུ་གྱུར་བ་ན།

ལུས་གནད་གང་རུང་གིས་ལུས་འགྱུལ་མེད་རོ་ལྟར་ཉལ་ནས་ངལ་གསོ་བ་དང་།

ངག་སྨྲ་མེད་པི་ཝང་སྐུད་ཆད་ལྟ་བུའི་ངང་དུ་ངག་གི་ངལ་གསོ་བ་དང་།

སེམས་བསམ་མེད་ལྐུགས་པ་ལྟ་བུ་སེམས་ཀྱི་ངལ་གསོ་བར་བྱའོ།།

༢ སོར་བཞག

རང་དོན་མཐར་ཕྱིན་ཆེད་དུ་ཉན་ཐོས་ཀྱི་ལྟ་སྟངས། གཞན་དོན་ལྷུན་གྱིས་འགྲུབ་ཕྱིར་བྱང་སེམས་ཀྱི་བལྟ་སྟངས། འཁོར་བ་སྒྲོལ་བྱེད་དུ་ཁྲོ་བོའི་བལྟ་སྟངས་སྟེ། མཁའ་འགྲོ་མ་མི་འགྱུར་དཔལ་སྒྲོན་གྱི་གསུངས་ཨ་ཧི་ཟབ་དོན་སྙིང་པོའི་ཁྲིད་དམིགས་ཟིན་བྲིས་ཀུན་བཟང་དགོངས་རྒྱུན་ལས།

The Actual Preliminaries

Here one must train in the 'three gates' preliminaries according to three stages: through striking the essential points by resting the three gates; through resting in one's natural state via the downwards, straight-ahead, and upwards gazes; and by means of perceiving and purifying* the three gates – body, speech, and mind - as vajra, mantra, and (ultimate) essence, respectively.

Stage 1: Striking or alighting upon the essential points

After one has trained in the outer rushen procedures of the three-fold Body, Speech, and Mind, when, in a common theme, one's body has become strained and worn out, when one's voice has become hoarse, and when one's mind has become overtaken with fleeting, flashing thoughts, lie down like a dead body in whatever position you like; relax your voice like a silent lute whose strings have been cut; and let your mind rest without thinking, like some kind of simpleton.

Stage 2: Resting naturally in one's own state

(Here there is the) the Shravaka gaze for the sake of one's self-perfection, the Bodhisattva gaze for the spontaneous realization of benefit for others, and the Wrathful gaze for the sake of liberation from Samsara. In Dakini Mingyur Paldron's Ati text, 'Samantabhadra's Mind-Ornament: Notes for Special Instructions on the Essence of the Profound Meaning', the rationale of these gazes is explained in more detail:

*The Tibetan word སྦྱང (jang) has the dual meaning of to purify and to train.

"དེའང་དང་པོ་ཉན་ཐོས་ཀྱི་ལྟ་སྟངས་ནི། སྟན་བདེ་བ་ལ་ལུས་གནད་ཆོས་བདུན་དང་ལྡན་པས།
མིག་སྣ་རྩེར་ཕབ་ལ།
མིག་འབྲས་མི་བསྒྱུར་ཞིང་རྫི་མ་ཐབ་ཐིབ་མི་བྱ་བར་ཟིམ་བུའི་མིག་གི་ལྟ་སྟངས་ལྷོད་དེ་ཅེ་རེ་བཞག ངག་རླུང་དནད་སོ་མར་བཞག སེམས་ཀྱི་གནད་སྤྱར་འདས་ཀྱི་རྗེ་མི་གཅོད། འདི་འདྲ་ཤིག་བྱས་བསམ་པ་དང་། ཕྱིས་མ་འོང་པའི་སྔུན་མི་བསུ་སྟེ་འདི་འདྲ་ཞིག་བྱེད་བསམ་པ་དང་། ད་ལྟ་འདི་ཡིན་འདི་མིན་སོགས་སེམས་ལ་ལས་གང་ཡང་མི་འཆོལ་བར་རྟོག་ཚོགས་ཀྱི་ཚོལ་འཕྲོ་ཐམས་ཅད་བ ཅད་དེ་ད་ལྟའི་རིག་པ་སྐད་ཅིག་མ་དེ་ཁའི་རང་ངོ་ལ་ཅེ་རེ་ལྟ་བཞག་བྱ།

དེ་ལ་གོམས་པ་ན། གཉིས་པ་བྱང་སེམས་ཀྱི་ལྟ་སྟངས་ནི།
ལུས་གནད་སྤྱར་ལྟར་ལས་མིག་གནས་ཐད་ཀའི་བར་སྣང་ལ་ལྟ་སྟངས་ཧར་རེ་གཏད། ངག་གནད་རླུང་སོ་མ་བཞག
སེམས་གནད་སྤྱར་བཞིན་དུས་གསུམ་གྱི་རྣམ་རྟོག་སྤྲངས་ལ་བཟོ་མེད་དུ་བཞག་གོ།

དེ་ལ་གོམས་པ་ན། གསུམ་པ་ཁྲོ་བོའི་ལྟ་སྟངས་ནི། ལུས་གནད་སྤྱར་ལྟར་རམ་རོལ་བའི་སྟབས་སམ། ཧག་གིས་ལངས་ལ་སེམས་གནས་ཆའི་ཚུགས་མ་ཞིག་པའི་ངང་ནས་མིགས་གི་ལྟ་སྟངས་བར་སྣང་བ་གྱེན་དུ་བགྲད་དེ་གཡས་གཡོན་དུ་ཧྲིག་ཧྲིག་བསྒྱུར་ཞིང་།
གོམས་པ་གྱ་ཚོམས་སུ་དོར་ལ་ངག་ཏུ་ཧ་ཧ་ཧི་ཧི་ཧུཾ་ཧུཾ་ཕཊ་ཕཊ་ཟེར་བ་ལ་སོགས་པའི་ཁྲོ་བོའི་གད་རྒྱངས་ཀྱི་སྒྲ་སྐད་བརྗོད་ཅིང་གནས་ཆའི་ཚུགས་མ་ཞིག་པར་སློབ་ཅིང་རིག་པ་ཧུར་ཕྱུང་སྟེ།

"So, first there's the Shravaka gaze: sitting comfortably, adopting the seven-point posture of Vairocana, bring your gaze down to the tip of your nose. Without moving your eyeballs or fluttering your eyelashes, stare fixedly and in a relaxed way with your eyes slightly open. Rest the vital points of speech-and-wind in a state of natural freshness, don't let your vital-point of mind chase after what is dead and gone. Don't welcome thoughts of the future and what is in front of you, do not sit thinking 'now, this is that or this isn't that' and so on. Thinking thus, without confusing your mind with any activity whatsoever, and having cut all searching and scattered thought patterns, remain gazing directly at your own nature, which is nothing other than awareness of the present moment.

Then, when you become used to that, there is the second, Bodhisattva gaze. With your body positioned as before, gaze straight ahead directly into space. Rest the vital points of speech and the winds in natural freshness. Abandoning conceptual thoughts of the three times, past, present and future as before, rest in uncontrived awareness.

Then when you become accustomed to that, there's the third way of looking, the Wrathful gaze. With your body posture like before, or else in the 'reveling posture'* or standing up straight and suddenly, establish yourself in a state of mental stability. Open your eyes wide and gaze upwards into space, and then move your eyes side-to-side, left and right. Stepping forward quickly and without hesitation, make loud, carrying cries of wrathful laughter, HA HA HI HI HUNG HUNG PHET PHET!, and so on. Train in establishing a foundation of mental stability and intensely awaken one's awareness (of the natural state).

* Refers to the posture of being seated with one leg tucked in and one leg slightly out in the way that Padmasambhava is commonly portrayed.

ཨོཾ

ཨ

ཧཱུྃ

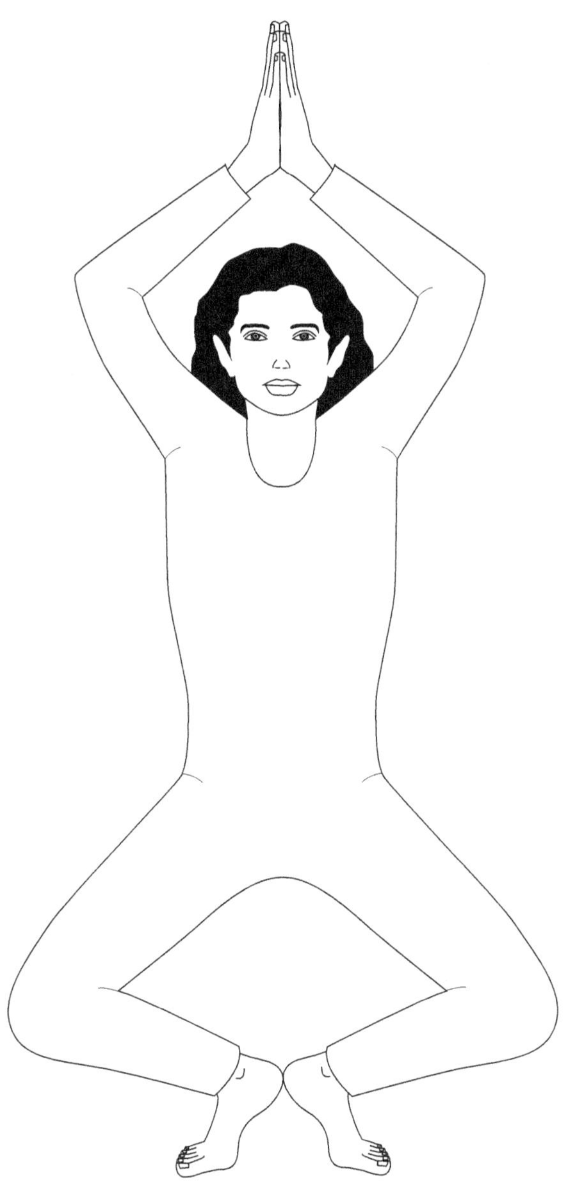

The Vajra Posture:
for the Body Training preliminary practice

རྩལ་སྦྱངས་པས་རང་བྱུང་རང་ཤར་སྤྲོས་བྲལ་བསལ་བཞག་མེད་པ་ཆུ་རླབས་རྒྱ་མཚོར་ཐིམ་པ་ལྟར་འགྱུར་བས། དེས་ནི་སྣང་རྐྱེན་ཇི་ཙམ་མང་བ་ཙམ་དུ་སྟོང་ཉིད་ཀྱི་ཡེ་ཤེས་ཀུན་གའཕེལ་བར་འགྱུར་ཏེ།

བུད་ཤིང་མང་ན་མེ་ལྕེ་མང་བ་བཞིན་ནོ། དེ་ལྟར་བགྲིས་པས་ཉན་ཐོས་ཀྱིས་རྣམ་པར་རྟོག་པ་འཇོམས་ཤིང་། སྒོ་གསུམ་གནས་པར་བྱེད། བྱང་སེམས་ཀྱིས་རྣམ་རྟོག་རགས་པ་འཇོམས་ཤིང་སྒོ་གསུམ་གནས་པར་བྱེད། ཁྲོ་བོས་རྣམ་རྟོག་སྦྲོམ་པོ་འཇོམས་ཤིང་བརྟན་པ་ལས་གྲོལ་བར་བྱེད་པའི་དགོས་པ་ཡོད་དོ།།

ཞེས་རྒྱས་པ་རྒྱུ་མཚན་དང་གསུངས་སོ།།

སྒོ་གསུམ་སྔོན་འགྲོ་ལ།

སྒོ་གསུམ་སྔོན་འགྲོ་ལ་ལུས་སྦྱང་སྟེ་ལུས་རྡོ་རྗེར་སྦྱང་པ། ངག་སྦྱང་སྟེ་ངག་ཧཱུྃ་དུ་སྦྱང་བ། སེམས་སྦྱང་སྟེ་བྱུང་གནས་འགྲོ་གསུམ་སྦྱང་བ་གསུམ་ལས།

ལུས་སྦྱང་ནི།

ལུས་རྡོ་རྗེར་སྦྱངས་པ་ནི།

ལག་གཉིས་སྤྱི་བོར་སྦྱར་ཤིང་རྐང་གཉིས་རྟིང་པར་ལྡངས་ཏེ་ལུས་རྡོ་རྗེའི་འདུག་སྟངས་སྦྱང་པ་སྟེ། རྒྱལ་དབང་ལྔ་པ་ཆེན་མོའི་རིགས་འཛིན་ཞལ་ལུང་ལས། "ལུས་ཀྱི་སྔོན་འགྲོ་རྡོ་རྗེའི་འདུག་སྟངས་དང་། ཁ་དོག་སྔོན་པོ་རྩེ་ལྔ་པ་མེ་འབར་བའི་འོད་ཟེར་གྱིས་ནད་གདོན་སྡིག་སྒྲིབ་བསྲེགས་ཏེ་རྡོ་རྗེ་ཁོང་སྟོང་དུ་བསམས་པས་ལུས་ཁང་རུལ་ཞིག་པ་ལྟ་བུ་དང་ཁོལ་བུར་ན་བ་དང་དྲོད་སྐྱེ་བ་དང་སེམས་མི་རྟོག་པའི་ངང་ལ་གནས་པ་ནི་ཚད་དོ། དགོས་པ་གསུམ་ནི་ཐུན་མོང་ལུས་ཀྱི་སྒྲིབ་པ་འདག བར་ཆས་ཞི ཞེན་པ་ལྡོག ཁྱད་པར་ལུས་འཁོར་བར་མི་ལྡུང་ཞིང་སྤྲུལ་སྐུར་གྲོལ། མཐར་སྐུ་རྡོ་རྗེའི་ཀློང་དུ་མྱ་ངན་ལས་འདའོ།།" ཞེས་གསུངས་སོ།།

By virtue of having cultivated one's creative potency, one will become like a wave merging into the ocean, arising and appearing spontaneously of one's own accord, unembellished, neither trying to hold onto anything nor cast it away. In this way, however much appearances multiply, so shall the wisdom of emptiness increase. When firewood increases flames increase in kind. Having acted in this way, by means of the Shravaka gaze all discursive thoughts will be vanquished and you will abide in the three gates. By means of the Bodhisattva gaze coarse discursive thoughts will be vanquished and you will abide in the three gates. By means of the Wrathful gaze rough ('thick') discursive thoughts will be vanquished and one will be liberated from the (illusion) of the permanence or solidity (of appearances).

Stage 3: The Preliminary Practices of the Three Gates:

The preliminaries of the three gates are three-fold, and includes: the training of Body, namely, training/purifying through the vajra-posture; the training of Speech, or training/purifying through HUNG, and the training of the Mind, known as the training/purifying by means of arising, abiding, and passing away.

a) Body Training:

With the 'training through the vajra body' one purifies oneself through the vajra posture, which involves placing both one's hands on the crown of one's head and lifting up both of one's heels (and balancing on one's toes etc.). As is explained in the Great and Victorious Fifth (Dalai Lama's) 'Oral Transmissions of the Vidyadharas (Awareness Holders)':

"The body-preliminary of the vajra posture entails imagining one's body as the cavity of a five-pronged, blue vajra of blazing clear-light that burns up sickness and (demonic) provocations, wrongdoings and obscurations. Thinking of one's body as a ruined, empty building, and (feeling) as if it's inflamed or irritated as if with sickness and that it produces heat, one abides in a state of non-conceptuality. There are three rationales for the practice: In general, it purifies obscurations and pacifies obstacles of the body and eliminates its attachments. In particular it prevents the body from falling into samsara and liberates one's body into an emanation body. Ultimately, it causes the body to pass beyond suffering into the Vajra-expanse (i.e. the profundity of the basic space of being, etc)."

ངག་སྦྱོང་ནི།

ངག་གི་སྒོ་ནས་ཧཱུྃ་སྦྱོང་ལ། རྒྱས་འདེབས། རྩལ་སྦྱོངས། མཉེན་བཙལ། ལམ་ཞུགས་བཅས་བཞི་ལ་བསླབ་པ་སྟེ།

དང་པོ་རྒྱས་འདེབས་པ་ནི། ཕྱི་སྣང་བ་དང་ནང་རང་ལུས་ལ་རྒྱས་འདེབས་པ་ཡིན་ཏེ། རྒྱལ་དབང་ལྔ་བ་ཆེན་མོའི་རིགས་འཛིན་ཞལ་ལུང་ལས། "དང་པོ་རྒྱས་འདེབས་ནི། སོ་དང་མཆུ་མ་རེག་ཙམ་དུ་རླུང་། ཞེས་པ།

ཧཱུྃ་གསུམ་གཅིག་ཏུ་བསྲེས་ལ་ཧཱུྃ་གི་གླུ་སྙན་ལ་རིང་བ་བླངས་པས་སྣང་བ་ཐམས་ཅད་ཧཱུྃ་སྤྱོན་དུ་རོང་རོང་མེར་མེར་ཡོད་པར་བསམས་པ་ནི་ཕྱི་སྣང་བ་ལ་རྒྱས་གདབ་པ་སྟེ་ཕྱི་ཧཱུྃ་དུ་རོང་ངེ་ཤར་བ་ནི་ཚད་དོ།། ཕྱིའི་ཧཱུྃ་དེ་དག་ཁ་དང་སྣའི་སྒོར་ཞུགས་ཏེ།

ལུས་ཀྱི་ནང་གི་ཧཱུྃ་གིས་མེར་ཁེངས་སྙམ་པ་ནི་ནང་ཕུང་པོ་རྒྱས་གདབ་པ་སྟེ་ལུས་གང་བ་དང་མི་བདེ་སྙམ་པ་ཚད་དོ།། དགོས་པ་ནི། ཕྱི་ནང་གི་སྣང་བ་ཐམས་ཅད་རང་བཞིན་མེད་པར་འགྱུར་རོ།།

b) Speech Training:

The purification of the Speech gate through the HUNG syllable is taught in four stages: applying the seal, training/purifying the creative potency, seeking the remedy, and entering the path.

i) The first, the 'applying the seal' practice, refers to the sealing of outer appearances and the inside of one's own body. As the Great and Victorious Fifth puts it in the 'Oral Transmissions of the Awareness-Holders':

"Firstly, the 'applying the seal' practice refers to the following: with one's teeth and lips just barely touching (i.e. slightly open), one unites one's vital energy (rlung), one's awareness (shes pa) and the HUNG together as one. By intoning a long, melodious HUUUUUNG and imagining all appearances as scintillating blue HUNG syllables, the seal will be applied to outer appearances, and outer (reality) will manifest as scintillating HUNG syllables. Then, after those outer HUNG syllables enter one's mouth and nostrils, one imagines that the inside of one's body is filled with the fire of the HUNG syllables. Imagining that one's body is uncomfortably saturated with this fire, one applies the seal to one's inner psycho-physical constituents.

The purpose of this practice is to transform all inner and outer appearances into emptiness, (i.e. their actual state 'devoid self-nature', lacking any inherent or independent existence).

Body Training (with Vajra Posture) and Speech Training (with the syllable HUNG).

གཉིས་པ་རྩལ་སྦྱངས་པ་ནི། ཧཱུྃ་གིས་སྤྲོ་སྡོད་དང་ནང་ལུས་འབྱུག་པ་ཡིན་ཏེ།
ཧཱུྃ་དྲག་ལ་དར་དང་ལྡན་པ་བརྗོད་ཅིང་ཧཱུྃ་མཐིང་ནག་མེ་འབར་བ་དེས་རི་ར་བ་ཁང་ཁྱིམ་ཐམས་
ཅད་ཕར་ཐལ་ཚུར་ཐལ་དུ་ཕུག་སྟེ་ཁྲོལ་མ་བཞིན་སོང་བར་བསམ་ལ།
ཕྱིའི་རྩལ་ཏེ་ཕྱིའི་ཡུལ་ཁྲལ་ཁྲོལ་དུ་སོང་སྙམ་བྱེད་པ་ནི་ཚད་དོ།།
ཧཱུྃ་དེས་རང་གི་ལུས་ཁྲོལ་མ་བཞིན་བཏང་བར་བསམ་པ་ནི་ནང་གི་རྩལ་ཏེ་ཆུ་ཟླ་ལྟར་སྣང་བ་
ཚད་དོ། དགོས་པ་ནི།
ཕྱི་ནང་གི་ཆོས་རྗེས་བཅས་སུ་སྣང་བ་ཐམས་ཅད་འོད་གསལ་འཇའ་ཚོན་ལྟར་གྲོལ་བར་འགྱུར་
རོ།།

གསུམ་པ་མཉེན་བཙལ་བ་ནི། ཧཱུྃ་ཤིང་བུར་ཀྲུས་འདེབས་པ་ཡིན་ཏེ།
རང་གི་མདུན་དུ་ཤིང་བུ་ཁྲུ་གང་བ་ཞིག་བཙུགས་པ་ལ་ཤེས་པ་གཏད་དེ་ཧཱུྃ་རིང་བར་བརྗོད་
པས་ཧཱུྃ་གི་ཐག་པ་ནར་ར་ར་སོང་སྟེ་ཤིང་ལ་དཀྲིས་ནས་སྟེང་དུ་ཡེར་རེ་འདུག་པ་ལ་མཉམ་པར་
བཞག ཡང་ནར་ར་ར་གྲོལ་ཏེ་ཚུར་བྱུང་ནས་སྙིང་གར་གནས་པར་བསམ།
ཡང་ན་ཤིང་བུའི་རྩེ་མོར་སླེབས་པ་དང་།
རྩ་བར་མར་ཕྱུངས་ཀྱིས་བབད་ཏེ་ཧཱུྃ་རྣམས་ཁྲོམ་ཚོགས་སུ་སྤྱོ་རོང་དེ་ཡོད་པར་བསམ། ཡང་ན་
ན་ར་ར་ཤིང་བུ་ལ་དཀྲིས། ཡང་ཤིག་པ་སོགས་ལ་བསླབ།
ཤེས་པ་གང་གཏད་དུ་ལྷམ་མེར་སྡོད་སྙམ་པ་ནི་ཚད་དོ།།
འདིའི་དུས་སུ་སྐྱེས་པ་རླུང་སྣ་བུག་གཡས་དང་བུད་མེད་ཡིན་ན་སྣ་བུག་གཡོན་ནས་འདྲེན་པ་
ནི་གནད་ཡིན་ནོ།། དེས་དམིགས་པ་གཞན་དུ་བསྒྱུར་ཐུབ་པའི་དགོས་པ་ཡོད་དོ།།

ii) The second practice of 'purifying the creative potency' refers to the piercing of the outer world and inner-body by means of HUNG. Having uttered HUNG! with a fierce roar, one imagines that one's house, the mountains surrounding and enclosing it, everything (in the world) has been pierced by blazing blue-black HUNG syllables that pass back and forth through everything, perforating (all existence) like a sieve. The outwardly directed creative force entails imagining that outer objects have been thoroughly perforated. (Conversely) by imagining that the inside of one's body has been pierced like a sieve by the HUNG syllables, the inner creative potency appears like the reflection of the moon in water."

"The purpose of the practice is to effect the liberation of all outer and inner phenomena which appear as corporeal things as rainbow-coloured clear light."

iii) "The third practice of 'seeking the remedy' is the applying of the seal to the HUNG stick. Plant a wooden stick of about one cubit's length (i.e. from the elbow to the tip of the middle finger) in front of you and focus your awareness firmly on it. Uttering an extended HUUUUUUNG send forth a string of HUNG syllables straight in front of you. These wrap around the stick and then, resting (your focus), luminous and open, atop the stick, remain in equanimity. Release the HUNG syllables once more in a straight line back in the direction they came, and imagine that they come to dwell in one's heart center. Or, alternatively, imagine that once the HUNGs reach the top of the stick, they descend to the base of the stick in a pile, and then gather together in a blue mass. Or else, having wrapped the syllables straight around the stick, train (like this) again and imagine that regardless of where one directs one's awareness it remains blazing and radiant."

"When you (do this practice), it's very important that you draw in the rlung through your right nostril if you're a man and through your left if you're a woman. In this way, you will be able to shift the object of your concentration."

བཞི་བ་ལམ་དུ་གཞུག་པ་ནི། ཧཱུྃ་ཕྱོགས་སུ་འགྲོ་བའི་དམིགས་སྦྱང་སྟེ།
རྒྱལ་དབང་ལྔ་པ་ཆེན་མོའི་རིགས་འཛིན་ཞལ་ལུང་ལས།
“རང་གི་མདུན་དུ་ཤིང་བུ་ཁྲུ་གང་བ་ཞིག་བཙུགས་པའམ་བསམ་ལ་ཧཱུྃ་ཞེས་བརྗོད་པས་སྙིང་ག་ནས་སེམས་ཀྱི་ངོ་བོ་ཧཱུྃ་ཞིག་བྱུང་། ཤིང་བུ་དེའི་རྩེར་ཡེར་རེ་བཞག ཡང་ཧཱུྃ་ཞེས་རང་གི་སྙིང་གར་ཐིལ་གྱིས་བྱུང་། དེ་ལྟར་ཕར་འགྲོ་ཚུར་ཡོང་ལ་ཤེས་པ་གཏད།
ཡང་ན་ཏང་གནས་པའི་ཨ་ཡུལ་ཐམས་ཅད་རི་ར་བ་ཁང་ཁྱིམ་སོགས་མེད་པར་ཁ་དོག་ལྗང་གུ་མེ་ལོང་གི་ངོས་ལྟར་འཇམ་པ་ཞིག་བསམ།
དེའི་སྟེང་དུ་སྙིང་ག་ནས་ཧཱུྃ་སྔོན་པོ་ཁྲུ་ཚད་ཙམ་པ་མདུན་ནས་ཕར་གསེགས་འགྲོས་ལྟ་བུའི་ལམ་ཕར་འཕྱོག་ཚུར་འཕྱོགས་ལ་རི་དང་ས་མཚམས་མ་ཟད་ཀྱི་བར་དུ་ཁྱིན་པར་བསམས་ལ་ཧཱུྃ་རིང་བར་བརྗོད། ཕ་རོལ་ཏུའང་མཐའ་མེད་མེད་པར་ཁྱིན་པ་ལ་སེམས་གཏད། དེ་བཞིན་ཕྱོགས་གཞན་ལ་སྦྱོར། དེས་དགའ་བ་དང་སྐྱི་བ་བ་སོགས་བྱུང་བ་ནི་ཉམས་སྐྱེས་པའི་ཚད་དོ།། དེས་ལུས་ངག་གི་ལྷ་སྲེལ་དུ་ཚུད་པའི་དགོས་པ་ཡོད་དོ།། སྤྱིའི་དགོས་པ་གསུམ་ནི། ཐུན་མོང་དག་སྒྲིག་འདུག་ཅིང་ཡོན་ཏན་ཐོབ་མངོན་ཞེན་ལྡོག
ཁྱད་པར་དག་འཁོར་བར་མི་ལྟུང་ཞིང་ཡོངས་སྐུར་གྲོལ། མཐར་གསུང་རྡོ་རྗེའི་ཀློང་དུ་སྨྲ་དན་ལས་འདའོ།། ཞེས་གསུངས་སོ།།

iv) The fourth practice of 'entering the path' refers to training/purifying one's attention as it goes toward the HUNG. The Great and Victorious Fifth explains in the 'Oral Transmissions of the Awareness-Holders':

"Erecting a wooden stick of one cubit's length in front of you and reflecting on it, say 'HUNG' and imagine that from one's heart-center a HUNG syllable of one's own heart-mind essence arises. Rest your awareness at the top of the stick, in perfect openness and clarity. Saying HUNG again, (the syllable) arises fully-formed in your heart-center. In that way, focus awareness on this back and forth (of thoughts etc). Or else, imagine then that all locations, — the mountains, enclosures, your home and so on are no more, and are smooth like the surface of a green-coloured mirror.

In addition, as you intone an extended HUUUUNG, imagine that from about one cubit's distance in front of the blue HUNG in your heart-center a slanting path flows outwards, twisting and turning hither and thither between not only mountains but also borderlands. Fix your attention on the far end of the path, going off endlessly (into the distance). In the same way, extend the path in other directions. The joy, arisings and so on born of this practice constitute meditative experiences arising in one's mental-continuum.

The point of this practice is to expand the path of body and speech. "There are three reasons for the practice: in general, it purifies the negativities of ordinary speech, makes manifest the obtainment of good qualities, and eliminates attachments. In particular, it prevents one's speech from falling into samsara and liberates it into the Sambhoga body. Ultimately, it causes one's speech to pass beyond suffering into the Vajra-expanse."

སེམས་སྐྱོང་ནི།

སེམས་བཙལ་སྐྱོང་སྟེ། སེམས་ཀྱི་བྱུང་གནས་འགྲོ་གསུམ་ལ་ལེགས་པར་རྩད་གཅོད་ཀྱི་དཔྱད་བསྒོམ་དཔྱིས་ཕྱིན་པ་བྱ་དགོས་སྟེ།། ཞབས་དཀར་ཚོགས་དྲུག་རང་གྲོལ་གྱི་ལྟ་བ་མཁའ་ལྡིང་གཤོག་བརླབ་ལས།

“རང་གི་སེམས་ཀྱི་རྩད་བཙར་མ་ཆོད་ན།། དགེ་སྦྱོར་གང་བྱས་གནད་དུ་མི་འགྲོ་སྟེ།།” ཞེས་དང་། སེམས་ཞེས་བྱ་བ་རིག་རིག་འཁྱུ་འཁྱུ་པོ།། བདས་ན་མི་ཟིན་ཡལ་ཡལ་བུན་བུན་པོ།། བཞག་ན་མི་སྡོད་ཚུབ་ཚུབ་ཡེར་ཡེར་པོ།། འདི་ཞེས་མཚོན་མེད་སྟོང་པ་ཕྱུང་ཆད་པོ།། བདེ་སྡུག་སྣ་ཚོགས་སྤྱོད་མཁན་རང་གི་སེམས།། དང་པོ་འདི་ནི་བྱུང་ས་གང་ནས་བྱུང་།། ཞེས་དང་། དང་པོ་གང་ནས་སྐྱེས་དང་ད་ལྟའི་དུས།། གང་ལ་གནས་དང་མགོ་དབྱིབས་ཇི་འདུག་ལྟོས།། ཐ་མར་རང་སར་ཞི་ནས་ཡལ་བའི་ཚེ།། གང་དུ་ཡལ་ནས་འགྲོ་སོགས་རྩད་བཙར་ཆོད།། འཆི་བའི་ཚེ་ན་ཇི་ལྟར་བྱས་ནས་འགྲོ།། ཞིབ་ཏུ་དཔྱོད་ལ་སྐྱེ་འཆི་འགྲོ་འོང་དང་།། ངོས་བཟུང་བྲལ་བའི་སྟོང་སངས་བརྗོད་མེད་དུ།། ངེས་པར་གཏན་ལ་མ་ཕེབས་བར་དུ་དཔྱོད།།”

ཅེས་གསུངས་པ་ལྟར་སེམས་ཀྱི་ཁོ་ཐག་ཆོད་པར་བྱའོ།།

c) Mind Training:

With the 'purification/training through looking for the mind' one ought to consummate the practice through thorough investigation, through analytical meditation on the arising, abiding, and passing away of the mind. As Shabkar Tsokdrug Rangdrol says in his 'Flight of the Garuda':

"If you do not inquire into your own mind, whatever virtuous spiritual practices you have undertaken will have no ultimate meaning. This thing called mind is full of lively and prying activity, if you chase after it you cannot grasp it, it vanishes and dissolves. If you just sit, it will not rest, but fidgets to and fro. This thing, this so-called mind of yours, is without exact location, is utterly empty and void, yet it is the experiencer of a myriad joys and sufferings. Look (and see): from whence does this mind first arise?"

And:

"From whence is it first born, where does it currently abide, what shape does it have? When ultimately thoughts have vanished from the basic ground of their own inherent condition, ask yourself, to where have they disappeared to, to where have they gone? Minutely analyze - when thoughts have expired, how is it that they have passed away? Analyze the birthing and the expiring, the coming and going of thoughts, investigate until you establish for yourself definitively mind's intangible emptiness and ineffable, totally liberated purity."

As Shabkar has written, so should you confirm definitively (the nature of) mind.

2

YUTHOK'S ATI YOGA PRIMORDIAL PURITY AND CUTTING THROUGH HARDNESS

ལེའུ་གཉིས་པ། ཀ་དག་ཁྲེགས་ཆོད།

ཀ་དག་ནི་གདོད་མ་ནས་སམ་ཐོག་མ་ནས་དག་པ་སྟེ་བསྒྲིབ་སླད་དང་གནོད་སྐྱོན་ཅི་ཡང་མ་ཞུགས་པའི་དོན་དང་། ཁྲེགས་ཆོད་ནི་གཉིས་འཛིན་ནམ་བདེན་འཛིན་མཁྲེགས་པོ་བཅད་ནས་ཆོད་པར་གྱུར་བའི་དོན་ཡིན་པས། རང་སེམས་ཐོག་མ་ནས་ཉོན་མོངས་ཀྱི་སླད་མེད་དག་པའི་གནས་ལུགས་རྟོགས་ན་བདེན་འཛིན་མཁྲེག་པོ་རང་བཞིན་གྱིས་ཆོད་པའམ་གྲོལ་འགྲོ་བས་སོ། འདི་ནི་རྫོགས་ཆེན་གྱི་ལྟ་བའི་མཐར་ཐུག་ཡིན་པས་ལྟ་བའི་མཐར་ཐུག་ཁྲེགས་ཆོད་ཀྱང་ཟེར་རོ།།

དེ་བཞིན་རྫོགས་པ་ཆེན་པོའི་སློབ་འགྲོ་ནི་རྟགས་དང་ཉམས་མྱོང་ཐོན་པར་སྦྱངས་རྗེས་རྫོགས་ཆེན་དངོས་གཞི་ཁྲེགས་ཆོད་ལ་འཇུག་ཤིན་ཏུ་སླ་བ་དང་། རྒྱང་བརྟན་པའི་སློ་ནས་གེགས་མེད་ཀ་དག་ཁྲེག་ཆོད་ལ་འཇུག་པ་སྟེ།

Chapter Two: Primordial Purity (Kadak) Cutting Through Hardness (Trekcho)

'Kadak' refers to that which is primordially or originally pure, and means that which has not undergone adulteration or damage in any way. 'Trekcho' has the meaning of that which 'cuts through', as in cutting through the 'hardness' of dualistic grasping and the fixation on reality as truly or permanently existent. If one realizes the originally pure natural state of one's own mind, which is free from the taint of afflictive emotions, the hardness or stubborness of one's clinging to reality as 'really real' will be severed or liberated naturally, of its own accord. Since this is the ultimate or consummate view of the Great Perfection, Trekcho is also referred to as the 'Cutting through Hardness Perfection of the View'. Thus, once one has practiced the preliminaries of the Great Perfection and obtained signs and meditative experiences of attainment, entering into the main practice of Trekcho is very easy, and one can enter into Primordial Purity Cutting through Hardness with a firm foundation and without impediments.

དེ་ཡང་འོད་གསལ་རྫོགས་པ་ཆེན་པོ་ལ་སྟོང་ཕྱོགས་ཀྱི་ཁྲེགས་ཆོད་དང་སྣང་ཕྱོགས་ཐོད་རྒལ་གཉིས་ལས་ཐོག་མར་ཁྲེགས་ཆོད་ཀྱི་སྐོར་ནི། རྫོགས་ཆེན་སློབ་དཔའ་རབ་རྡོ་རྗེའི་ཚིག་གསུམ་གནད་བརྡེག་གི་གཞུང་། ངོ་རང་ཐོག་ཏུ་སྤྲད། ཐག་གཅིག་ཐོག་ཏུ་བཅད། གདིང་གྲོལ་ཐོག་ཏུ་བཅའ་ཞེས་གསུངས་པ་བཞིན། ཐོག་མར་ངོ་སྤྲོད་དང་། དེ་ནས་ཐག་གཅོད་དང་རྗེས་སུ་གྲོལ་ཚད་གསུངས་པ་ཡིན་ཏེ། གཡུ་ཐོག་སྙིང་ཐིག་ལུགས་ལ་དང་པོ་གཞི་ངོས་བཟུང་པ། དེ་ནས་ཕྱི་ནང་དང་བྱེད་ལས་ངོ་སྤྲོད་པ་དང་། ངོ་སྤྲོད་དངོས་ལ། སྐུ་དང་ཡེ་ཤེས། ཐུང་པོ། འབྱུང་བ། མཆོན་བྱེད་དང་བཅས་གནད་ཚང་བ་དང་། ཐག་གཅིག་ཐོག་ཏུ་བཅད་ནས་ཉམས་སུ་ལེན་ཐབས་བཅས་གསུངས་པ་ཡིན་ཏེ།

རྗེ་བཙུན་གཡུ་ཐོག་པས། "དེ་ལྟར་ཕྱི་ནང་གསང་བའི་ལྟ་ཆེན་ལྟ་ལ། འཁོར་འདས་གང་ཡང་མ་ཚང་བ་མེད་ཅིང་། ཐམས་ཅད་ཚང་བ་སྟེ། དེ་བཞིན་དུ་རྣལ་འབྱོར་པ་རང་ལ་ཐམས་ཅད་ཚང་ཞིང་ཡོངས་སུ་རྫོགས་ལ། དེ་དག་ངོ་མ་ཤེས་པས། ཕན་རྩུན་ཡུལ་དང་ཡུལ་ཅན་དུ་ཕྱེད། དེ་དག་སྣང་སྣང་གི་འཛིན་པ་ཞུགས་པས་བཅིངས། བཅིངས་པས་འཁོར་བར་འཁོར་ཞིང་གྲོལ་དུས་མེད་པས་སྡུག་བསྔལ་བའོ། ། དེ་དག་ཀྱང་བླ་མས་ངོ་སྤྲད་དེ། རང་ལ་ཡོད་པ་རང་གིས་གོ་ཞིང་རྟོགས་པར་བྱས་པས། འཁོར་འདས་ཐམས་ཅད་རང་ལ་ཚང་བ་ཐག་ཆོད། ། གཞན་ནས་མ་བྱུང་བ་ཐག་ཆོད། ཡེ་གདོད་མ་ནས་ལྷུན་གྱིས་གྲུབ་པ་གདེང་ཐོབ། སྣང་སྣང་དགག་སྒྲུབ་རེ་དོགས་ལ་སོགས་པ་གཉིས་འཛིན་གྱི་མཐའ་ལས་འདས་པ་ཐག་ཆོད་པ་སྟེ། དེ་ལྟ་བུའི་རྩལ་གྱིས་ངོ་འཕྲོད་པར་བྱའོ། ། "

The Great Perfection of Clear Light has two dimensions: Trekcho or 'Cutting through Hardness' which focuses on emptiness, and Togal or 'Direct Crossing' which focuses on appearances. First, when it comes to Trekcho, (we can look at this) in accordance with the 'Three Statements that Strike the Vital Points' scripture that was taught by the founder of Dzogchen, Garab Dorje. Garab Dorje's three axioms are:

1) 'Direct Introduction to one's true nature'
2) 'Directly and definitely deciding upon this state'
3) 'Gaining confidence in the immediacy of Liberation'

First, introduction or 'pointing out' is taught, then deciding or confirming, then (confidence in) liberation. In the Yuthok Nyingthig system, the 'recognizing of the basis' is taught first, then the outer, inner, and activity pointing out; then the actual pointing out. All the essential points of the body and wisdom, the psycho-physical constituents, the elements, and the 'symbols' or lights are included. Once one has absolutely determined (the basic nature of mind) the so-called 'mode of practice' is then explained.

As Venerable Yuthok said:

"So it is that the five outer, inner, and secret groups of five substances are wholly and fully a part of Samsara and Nirvana, of cyclical existence and its liberation, everything is included. The individual yogi thus contains in himself all things completely. By not recognizing this, we have separated object and subject from one another, and having become fixated on taking up and/or rejecting these, we have bound ourselves (to Samsara). Being bound, we cycle through cyclical existence, and suffer without any moment of release. After the guru points these (things) out, and you have realized that (everything) exists within you, confirm conclusively that you comprise all of Samsara and Nirvana. Confirm for yourself definitively that nothing arises from any other (source). Gain confidence in the primordial, spontaneous presence.

Resolve to pass beyond the limits of dualistic thinking, with its clinging to what is desirable and casting away of what is not, its negations and affirmations, its hopes and fears. In this way, be introduced to (and recognize the nature of your own mind)."

ཞེས་དང་། "སྨིན་གྲོལ་འཁོར་འདས་རང་གྲོལ་སྐད་ཅིག་སྨིན་ཅིང་གྲོལ་བ། བསྐྱེད་རྫོགས་འཁོར་འདས་རང་གྲོལ་མཐའ་ལས་འདས་པ། ལམ་བརྒྱ་འཁོར་འདས་རང་གྲོལ་ལྷུན་གྱིས་གྲུབ་པའོ།། གོང་ན་ཆེན་པོ་དེ་ལྟ་བུའི་གནད་ཀྱིས་ཟིན་པ་ལ། ཉམས་ལེན་མཐར་ཐུག་ཟེར་རོ། །" ཞེས་གསལ་དུ་གསུངས་པ་ལས་རྟོགས་ཐུབ་པས། སྟོན་རྒྱལ་གཡུ་ཐོག་པའི་རྫོགས་ཆེན་གྱི་དགོངས་པ་ནི་སྟོན་པ་དགའ་རབ་རྡོ་རྗེའི་གསང་ལམ་འཁྲུལ་མེད་དུ་སྟོན་པ་ཞེས་ཐུབ་བོ།།

ཀ། ངོས་བཟུང་པ།

གཞི་དུས་ཀྱི་འབྱུང་བ་ལྔ་དང་ཕུང་པོ་ལྔ་། ལམ་དུས་ཀྱི་མཆོན་བྱེད་དམ་འོད་ལྔ་། འབྲས་དུས་ཀྱི་ཡེ་ཤེས་ལྔ་དང་སྐུ་ལྔའི་ཀྲང་གྲངས་བསྟན་པའམ་དེ་རྣམས་ངོས་ཟིན་པར་བྱ་སྟེ།

སྐུ་ལྔ་། ཆོས་སྐུ། ལོངས་སྐུ། སྤྲུལ་སྐུ། མངོན་པར་བྱང་ཆུབ་སྐུ། མི་འགྱུར་རྡོ་རྗེའི་སྐུ་བཅས་ལྔའོ།།

ཡེ་ཤེས་ལྔ་། ཆོས་དབྱིངས་ཡེ་ཤེས། མེ་ལོང་ཡེ་ཤེས། མཉམ་ཉིད་ཡེ་ཤེས། སོར་རྟོག་ཡེ་ཤེས། བྱ་གྲུབ་ཡེ་ཤེས་བཅས་ལྔའོ།

ཕུང་པོ་ལྔ་། གཟུགས། རྣམ་ཤེས། ཚོར་བ། འདུ་ཤེས། འདུ་བྱེད་བཅས་ལྔའོ།།

འབྱུང་བ་ལྔ་། ནམ་མཁའ། ས། ཆུ། མེ་དང་རླུང་བཅས་ལྔའོ།།

མཆོན་བྱེད་ལྔ་། འདི་ལ་འོད་ལྔ་ཡང་ཟེར་ཏེ། མཐིང་ག དཀར་པོ། སེར་པོ། དམར་པོ། ལྗང་གུ་བཅས་ལྔའོ།།

སྐུ་དང་ཡེ་ཤེས་དང་། ཕུང་པོ་དང་འབྱུང་བ་ལྔ་དང་མཆོན་བྱེད་བཅས་ལ་འང་ཕྱི་ནང་གསང་གསུམ་བཅས་ལྔ་ཚན་ལྔ་སྟེ་བསྡོམ་ཚན་བདུན་ཅུ་དོན་ལྔར་དབྱེ་བ་ཡིན་ནོ།།

And:

"Ripening and liberating in an instant (via) the Ripening and Liberating (teachings) of the Self-Liberation of Samsara-Nirvana, going beyond the development and completion stages of the Self-Liberation of Samsara-Nirvana, realizing spontaneously the hundred paths of the Self-Liberation of Samsara-Nirvana - grasping the great, essential meaning as laid out above is called 'the consummation of the practice"

If one is able to grasp this clearly laid out teaching then one will be able to appreciate that Yuthok, the King of Medicine's (enlightened) perspective on Dzogchen represents the unmistaken secret path of the great Master Garab Dorje.

1) Recognizing

This is the range of things that it is taught that one should recognize: the five natural elements which are of the 'time of the ground'; the five psycho-physical aggregates; the five symbols or signifiers of the 'time of (being on) the path', a.k.a. the five lights; the five wisdoms that are of 'the time of fruition'; and the five kayas.

The five kayas are: the dharmakaya, sambhogakaya, nirmanakaya, the body of the direct (perception) of a Bodhisattva, and the unchangeable vajrakaya. The five wisdoms are: the wisdom of the expanse of absolute-reality (dharmadhatu), the mirror-like wisdom, the wisdom of equality, the discriminating wisdom, and the all-accomplishing wisdom. The five aggregates are: physical form, consciousness, sensation, perception, and conditioned formations. The five elements are: space, earth, water, fire, and wind. The five symbols (this is another way of referring to the five lights) are: deep blue, white, yellow, red, and green (light). The five-fold bodies, wisdoms, aggregates, elements and lights are (further) divided into inner, outer, and secret categories, which separates out altogether into 75 identifyers (See Appendices C).

ཁ། ངོ་སྤྲོད་པ།

སྤྱིའི་ངོ་སྤྲོད་ལ་ཕྱི་ནང་སྣོད་བཅུད་དང་བྱེད་ལས་ཀྱི་སྒོ་ནས་གསུངས་སྟེ།

ཐ་མལ་གྱི་ཕྱི་འཇིག་རྟེན། དག་པའི་ཞིང་ཁམས་དང་གཞལ་ཡས་ཁང་དུ་ངོ་སྤྲོད་པ།

ཐ་མལ་གྱི་ནང་སེམས་ཅན། ཡེ་ཤེས་ཀྱི་ལྷ་ཚོགས་དང་འཕགས་ཚོགས་སུ་ངོ་སྤྲོད་པ།

མ་དག་པའམ་འཁྲུལ་བའི་བྱེད་ལས་འཁྲུལ་བ། དག་པའི་ཐུགས་རྗེ་དང་བརྩེ་བས་སྐྱོང་བར་ངོ་སྤྲོད་པའོ།

2) Identifying (a.k.a. 'Recognizing' or 'Pointing out')

The general identifying/pointing out is taught on the inner and outer level of the (inanimate and animate) universe and its activities. The ordinary external world is identified as the pure-lands and as celestial mansions beyond measure. Ordinary (sentient beings) within the world are identified as the assembly of wisdom-deities and the gathering of noble beings. Impure or deluded actions are identified as pure compassion and nurturing love.

གཡུ་ཐོག་རྫོགས་ཆེན་འཁོར་འདས་རང་གྲོལ་ཆེན་མོའི་རྒྱ་བར་ "ངོ་སྤྲོད་པར་བྱ་བ་ནི། སྣང་སྲིད་འཁོར་འདས་ཀྱིས་བསྡུས་པའི་ཆོས་ཐམས་ཅད། བྱེ་བྲག་རྣམ་གྲངས་རྒྱུ་དང་མཚན་ཉིད་ལ་སོགས་རྒྱས་པར་བཤད་ན་བསམ་གྱིས་མི་ཁྱབ་ཀྱང་། དོན་མདོར་བསྡུས་ན། ཕྱི་ནང་སྣོད་བཅུད་བྱེད་ལས་གསུམ་དུ་འདུས་ཤིང་། འཁོར་བ་པའི་ཕྱི་སྣོད་ཀྱི་འཇིག་རྟེན་ཁམས། ནང་བཅུད་ཀྱི་སེམས་ཅན་གྱི་རིགས། བྱེད་ལས་འཕྲུལ་བའི་བྱ་བ་འབའ་ཞིག་ལ་སྤྱོད་པའོ། །འཇིག་རྟེན་འདས་པའི་ཕྱི་སྣོད་ཞིང་ཁམས་དང་གཞལ་ཡས། ནང་བཅུད་སེམས་ཅན་གྱི་ཡེ་ཤེས་ཀྱི་ལྷ་དང་འཕགས་ཚོགས། བྱེད་ལས་བརྩེ་བའི་ཐུགས་རྗེ། མཛད་པའི་ཕྲིན་ལས་ལས་འགྲོ་དོན་ལ་སྤྱོད་པའོ། །དེ་ཐམས་ཅད་རྣལ་འབྱོར་པ་རང་ཉིད་ལ་ཚང་སྟེ། སྣོད་ལུས་བཅུད་སེམས། བྱེད་ལས་འདུ་ཤེས་དང་འདུ་བྱེད་ཀྱི་ལུ་གུ་རྒྱུད་ལ་སྤྱོད་པའོ། ། མཚན་ཉིད་འཛིན་པའི་ཡེ་ཤེས་ནི། སྣང་སྲིད་འཁོར་འདས་ཀྱིས་བསྡུས་པའི་ཆོས་ཐམས་ཅད་རང་བཞིན།། མཚན་ཉིད་ཀྱི་རྒྱབ་ཆོད་པའོ།། མངོན་སུམ་རང་སྣང་གི་ཡེ་ཤེས་དེ་དག་ཐམས་ཅད་གཞན་གང་ནས་ཀྱང་མ་བྱུང་ཞིང་རང་ལ་ཞུགས། རང་ལས་འཆར་རང་ལས་གནང་པ་ལས་ཀྱང་། རང་གི་མངོན་སུམ་དུ་བལྟར་ཡོད། སྤྱོད་དུ་ཡོད། བརྟེགས་ཏུ་ཡོད། ལམ་གྱི་འཆར་སྒོམ་འགགས་པར། འཕེལ་ཞིང་ཚད་དང་བཅས་པ་ཡོད། དེ་ལྟར་ཡོད་པ་དེ། བྱས་བྱུང་ཅན་ཡིན་ནམ་ཞེ་ན། དེ་ནི་མ་ཡིན་ཏེ། ཡེ་གདོད་མ་ནས་ཡོངས་ལ་ཁྱབ་ཅིང་། གསལ་སྟོང་དབྱེར་མེད་དུ་འཕོ་འགྱུར་མེད་པའོ། །"

ཞེས་ཤིན་ཏུ་གསལ་བར་གསུངས་པ་དང་།

In the root-text of Yuthok's Great Perfection 'Great Self-Liberation of Samsara-Nirvana' this is laid out very clearly:

"Regarding that which ought to be pointed out: if one were to elaborate upon the particularities, enumerations, and defining characteristics of all phenomena or dharmas – those appearances and arisings which together comprise all of Samsara and Nirvana - the mind could hardly encompass them. Still, if one were to summarize these briefly, they would comprise three categories: the outer 'container, 'inner 'contents', and the actions or activities. The 'outer container' of samsara is nothing but our world-system, the 'inner contents' are nothing but the various kinds of sentient beings (that exist within it), and the 'activities' are nothing but the deluded actions or behavior (of these beings). The outer container of the trans-mundane world is the pure-lands and inestimable celestial mansions, the 'inner content' sentient beings within these are the wisdom-deities and noble assemblies, and their actions are loving compassion, are the conduct that derives from the enlightened activities done for the sake of sentient beings. All of these are contained within the yogi's own being.

His body is the universe, his mind its inhabitants, its activities are his conduct, the interlocking chain of his perceptions and conditioned mental formations. The (primordial) wisdom that apprehends the attributes is the nature of all the collected phenomena, all the arisings and appearances of Samsara and Nirvana, and it cuts through to the root of the attributes.

All these directly perceived self-manifesting wisdoms abide in one's own mind and arise from no other source. They appear from one's own mind and act from one's own mind. They're observed directly by one's own mind, used by it, lifted up by it, conceptual experiences on the path proliferate unobstructedly in accordance with it. This being so, if one were to ask whether one's mind was something that was produced or that emerged, (the answer would have to be) no. (One's mind) is primordially all-pervasive, it is indivisible clarity-emptiness that neither shifts nor changes."

གཞན་ཡང་ངོ་སྤྲོད་དང་མ་སྤྲད་པ་དང་མ་འཕྲོད་པ་སོགས་ཀྱི་སྐོར་ལ་ སློབ་དཔོན་ཀུན་བཟང་ཐོག་མའི་རྫོགས་ཆེན་འཁོར་འདས་རང་གྲོལ་ལས་འདི་ལྟར་གསུངས་སྟེ།

“དེ་ཐམས་ཅད་རྣལ་འབྱོར་བ་རང་ལ་ཚང་ཞིང་། སྟོན་ལུས། བཅུདསེམས། བྱེད་ལས་འདུ་ཤེས་དང་། འདུ་བྱེད་ཀྱི་ལུ་གུ་རྒྱུད་ལ་སྤྲོད་ཅིང་ངོ་མ་སྤྲད་ཅིང་། མ་འཕྲོད་ན་འཁོར་བ་པ་ངོ་སྤྲད་ཅིང་། འཕྲོད་ན་མྱ་ངན་ལས་འདས་པའོ།། ངོ་སྤྲད་པ་དེ་འཕྲོད་པར་བྱེད་པ། ཡང་གང་གིས་སྤྲོད་ན། བླ་མ་མཚན་ཉིད་དང་ལྡན་པས་སྤྲོད། གང་ལ་སྤྲོད་ན། བླ་མེད་བྱང་ཆུབ་སྒྲུབ་པ་དོན་དུ་གཉེར་བའི་སྐལ་ལྡན་ལ་སྤྲད། ཇི་ལྟར་སྤྲོད་ན། འོག་ནས་འབྱུང་བ་ལྟར་སྤྲོད་དོ།། སྤྲོད་པའི་ཡོན་ཏན་ནི། མྱང་འདས་ཐོབ། མ་སྤྲད་པའི་སྐྱོན་འཁོར་བ་ནས་མི་ཐར་བས། ངེས་པར་དུ་ངོ་སྤྲོད་པ་གལ་ཆེའོ།། དེ་ཡང་ངོ་སྤྲད་པས་འཕྲད་པས་ཉམས་སུ་ལེན་པ་དང་། ངོ་འཕྲོད་ཀྱང་ཉམས་སུ་མི་ལེན་པ་དང་། ངོ་སྤྲོད་པས་མ་འཕྲོད་པ་དང་། ངོ་སྤྲད་པས་འཕྲོད་པ་ནི། རང་ངོ་རང་གིས་ཤེས་པའོ། །འཕྲོད་པས་ཉམས་སུ་ལེན་པ་ནི། རང་ངོམ་རང་གིས་ཤེས་ནས་འཁྲུལ་པའི་རྗེས་སུ་མི་འབྲང་བའོ། ། ངོ་འཕྲས་པས་ཉམས་སུ་མི་ལེན་པ་ནི། གོ་ཡུལ་དུ་ལུས་ནས་རང་གི་རྒྱུད་ཐོག་ཏུ་མི་ཕེབས་པའོ།། ངོ་སྤྲོད་པས་མ་འཕྲོད་པ་ནི། ཚིག་རྣ་བར་ཐོས་པས་བློ་འདྲིད་དེ། དོན་ཡིད་ལ་མ་ངེས་པས། ཉམས་སུ་ལེན་རྒྱུ་མེད། དཔེར་ན་སྦྲུམ་བུ་བཟོ་ཉེས་པ་དང་འདྲ། ངོ་ཡེ་ནས་མ་སྤྲད་པ་ནི། སྦྲུམ་བུ་བཟོ་མ་བྱས་པ་དང་འདྲ་སྟེ། སྦྲུམ་བུ་དེ་མཁས་པའི་ལག་ཏུ་སླེབས་ནས། ཇི་ལྟར་འདོད་པ་བཞིན་འབྱུང་ལ། ལན་གཅིག་བཟོ་ཉེས་པ་སྟེ། བཅས་བཅོས་བྱ་ར་མི་བཏུབ་པ་དང་མཚུངས་ཏེ། ངོ་སྤྲོད་བཏབ་ལམ་ཐེབས་པས། ལྟ་སྤྱོད་ཡ་བྲལ་དུ་སོང་ན་གྲོལ་དུས་མི་འབྱུང་ངོ་། དེ་ན་ངོ་འཕྲོད་པར་གདབ། ཐོབ་ནས་རང་རྒྱུད་དང་འདྲེས་པར་ཉམས་སུ་ལེན་པར་བྱེད་པ་གནད་ཆེ།།” ཞེས་པ་ནི་ཐོག་མའི་གོ་བ་ལ་ཧ་ཅང་གལ་ཆེ་བ་དང་།

Moreover, Yuthok the King of Medicine's Great Perfection of the Self-Liberation of Samsara-Nirvana also states, on the subject of what has been pointed out, not pointed out, recognized and not recognized, and so on:

"All of this is contained in the yogi's own being. The universe is his body, its inhabitants his mind, its activities are his own conduct, the interconnected chain of his perceptions and conditioned mental formations. If this hasn't been pointed out or recognized as being so, then one (remains) a wanderer in samsara, if it has, then one passes beyond suffering to Nirvana. What is pointed out must be recognized - whoever does the pointing out should be a properly qualified lama, and whomever receives it should be one of those fortunate ones aspiring to attain the unparalleled (state of the) Bodhisattva. The way one should point is as follows:

Given that the advantage of identifying is obtaining Nirvana, and the defect of not having identified is that you will not be freed from Samsara, identifying is necessarily very important. (There are a number of possibilities): being introduced, recognizing and then practicing; recognizing and nonetheless not practicing; and being introduced but not recognizing. Being introduced and recognizing means comprehending one's own essential nature oneself. Recognizing and then putting into practice means that once one has comprehended one's own nature oneself, one will no longer follow after delusions. Recognizing but not practicing is when one is left with purely theoretical knowledge which doesn't enter into one's (mental) continuum. When one has been introduced but has not recognized, one has heard the words (of the teachings) with one's ears, but they have slipped from one's mind, their meaning hasn't been assimilated into one's mind, and one doesn't bother to practice. This can be likened metaphorically to a defective roll of woollen cloth. Never having been introduced at all, from the very beginning, would be like if the cloth had never been made in the first place. Equally, even if this cloth came into the hands of an expert, it being defective from the start, he would not succeed in repairing it, no matter however much he might want to. If one has managed to receive some introduction but one's View and Conduct diverge from each other, the moment of liberation will not arise. Thus, it's vital that one finds a way to really recognize (what has been pointed out) and that one then practices with this recognition thoroughly merged with one's own mind-stream."

Understanding this from the very beginning is extremely important.

རྫོགས་ཆེན་ལྟ་བ་མཁའ་ལྡིང་གཤོག་བརླབ་ཏུ་འང་། "ངོ་སྤྲོད་མ་ཐེབས་ཉམས་སུ་ལེན་པ་དེ།། དཔེར་ན་ཆོས་པ་གཅིག་ནས་འཕྱུག་པ་ན།། བཅོ་ལྔའི་བར་དུ་འཕྱུག་པ་ཇི་བཞིན་ནོ།། ཀུན་རྫོབ་ཆོས་རྣམས་ཐམས་ཅད་བདེན་མེད་དུ།། མ་རྟོགས་སྟོང་ཉིད་རྟོགས་ཟེར་རྫུན་ཆེན་ཡིན།། དེས་ན་ངོ་སྤྲོད་འདི་བཞིན་དང་པོའི་དུས།། བླ་མའི་དྲུང་དུ་སྤྲོད་ལ་གནས་ལུགས་ཀྱི།། སྟེང་དུ་གཏན་ལ་ཕེབས་དང་གོལ་ས་མེད།། དེའི་ཕྱིར་སྐལ་ལྡན་བུ་རྣམས་སྙིང་ལ་ཆོངས།། ཞེས་ཐོག་མའི་ངོ་སྤྲོད་མ་འཁྲུལ་དགོས་པ་གསལ་དུ་གསུངས་པ་ནི་ལེགས་བཤད་བླ་ན་མེད་པའོ།།

ག ངོ་སྤྲོད་དངོས།

དེ་ཡང་ངོ་སྤྲོད་དངོས་འདི་བྱེ་བྲག་ངོ་སྤྲོད་རྒྱས་པར་བསྟན་པ་ནི་ལྔ་ཚན་ལྔས་བསྟན་ཏེ། སྐུ་ལྔ། ཡེ་ཤེ་ལྔ། ཕུང་པོ་ལྔ། འབྱུང་ལྔ་དང་མཚོན་བྱེད་དམ་འོད་ལྔ་བཅས་གཤམ་དུ་བསྟན་བྱ་སྟེ།

དང་པོ། སྐུ་ལྔ་ལ་ཕྱི་ནང་གསང་གསུམ་དང་།

ཕྱིའི་སྐུ་ལྔ་ནི་རིགས་ལྔ་ལས་བྱུང་བའི་སྐུ་ལྔ་སྟེ། རིག་པའི་ཡེ་ཤེས་རྣམ་པར་སྣང་། རིག་པའི་ཡེ་ཤེས་སྣང་བ་མཐའ་ཡས། རིག་པའི་ཡེ་ཤེས་རྡོ་རྗེ་སེམས་དཔའ། རིག་པའི་ཡེ་ཤེས་རིན་ཆེན་འབྱུང་ལྡན། རིག་པའི་ཡེ་ཤེས་དོན་ཡོད་གྲུབ་པ་བཅས་སོ།།

ནང་གི་སྐུ་ལྔ་ནི། སྐུའི་ཚོ་འཕྲུལ་ལས་བྱུང་བའི་ལམ་རྟགས་ཀྱི་སྐུའི་འཁོར་ལོ། གསུང་པད་མ། ཐུགས་རྡོ་རྗེ། ཡོན་ཏན་རིན་ཆེན། འཕྲིན་ལས་སྣ་ཚོགས་རྡོ་རྗེ་བཅས་སོ།།

གསང་བའི་སྐུ་ལྔ་ནི། གདུལ་བྱ་སེམས་ཅན་གྱི་དོན་མཛད་པ། ཆོས་སྐུ། ལོངས་སྐུ། སྤྲུལ་སྐུ། མངོན་པར་བྱང་ཆུབ་སྐུ་དང་མི་འགྱུར་རྡོ་རྗེའི་སྐུ་བཅས་ལྔའོ།།

In the 'Great Perfection's View, the Flight of the Garuda' the need to identify the nature of things without confusion right from the start is explained clearly through the following unsurpassed piece of advice:

"Practicing without having first identified (the nature of things) is like having lost your way on the first day of the month and then still finding yourself wandering in the wrong direction (two weeks later) on the fifteen! All relative phenomena are untrue, they do not truly (i.e. intrinsically) exist - saying that one has realized emptiness without having actually done so is a great falsehood. So, make sure you identify right from the start in this way: while sitting (right there) in front of the guru, confirm for yourself the true nature of reality, and don't go astray. On account of this, oh you fortunate ones, take this advice to heart!"

3) Actual Identifying/Pointing Out

The Actual Identifying is a specific, more extended pointing out teaching, which involves the five categories of five phenomena: the five bodies, the five wisdoms, the five aggregates, the five elements and five symbols or lights, which will be explained below.

a) There are the five kayas, which have three levels, outer, inner and secret. The five outer bodies are the five kayas that emerge from the five Buddha-families: the primordial wisdom of natural awareness (rigpa) Vairocana of the Body-family, and the wisdom of awareness of the Amitabha, Vajrasattva, Ratnasambhava, and Amoghasiddhi families.

The five inner kayas are: the chakra of the Body of the signs (of progress) on the path that emerges from the bodily miraculous display, the Lotus of Speech, the Vajra of Mind, the Precious Jewel of Good Qualities, and the Vajra of Manifold Activities.

The five secret kayas are: the deeds done on behalf of sentient beings to be 'tamed' (by the Dharma), the manifest Bodhikaya of absolute reality or truth (Dharmakaya), the Sambhogakaya, the Nirmanakaya, and the unchanging Vajrakaya.

དེ་ལྟར་སྐུ་ལྔ་པོ་གཞན་ཞིག་ནས་བྱུང་བ་མ་ཡིན། རྣལ་འབྱོར་པ་རང་གི་ལུས་ངག་ཡིད་གསུམ་ལ་ཚང་། ཕྱི་ཡི་སྐུ་ལྔ་ལུས་ལ་ཚང་། ནང་གི་སྐུ་ལྔ་ངག་ལ་ཚང་། གསང་བའི་སྐུ་ལྔ་སེམས་ལ་ཚང་སྟེ། འཁོར་འདས་རང་གྲོལ་ཆེན་མོའི་ཀྱ་བར། “ ངོ་སྤྲོད་དངོས་ནི། དང་པོ་སྐུ་ལྔ་ལ་ཕྱི་ནང་གསང་བ་གསུམ་སྟེ།

ཕྱིའི་སྐུ་ལྔ་ནི། རིགས་ལྔ་ལས་བྱུང་བའི་སྐུ་ལྔ་སྟེ། རིག་པའི་ཡེ་ཤེས་སྐུའི་རིགས་ལས་བྱུང་བའི་སྐུ་རྣམ་པར་སྣང་མཛད། རིག་པའི་ཡེ་ཤེས་གསུང་གི་རིགས་ལས་བྱུང་བའི་གསུང་སྣང་བ་མཐའ་ཡས། རིག་པའི་ཡེ་ཤེས་ཐུགས་ཀྱི་རིགས་ལས་བྱུང་བའི་ཐུགས་རྡོ་རྗེ་སེམས་དཔའ་དང་། རིག་པའི་ཡེ་ཤེས་ཡོན་ཏན་གྱི་རིགས་ལས་བྱུང་བའི་རིན་འབྱུང་། རིག་པའི་ཡེ་ཤེས་ཀྱི་འཕྲིན་ལས་ཀྱི་རིགས་ལས་དོན་གྲུབ་རིག་པའི་ཡེ་ཤེས་སོ།།

ནང་གི་སྐུ་ལྔ་ནི། ཆོ་འཕྲུལ་རྟགས་ཀྱི་སྐུ་ལྔ་སྟེ། སྐུའི་ཆོ་འཕྲུལ་ལས་བྱུང་བའི་ལམ་རྟགས་ཀྱི་འཁོར་ལོ། དེ་འགྲེ་བར། གསུང་གི་ཆོ་འཕྲུལ་ལས་བྱུང་བའི་ལམ་རྟགས་ཀྱི་པདྨ། ཐུགས་ཀྱི་ཆོ་འཕྲུལ་ལས་བྱུང་བའི་ལམ་རྟགས་ཀྱི་རྡོ་རྗེ། ཡོན་ཏན་གྱི་ཆོ་འཕྲུལ་ལས་བྱུང་བའི་ལམ་རྟགས་ཀྱི་རིན་ཆེན། འཕྲིན་ལས་ཀྱི་ཆོ་འཕྲུལ་ལས་བྱུང་བའི་ལམ་རྟགས་ཀྱི་སྣ་ཚོགས་རྡོ་རྗེ་བཅས་སོ།།

གསང་བའི་སྐུ་ལྔ་ནི། གདུལ་བྱ་སེམས་ཅན་གྱི་དོན་མཛད་པ། སྟོན་པ་སངས་རྒྱས་ཀྱི་སྐུ་ལྔ་སྟེ། སྔར་བསྟན་པའི་ཆོས་སྐུ་ལ་སོགས་པ་ལྔའོ། །

In this way have the five kayas emerged, they have no other source. All are encompassed by the yogi's own body, speech, and mind. The five outer kayas are contained within the yogi's body, the inner kayas by his speech, the five secret kayas by his mind. This is elaborated upon in the root-text of the Great Self-Liberation of Samsara-Nirvana:

"On the actual pointing out: First there are the five kayas in their inner, outer and secret aspects. The five outer kayas are the five kayas that emerge from the five Buddha-families - The primordial wisdom of natural awareness of the Body (aspect) of Vairocana that arises from the Body-family of the wisdom of awareness; the primordial wisdom of natural awareness of the Speech aspect of Amitabha who derives from the Speech-Family of the wisdom of awareness, the primordial wisdom of natural awareness of the Mind aspect of Vajrasattva who emerges from the Mind-Family of the wisdom of awareness, the primordial wisdom of natural awareness of Ratnasambhava who comes from the family of Good Qualities, the wisdom of natural awareness of Amoghasiddhi of the family of enlightened activities.

The five inner bodies are the five bodies of the miraculous signs: the chakra of the signs of progress on the path that comes from the miraculous (power/ display) of Body, from this proceed the Lotus of the signs that emerge from the miraculous display of Speech, the Vajra of the signs that emerge from the miraculous display of Mind, the Precious Jewel of the signs that come from the miraculous display of Good Qualities, and the Manifold-Vajra of the signs that emerge from the miraculous display of Enlightened Activities. The five secret bodies are the deeds done on behalf of sentient beings who are to be tamed, and the five bodies of the Great Master Buddha, the five bodies of absolute reality and so on, as previously taught."

དེ་ལྟར་སྐུ་ལྔ་པོ་གཞན་ཞིག་ནས་བྱུང་བ་མ་ཡིན་ཞིང་། རྣལ་འབྱོར་པ་རང་གི་ལུས་ངག་ཡིད་གསུམ་ལ་ཚང་། ཇི་ལྟར་ཚང་ན། ཕྱི་སྐུ་ལྔ་ལུས་ལ་ཚང་སྟེ། ཁམས་ཀུན་ཆང་བ་རྒྱུན་གྱི་ཐིག་ལེ་རྣམ་པར་སྣང་མཛད། ཁྲག་དང་ཆུ་སེར་མི་བསྐྱོད་པ། ཤ་རིན་འབྱུང་། པགས་པ་བཀྲག་མདངས་སྣང་བ་མཐའ་ཡས། སྐྲ་དང་བ་སྤུ་དོན་གྲུབ། ནང་གི་སྐུ་ལྔ་ངག་ལ་ཚང་སྟེ། སྐད་ཀྱི་སྣང་བ་ལྟང་དེ་གྲགས་པ་འཁོར་ལོ། ཚིག་འབྲུ་མི་བསྐྱོད་པ། སྙན་པར་སྨྲ་བ་པདྨའོ། །དོན་བསྟན་པ་སྟོན་ཞིང་། དབུགས་ཀྱི་རྟ་ལས་བྱུང་བ་རྒྱ་གྲམ་མོ། །

གསང་བའི་སྐུ་ལྔ་སེམས་ལ་ཚང་སྟེ། སེམས་ཀྱི་ངོ་བོ་སྟོང་བ་ཆོས་སྐུ། རང་བཞིན་གསལ་བ་ལོངས་སྐུ། སྣང་བ་རིག་བྱེད་དུ་སྣང་བ་སྤྲུལ་སྐུ། དེ་གསུམ་ཀའི་དབྱིངས་མི་གཡོ་མི་འགྱུར་བ་རྡོ་རྗེའི་སྐུ། མཁྱེན་བརྩེ་དང་ལྡན་པ་མངོན་པར་བྱང་ཆུབ་སྐུ་དང་། དེ་ལྟར་ན་ཕྱི་ནང་གསང་བའི་སྐུ་ཐམས་ཅད་རྫོགས་ཤིང་རང་ལ་ཚང་བས། གཞན་ནས་བཙལ་དུ་མེད་པའོ། །"ཞེས་རྒྱས་པར་གསུངས་སོ།།

"In this way have the five kayas emerged, they have no other source. All are encompassed by the yogi's own body, speech, and mind. The way they are encompassed is that the five outer bodies are contained within the yogi's body - the thigle or light-spheres of his mental continuum which hold all his basic bodily constituents are Vairocana, his blood and lymph are Akshobhya, his flesh is Ratnasambhava, his skin and inner vitality (expressed through the complexion) are Amitabha, his head and body hair are Amoghasiddhi.

The five inner kayas are encompassed by his voice. The clarity and renown of his voice is Chakra ('The Wheel'), his words are Akshobhya, his pleasant speech is Lotus, the meaning of the teachings is the Teacher (Buddha), and the crossed double-vajras come from the flow or rhythm of his breath, which expresses this meaning.

The five secret kayas are encompassed by his mind. The empty-essence of his mind is the Dharmakaya, the clear nature is the Sambhogakaya, the radiance of his intellect or 'cognizing awareness' is the Nirmanakaya, the basic, unmoving and unchanging expanse of all three is the Vajrakaya, and the mind's inherent wisdom and compassion are the manifest Bodhikaya.

Thus, since all of the outer, inner and secret kayas are perfected within and encompassed by the yogi's own being, there is nowhere else one need to search (to find their origin)."

གཉིས་པ། ཡེ་ཤེས་ཕྱི་ནང་གསང་གསུམ་སྟེ།

ཕྱིའི་ཡེ་ཤེས་ནི། ཆོས་དབྱིངས་ཡེ་ཤེས། མེ་ལོང་ཡེ་ཤེས། མཉམ་ཉིད་ཡེ་ཤེས། སོར་རྟོག་ཡེ་ཤེས་དང་བྱ་གྲུབ་ཡེ་ཤེས་བཅས་ལྔའོ།།

ནང་གི་ཡེ་ཤེས་ནི། ཤེས་པ་བསྡུས་པ་ཡེ་ཤེས། ཇི་ལྟ་བ་མཁྱེན་པའི་ཡེ་ཤེས། ཇི་སྙེད་མཁྱེན་པའི་ཡེ་ཤེས། སྤྲོས་པའི་ཡེ་ཤེས། མཛད་པ་མཐར་ཕྱིན་གྱི་ཡེ་ཤེས་བཅས་ལྔའོ།།

གསང་བའི་ཡེ་ཤེས་ནི། ངོ་བོ་ཀ་དག་གི་ཡེ་ཤེས། རང་བཞིན་ལྷུན་གྲུབ་ཀྱི་ཡེ་ཤེས། ཐུགས་རྗེ་ཀུན་ཁྱབ་ཀྱི་ཡེ་ཤེས། མཚན་ཉིད་འཛིན་པའི་ཡེ་ཤེས་དང་མངོན་སུམ་རང་སྣང་གི་ཡེ་ཤེས་བཅས་ལྔའོ།།

b) The three outer, inner, and secret wisdoms:

The outer wisdoms are: the wisdom of the dharmadhatu, the mirror-like wisdom, the wisdom of equality, discriminating wisdom, and the all-accomplishing wisdom.

The inner wisdoms are: the condensed cognition wisdom, the wisdom that sees things as they really are, the wisdom that knows all that exists, the elaborated or embellished wisdom, and the wisdom of perfected activity.

The secret wisdoms are: the wisdom of the essence of primordial purity, the wisdom of the spontaneously present nature (of being), the wisdom of all-pervading compassion, the wisdom that apprehends the attributes, and the directly perceived, self-manifesting wisdom.

གཡུ་ཐོག་རྫོགས་ཆེན་འཁོར་འདས་རང་གྲོལ་ཆེན་མོའི་རྒྱ་བར་”ཡེ་ཤེས་ལྔ་ལ་ཕྱི་ནང་གསང་པ་གསུམ་སྟེ།

ཕྱིའི་ཡེ་ཤེས་ལྔ་ནི། ཆོས་དབྱིངས་ཡེ་ཤེས། མེ་ལོང་། མཉམ་ཉིད། སོར་རྟོག བྱ་གྲུབ། ནང་གི་ཡེ་ཤེས་ལྔ་ནི། ཤེས་པ་བསྡུས་པ་ཡེ་ཤེས། ཤེས་པ་འཕྲོ་བའི་ཇི་ལྟར་བར་མཁྱེན་པའི་ཡེ་ཤེས། ཇི་སྙེད་པ་གཟིགས་པའི་ཡེ་ཤེས། མཛད་པ་མཐར་ཕྱིན་པའི་ཡེ་ཤེས་གསང་བའོ། ། ངོ་བོ་ཀ་དག་གི་ཡེ་ཤེས། རང་བཞིན་ལྷུན་གྲུབ་ཀྱི་ཡེ་ཤེས། ཐུགས་རྗེ་ཀུན་ཁྱབ་ཀྱི་ཡེ་ཤེས། མཚན་ཉིད་འཛིན་པའི་ཡེ་ཤེས། མངོན་སུམ་རང་སྣང་གི་ཡེ་ཤེས་ཏེ། དེ་ལྟར་ཡེ་ཤེས་རྣམས་ཀྱང་གཞན་གང་ནས་མ་བྱུང་། རང་ལ་རང་ཆས་སུ་ཚང་ཞིང་། ཇི་ལྟར་ཚང་བ་ནི། ཆོས་དབྱིངས་ཡེ་ཤེས་ནི། རང་གི་སེམས་ཉིད་ལ་མཐའ་དབུས་མེད་པའོ།། མེ་ལོང་ལྟ་བུའི་ཡེ་ཤེས། སེམས་ཀྱི་སྣང་ཆ་ལ་མ་བསྒྲིབས་པར་སྣང་ལ་རང་བཞིན་མ་གྲུབ་པར་གསལ་བའོ། ། མཉམ་ཉིད་ཡེ་ཤེས་སེམས་སྤྲོས་པའི་མཐའ་ཐམས་ཅད་དང་བྲལ་བ། མཉམ་པ་ཉིད་དུ་གནས་པའོ། ། སོ་སོར་རྟོག་པའི་ཡེ་ཤེས་ནི། གང་ལ་གང་འདུལ་གྱི་ཆོས་ཐམས་ཅད་སེམས་ཉིད་ཀྱི་ཀློང་དུ་རིམ་པ་མ་འདྲེས་པར་སོ་སོར་གསལ་བའོ། ། བྱ་བ་གྲུབ་པའི་ཡེ་ཤེས་ནི། འབད་རྩོལ་དང་བྲལ་ཞིང་། ཆོས་ཀུན་སེམས་ཉིད་ཀྱི་རང་བཞག་རང་གྲོལ་རང་ལ་རྫོགས་པའོ། །

The root text of Yuthok's Great Perfection Self-Liberation of Samsara-Nirvana says:

"The five wisdoms have three aspects, outer, inner and secret. The five outer wisdoms are the wisdom of the dharmakaya, of the mirror, equality, discriminating wisdom, and the all-accomplishing wisdom. The five inner wisdoms are condensed cognition wisdom, the wisdom that knows things (qualitatively) as they are that extends from cognition, the wisdom that sees (quantitatively) all that there is, and the wisdom of perfected activity. The secret ones are the wisdom of the essence of primordial purity, the wisdom of spontaneously present nature, the wisdom of all-pervading compassion, the wisdom that apprehends the attributes, and the directly-perceived, self-displaying wisdom.

Such are the wisdoms, which have no other origin. They are encompassed by and entirely inherent to one's mind. The way that they are encompassed is like this: The wisdom of the dharmakaya is one's very mind itself, which has neither limit nor center; the mirror-like wisdom is the mind's perceiving or manifesting aspect which is unobscured and whose manifestations are clear and without self-nature, the wisdom of equality is the mind which is devoid of all conceptually-elaborated limitations, and which abides in the perfect equanimity (of absolute being/emptiness); the discriminating wisdom is that which clearly (sees) all and every phenomenon to be tamed as it is, as the vast expanse of mind's own nature, unadulterated by stages; and the all-accomplishing wisdom is the mind-essence of all phenomena, that is devoid of striving, that is self-abiding, self-liberating and perfect in itself."

ཤེས་པ་བཏུས་པའི་ཡེ་ཤེས་ནི། གདུལ་བྱའི་བསམ་པ་མཁྱེན་ཅིང༌། གཞན་དོན་ཡོང་དུ་རྒྱུད་པས་ཆོས་ཐམས་ཅད་ཀྱི་རང་བཞིན་ཤེས་པ་འགྱུར་བའོ། ། སྦྱོར་པའི་ཡེ་ཤེས་ནི། འཁོར་འདས་ཀྱི་ཆོས་ཐམས་ཅད་རང་བཞིན་ལྷུན་གྱིས་གྲུབ་པར་ཤེས་པའོ། ། ཇི་ལྟ་བ་མཁྱེན་པའི་ཡེ་ཤེས་ནི། བདག་གི་དངོས་པོ་གཤིས་ཀྱི་གནས་ལུགས་ཤེས་ཏེ། རང་དོན་རྟོགས་པ་ལས་འབྲུལ་བའི་རྒྱུ་ཟད་པའོ།། ཇི་སྙེད་པ་གཟིགས་པའི་ཡེ་ཤེས་ནི། རང་དོན་ཚད་ལ་ཕབས་ནས་གཞན་དོན་ཐུགས་རྗེའི་རོལ་པས་འཛད་པ་མེད་པའོ།། མཛད་པ་མཐར་ཕྱིན་པའི་ཡེ་ཤེས་ནི། རང་གཞན་མ་ལུས་པའི་དོན་མཛད་པ་ཐམས་ཅད་མཐར་ཕྱིན་པའོ། ། ངོ་བོ་ཀ་དག་གི་ཡེ་ཤེས་ནི། མ་རིག་པ་མིང་ཙམ་ཡང་མེད་ཅིང་གྲངས་ལས་འདས་པའོ། ། རང་བཞིན་ལྷུན་གྲུབ་ཀྱི་ཡེ་ཤེས། མི་སྐྱེ་མི་འགག་པར། ཅིའི་ངོ་བོ་སྒྲུང་མི་དགོས་ཤིང༌། ཡུལ་ཐམས་ཅད་ངེས་པ་མེད་པའོ།། ཐུགས་རྗེ་ཀུན་ཁྱབ་ཀྱི་ཡེ་ཤེས། རང་གི་གསལ་བའི་བདག་ཉིད་ཅན་ལས། རང་བཞིན་ཤུགས་ཀྱིས་ཐུགས་རྗེ་འགག་པ་མེད་པར་འཆར་ནས་འགྲོ་དོན་བྱེད་པར་འགྱུར་རོ། ། ཞེས་གསུངས་སོ།།

"The condensed wisdom is the knowledge of the thoughts of beings-to-be-tamed, which realizes the nature of all phenomena, and is concerned only with the welfare of others; the elaborated wisdom is that which comprehends spontaneously and perfectly the nature of all phenomena of Samsara and Nirvana; the wisdom which sees things as they are is that which realizes the ultimate nature of the basis of the phenomenon of self and which exhausts the causes of delusion that comes from self-interest; the wisdom that sees all that exists is that which, having perfected one's own interests, displays compassion for others inexhaustibly; the wisdom of the perfection of activity is the consummation of all actions on behalf of both self and others without exception.

The wisdom of the essence of primordial purity is unfathomable, and that for which ignorance doesn't even nominally exist; the wisdom of the spontaneously present nature is without birth or cessation - it has no need to avoid anything, and it is wholly devoid of fixation on any object; the wisdom of all-pervading compassion is that which, from one's own clear being, by the force of one's naturally appearing unobstructed compassion, acts on behalf of all sentient beings."

གསུམ་པ། ཕུང་པོ་ལྔ་ལ་ཕྱི་ནང་གསང་གསུམ་སྟེ།

ཕྱིའི་ཕུང་པོ་ལྔ་ནི། གཟུགས། སྒྲ། དྲི། རོ། རེག་བྱའོ།

ནང་གི་ཕུང་པོ་ལྔ་ནི། མིག རྣ། སྣ། ལྕེ་དང་ལུས་སོ།

གསང་བའི་ཕུང་པོ་ལྔ་ནི། མིག་གི་དབང་ཤེས། རྣའི་དབང་ཤེས། སྣའི་དབང་ཤེས། ལྕེའི་དབང་ཤེས་དང་ལུས་ཀྱི་དབང་ཤེས་བཅས་ལྔའོ།

གཡུ་ཐོག་རྫོགས་ཆེན་འཁོར་འདས་རང་གྲོལ་ཆེན་མོའི་རྒྱབ་ནས། “ ཕུང་པོ་ལྔ་ལ་ཕྱི་ནང་གསང་བ་གསུམ་སྟེ། ཕྱི་ཡུལ་གྱི་ཕུང་པོ་ལྔ། ནང་ཡུལ་གྱི་ཕུང་པོ་ལྔ། གསང་བ་དེར་འཛིན་གྱི་ཕུང་པོ་ལྔ། དེ་དག་ཀུང་རང་ལ་ཚང་སྟེ། ཕྱི་ཡུལ་གྱི་ཕུང་པོ། གཟུགས་སྒྲ་དྲི་རོ་རེག་བྱ་ལྔ་པོ་རང་ལས་བྱུང་། ནང་ཡུལ་ཅན་གྱི་ཕུང་པོ། མིག རྣ་བ། སྣ། ལྕེ། ལུས་ལྔ་ནི་རང་ལ་ཡོད། གསང་བ་དེར་འཛིན་གྱི་ཕུང་པོ་དབང་ཤེས། སྟོང་བྱེད་ཀྱི་ཚོར་བ་ལྔ་ཡང་རང་ལ་ཡོད། རང་ལས་བྱུང་སྟེ། དེ་ལྟར་ན་རང་ལ་གནས་སྐབས་སུ་བྱུང་བ་མ་ཡིན། ཡེ་ནས་ཚང་ཞིང་དེ་དག་ཀུང་སྤྱང་བླང་ལས་འདས་པའོ། “ཞེས་གསུངས་སོ།།

c) There are three aspects to the five psycho-physical aggregates: outer, inner, and secret.

The five outer aggregates are: form, sound, smell, taste and touch.

The five inner aggregates are: the eyes, the ears, nose, tongue, and skin.

The five secret aggregates are: the faculties or consciousness of seeing, hearing, smelling, tasting, and touching.

In the root-text of Yuthok's Great Perfection Self-Liberation of Samsara-Nirvana it is explained thus:

"There are three aspects to the five aggregates, inner, outer, and secret - five external-object aggregates, five internal-object aggregates, and five secret grasped-at (apprehended) aggregates. These are all part of one's own being. The aggregates of external-objects - form, sound, smell, taste, touch - all five arise from one's own being. The inner-object aggregates of eyes, ears, nose, tongue and skin are of one's own mind or being. The secretly apprehended aggregates, the sensory faculties of experiencing, doing and feeling, all five also exist in one's own being. They have thus not emerged temporarily but have existed in one's being from the primordial beginning and exist beyond all attachment and detachment, all taking up and casting aside."

བཞི་པ། འབྱུང་བ་ལྔ་ལ་ཕྱི་ནང་གསང་བའི་འབྱུང་བ་ལྔ་སྟེ།

ཕྱིའི་འབྱུང་བ་ལྔ་ནི། ས། ཆུ། མེ། རླུང་། ནམ་མཁའ་བཅས་ལྔའོ།

ནང་གི་འབྱུང་བ་ལྔ་ནི། སེམས་ནམ་མཁའ། ཁྲག་ཆུ། ཤ་རུས་ས། དྲོད་མེ། དབུགས་རྒྱུ་བ་རླུང་བཅས་སོ།

གསང་བའི་འབྱུང་བ་ལྔ་ནི། སེམས་ཀྱི་ངོ་ཅིར་ཡང་མ་གྲུབ་པར་སྟོང་པ་ནམ་མཁའ། སེམས་ཀྱི་རང་བཞིན་མ་སྒྲིབ་པ་ས། གསལ་ཞིང་ཚོར་བ་རགས་པ་དང་བཅས་པ་མེ། ཡོང་ལ་ཁྱབ་ཅིང་གཤེར་འཛིན་པ་ཆུ། སེམས་ཀྱི་རྣམས་པ་འགྱུར་མེད་མ་འགག་པ་རླུང་བཅས་ལྔའོ།།

གཡུ་ཐོག་རྫོགས་ཆེན་འཁོར་འདས་རང་གྲོལ་ཆེན་མོའི་རྒྱ་བར་ "འབྱུང་བ་ལྔ་ལ་ཕྱི་ནང་གསང་བ་གསུམ་སྟེ། ཕྱིའི་འབྱུང་བ་ལྔ་ནི། ནམ་མཁའ་ལ་སོགས་པ་ལྔ། ནང་གི་ནི། སེམས་ནམ་མཁའ། ཁྲག་ཆུ། ཤ་རུས་ས། དྲོད་མེ། དབུགས་རྒྱུ་བ་རླུང་ངོ་། ། གསང་བའི་འབྱུང་བ་ལྔ་ནི། སེམས་ཀྱི་ངོ་བོ་ཅིར་ཡང་མ་གྲུབ་པར་སྟོང་པ་ནམ་མཁའ། སེམས་ཀྱི་རང་བཞིན་མ་སྒྲིབ། གསལ་ཞིང་ཚོར་བ་རགས་པ་དང་བཅས་པ་མེ། ཡོངས་ལ་ཁྱབ་ཅིང་གཤེར་འཛིན་པས་ཆུ། སེམས་ཀྱི་རྣམ་པ་འགྱུར་མེད་མ་འགགས་པས་རླུང་། དེ་རྣམས་ཀུན་དབྱིབས་གཅིག་གི་ངང་དུ་གནས་ཤིང་གཡོ་བ་མེད་པ་སྟེ། དེ་ལྟར་ཡང་མཐར་རང་ལས་བྱུང་། རང་ལ་གནས། རང་གི་ཀློང་ལས་མ་འདས་ཤིང་། སྤང་ལེན་ལས་འདས་ཏེ་སྤོ་མི་འཚལ་ཞིང་། བླང་མི་འཚལ་ཏེ་ཡེ་ནས་ཡོད་པའོ། ཞེས་གསུངས་སོ།། །།

d) The 'five elements' are the outer, inner, and secret elements.

The five outer elements are earth, water, fire, wind, and space.

The five inner elements are mental-space; the water of the blood; the earth of flesh and bone; the fire of body-heat/temperature; and the wind that is the air-current we breathe.

The five secret elements are the empty space of mind's essence, which cannot be established as anything at all; the earth or ground that is the mind's undefiled nature; the fire that comes with clear and radiant feeling; the water of all-pervading produced moisture; and the wind of mind in its unobstructed, unchanging aspects.

The root-texts of Yuthok's Great Perfection Self-Liberation of Samsara-Nirvana says:

"There are three aspects of the five elements: outer, inner and secret. The five outer elements are space etc. The inner are the mind's space, blood's water, flesh and bone's earth, body heat's fire and the wind of the breath. The five secret elements are the empty space of the essence of mind, which cannot be established as anything at all, (the earth) that is the undefiled or unobscured nature of mind, the fire that goes along with clear and radiant gross feeling, the water of all-pervading, produced moisture, and the wind of the mind's unchanging and unobstructed aspects. All these abide in a single shape or form, unwaveringly. Thus, do they ultimately emerge from one's own being and abide in one's being; they do not pass beyond the vast expanse of one's own being. They have gone beyond all taking up and casting aside - they exist primordially, and (nothing to) hold onto or cast away can be found in them."

ལྟ་བ། མཚོན་བྱེ་ལྟ་ལ་ཕྱི་ནང་གསང་གསུམ་སྟེ།

ཕྱི་མཚོན་བྱེད་ལྟ་ནི། མདོག་ལྟའམ་འོད་ལྟ་ལ་གོ་སྟེ། འོད་དཀར་པོ། འོད་སེར་པོ། དམར་པོ། འོད་ལྗང་གུ། འོད་སྔོན་པོ་བཅས་སོ།

ནང་གི་མཚོན་བྱེད་ནི། རུས་པ་སོགས་དཀར་པོའི་མདངས་ཅན། སྐྲ་ལ་སོགས་པ་སྤུ་རྟགས་ཀྱི་རིམ་པ་སྔོན་པོ། མཁྲིས་པ་ལ་སོགས་སེར་པོ། ཤ་ཁྲག་ལ་སོགས་དམར་པོ། རླངས་ལ་སོགས་རླུང་གི་རྒྱུ་བ་ལྗང་གུ་བཅས་ལྟའོ།།

གསང་བའི་མཚོན་བྱེད་ལྟ་ནི།

སེམས་ཀྱི་འཕྲོ་རྟོག་དགའ་བ་ལ་སོགས་སྤྲོ་བ་དཀར་པོ། ཆགས་པ་དང་སྲེད་པའི་འདུ་ཤེས་དམར་པོ། སྡང་ཞེན་འཁོན་འཛུག་གི་རྣམ་པས་བྱེ་བྲག་འབྱེད་པ་སྔོན་པོ། རྟོག་པ་ཕྲ་རགས་སྤྲོམ་པ་ལ་སོགས་ཀྱི་འདུ་འཕྲོད་དཔག་ཏུ་མེད་པ་ལྗང་གུ། གཉིད་མི་གཡོ་བར་གནས་པ་སེར་པོའི་མཚོན་བྱེད་ཡིན་ནོ། །

e) The five symbols have three aspects, outer, inner and secret.

The five outer symbols refer to the five colours or lights, which include white, yellow, red, green, and deep blue.

The five inner symbols are: the white tone of the bones and (other white substances); the blue stage of the marks of body and head hair; the yellow of bile, and similarly yellow substances; the red of flesh and blood and the like; the green of the flow of the vital-winds (connected with) the breath, and so on.

The five secret symbols are: the white transference of discursive thoughts into bliss; the red perception of desire and lust; the blue of differentiating between characteristics to be adopted and rejected, to be 'encountered and be involved with'; the green of the assembling of subtle and gross discursive thoughts without measure; and the yellow symbol/light of abiding deeply without wavering.

དེ་ཡང་གཡུ་ཐོག་རྫོགས་ཆེན་འཁོར་འདས་རང་གྲོལ་ཆེན་མོའི་རྒྱ་བར་འདི་ལྟར་”མཆོད་བྱེད་ལྷ་ནི་ཕྱི་ནང་གསང་བ་གསུམ་སྟེ། ཕྱི་མཆོད་བྱེད་དཀར་པོ་ལ་སོགས་ཁ་དོག་ལྔ། ནང་གི་མཆོད་བྱེད་ལྔ་ལ། རུས་པ་ལ་སོགས་དཀར་པོའི་མདོག་ཅན། སྐྲ་ལ་སོགས་སྤུ་རྟགས་ཀྱི་རིམ་པ་སྔོན་པོའི་མདོག་ཅན། མཁྲིས་པ་ལ་སོགས་སེར་པོ། ཤ་ཁྲག་ལ་སོགས་དམར་པོ། བརླངས་ལ་སོགས་རླུང་གི་རྒྱུ་རྡུབ་ལྗང་གུ། གསང་བའི་མཆོད་བྱེད། སེམས་ཀྱི་འཕྲོ་རྟོག་དགའ་བ་ལ་སོགས། སྡོ་བ་དཀར་པོའི་མཆོད་བྱེད། ཆགས་པ་དང་སྲེད་པའི་འདུ་ཤེས་དམར། སྤང་ལེན་འཕྲོད་འཛུག་གི་རྣམ་པས། བྱེ་བྲག་འབྱེད་པ་སྔོན་པའི། རྟོག་པ་ཕྲ་རགས་སྒྲིམ་པ་ལ་སོགས་ཀྱི། འདུ་འཕྲོད་དཔག་ཏུ་མེད་པ་ལྗང་གུ། གཏིང་མི་གཡོ་བར་གནས་པ་སེར་པོའི་མཆོད་བྱེད་དེ། དེ་ལྟར་མཆོད་བྱེད་ཐམས་ཅད་ཀྱང་། རང་ལས་བྱུང་ཞིང་རང་སྣང་གི་བྱ་རྒྱུ་ཙམ་ལས། གཞན་ནས་བྱུང་བ་མ་ཡིན་པའོ། །” ཞེས་དང་།

དེ་ལྟར་ཕྱི་ནང་གསང་བའི་ལྔ་ཚན་ལྔ་ལྔ་ལ། འཁོར་འདས་གང་ཡང་མ་ཚང་བ་མེད་ཅིང་། ཐམས་ཅད་ཚང་བ་སྟེ། དེ་བཞིན་དུ་རྣལ་འབྱོར་པ་རང་ལ་ཐམས་ཅད་ཚང་ཞིང་ཡོངས་སུ་རྫོགས་ལ། དེ་དག་ངོ་མ་ཤེས་པས། ཕན་ཚུན་ཡུལ་དང་ཡུལ་ཅན་དུ་ཕྱེད། དེ་དག་ལ་སྤང་བླང་གི་འཛིན་པ་ཞུགས་པས་བཅིངས། བཅིངས་པས་འཁོར་བར་འཁོར་ཞིང་གྲོལ་དུས་མེད་པས་སྡུག་བསྔལ་བའོ། ། ཞེས་བསྟན་ནོ།།

དེ་དག་ཀྱང་བླ་མས་ངོ་སྤྲད་དེ། རང་ལ་ཡོད་པ་རང་གིས་གོ་ཞིང་རྟོགས་པར་བྱས་པས། འཁོར་འདས་ཐམས་ཅད་རང་ལ་ཡོད་པ་ཐག་ཆོད། གཞན་ནས་མ་བྱུང་བ་ཐག་ཆོད། ཡེ་གདོད་ནས་ལྷུན་གྱིས་གྲུབ་པ་གདེང་ཐོབ། སྤང་བླང་དགག་སྒྲུབ་རེ་དོགས་ལ་སོགས་པ་གཉིས་འཛིན་གྱི་མཐའ་ལས་འདས་པ་ཐག་ཆོད་པ་སྟེ། དེ་ལྟ་བུའི་ཚུལ་གྱིས་ངོ་འཕྲོད་པར་བྱའོ། །

The root-text of Yuthok's Great Perfection Great Self-Liberation of Samsara-Nirvana teaches this as follows:

"The five symbols have three aspects, outer, inner, and secret. The five outer symbols are the five colours, such as white, and so on. The five inner symbols are the white-coloured bones and so on; the blue-coloured stages of the marks of the (body-)hair, head-hair and so on; the yellow bile etc; the red flesh and blood; the green breath and inhaled wind etc. The secret symbols are the symbol of the white transference of the mind's discursive thoughts into bliss; the red perception of desire and lust; the blue of differentiating between characteristics to be adopted and rejected, ('encountered and involved with'); the green of the assembling of subtle and gross discursive thoughts without measure; and the yellow of abiding deeply without wavering. In this way, all of the symbols emerge from one's own being and have no other origin aside from the activities of mind's own manifestations."

And also:

"Thus, there is nothing at all in Samsara and Nirvana that is not encompassed by the five categories of five things in their outer, inner and secret aspects. Everything is contained in them. In this way, everything is contained wholly and completely in the yogi's being. By not recognizing this, by separating object and subject from one another, by becoming fixated on taking up and/or rejecting these, we have bound ourselves (to Samsara). Being bound, we cycle through cyclical existence, and suffer without any moment of release.

Nevertheless, once this has been pointed out by the guru, once one realizes all this comes from one's own mind, once one confirms for oneself that everything in Samsara and Nirvana exists in one's own being, that it has no other origin, one will gain the confidence of the primordial, spontaneously-present (nature of mind). Resolve to pass beyond the limits of dualistic thinking, with its clinging to what is desirable and casting away of what is not, its negations and affirmations, its hopes and fears. In this way should one be introduced (to and recognize the nature of one's own mind)."

ངོ་འཕྲོད་ཅིང་ཐག་ཆོད་པའི་ཕན་ཡོན་ནི།

དེ་ལྟར་ངོ་འཕྲོད་པས་འཁོར་བ་མ་སྤངས་གནས་སུ་དག་ཅིང༌། འདོད་ཆགས་ཞེ་སྡང་གཏི་མུག་ང་རྒྱལ་ཕྲག་དོག་ལ་སོགས་རང་སར་གྲོལ་ནས་ཡེ་ཤེས་ལྔ་ལ་སོགས་པར་འགྱུར་པས་སྟེ།

སྙིང་ག་ཆོས་ཀྱི་འཁོར་ལོ་ནས་ཞེ་སྡང་མེ་ལོང་ལྟ་བུའི་ཡེ་ཤེས་སུ་གྲོལ་ཏེ། རང་གི་ཡིད་ཀྱི་སྒྲིབ་པ་བྱང༌། སངས་རྒྱས་ཀྱི་ཐུགས་ཀྱི་ཡོན་ཏན་ཐོབ། གཟུགས་ཀྱི་ཕུང་པོ་རྡོར་སེམས་སུ་གྱུར། ཆུའི་ཁམས་མ་མ་ཀིའི་རང་བཞིན་དུ་དག སངས་རྒྱས་རྡོ་རྗེ་རིགས་ཀྱི་ཐུགས་འཁྲུལ་བ་མེད་པ་ཐོབ་ནས་འགྲོ་དོན་བྱེད་པར་འགྱུར།

མགྲིན་པ་ལོངས་སྤྱོད་འཁོར་ལོ་ནས་འདོད་ཆགས་སོ་སོར་རྟོག་པའི་ཡེ་ཤེས་སུ་གྲོལ་ཏེ། ངག་གི་སྒྲིབ་པ་དག གསུང་གི་ཡོན་ཏན་ཐོབ། འདུ་ཤེས་ཕུང་པོ་སྣང་བ་མཐའ་ཡས་སུ་གྱུར། མེའི་ཁམས་གོས་དཀར་མོ་ཉིད་དུ་གནས་དག པད་མ་རིགས་ཀྱི་གསུང་འགག་པ་མེད་པ་ཆོས་ཀྱི་སྒྲ་དབྱངས་ཐོབ་ནས་འགྲོ་དོན་བྱེད་པར་འགྱུར་རོ། །

སྤྱི་བོ་བདེ་ཆེན་འཁོར་ལོ་ནས་གཏི་མུག་ཆོས་དབྱིངས་ཡེ་ཤེས་སུ་གྲོལ་ཏེ། རང་གི་ལུས་ཀྱི་སྒྲིབ་པ་དག སངས་རྒྱས་ཐམས་ཅད་ཀྱི་སྐུའི་ཡོན་ཏན་ཐོབ། རྣམ་ཤེས་ཕུང་པོ་རྣམ་སྣང་དུ་གྱུར། ནམ་མཁའི་ཁམས་ཆོས་ཀྱི་དབྱིངས་ཕྱུག་མར་གནས་དག དེ་བཞིན་གཤེགས་པའི་སྐུ་འགྱུར་བ་མེད་པ་ཆོས་ཀྱི་སྐུ་ཐོབ་ནས་འགྲོ་དོན་བྱེད་པར་འགྱུར་རོ། །

The benefits of pointing out and confirming are as this: once one has been introduced in this way, once one has purified Samsara in its basic state without rejecting it (i.e. has allowed it to rest in the perfection of its innate being), and once desire, anger, ignorance, pride, and jealousy have been liberated in their own ground, they will be transformed into the five wisdoms in the following way:

From the 'dharma' chakra of absolute reality in one's heart-center anger will be liberated into mirror-like wisdom. The obscurations of one's mind will be purified and one will obtain the superior qualities of Buddha-mind. One's bodily aggregates will be transformed into Vajrasattva. Having transmuted one's water-element into the nature of Mamaki, and having obtained the undeluded Mind of the Vajra Buddha-family, one will act on behalf of all sentient beings.

From the throat chakra of enjoyment, desire will be liberated into the discriminating wisdom. Obscurations of the voice will be purified and one will obtain the superior qualities of Speech. The aggregates of perception will be transformed into Amitabha. Having transmuted and purified the fire-element into its innate being as Pandaravasini, 'The White-Clad Lady', and having obtained the dharma-melody of the unobstructed Speech of the Lotus Buddha-family, one will act on behalf of all sentient beings.

From the head chakra of great bliss, ignorance will be liberated into the wisdom of the dharmadhatu. The obscurations of one's body will be purified and one will obtain the superior qualities of the bodies of all the Buddhas. One's aggregates of consciousness will be transformed into Vairocana. Having transmuted one's space-element into its innate being as 'The Rich Lady of the Dharma-Expanse' (Choying Chugma), and having obtained the unchanging reality-body of the tathagathas, one will act on behalf of all sentient beings.

ལྟེ་བ་སྤྲུལ་བའི་འཁོར་ལོ་ནས་ང་རྒྱལ་མཉམ་པ་ཉིད་ཡེ་ཤེས་སུ་གནས་གྲོལ་ཏེ། ལུས་ངག་ཡིད་གསུམ་གྱི་སྒྲིབ་པ་དག སངས་རྒྱས་ཐམས་ཅད་ཀྱི་ཡོན་ཏན་ཆེ་བའི་ཡོན་ཏན་ཐོབ། ཚོར་བའི་ཕུང་པོ་རིན་ཆེན་འབྱུང་ལྡན་དུ་བྱང་ཆུབ། སའི་ཁམས་སྤྱན་མར་གནས་དག རིན་ཆེན་འབྱུང་ལྡན་གྱི་ཡོན་ཏན་ཐམས་ཅད་མཁྱེན་པ་ཉིད་ཐོབ་ནས་འགྲོ་དོན་བྱེད་པར་འགྱུར་རོ། །

གསང་གནས་བདེ་སྐྱོང་འཁོར་ལོ་ནས་ཕྲག་དོག་བྱ་གྲུབ་ཡེ་ཤེས་སུ་གྲོལ་ཏེ། ཉོན་སྒྲིབ་དང་ཤེས་སྒྲིབ་དག སངས་རྒྱས་ཐམས་ཅད་ཀྱི་འཕྲིན་ལས་ཀྱི་ཡོན་ཏན་ཐོབ། འདུ་བྱེད་ཕུང་པོ་བཅོམ་ལྡན་དོན་ཡོད་གྲུབ་པ་ཉིད་དུ་བྱང་ཆུབ། རླུང་གི་ཁམས་དམ་ཚིག་སྒྲོལ་མར་གནས་དག་སངས་རྒྱས་ལས་ཀྱི་རིགས་ཀྱི་ཕྲིན་ལས་ཐོགས་པ་མེད་པ་འགྲུབ་ནས་འགྲོ་དོན་བྱེད་པར་འགྱུར་ཏེ།

From the navel chakra of magical-emanation, pride will be liberated in its own being into the wisdom of absolute equality. The obscurations of body, speech, and mind will all be purified and one will obtain the greater superior qualities of all the Buddhas. The aggregates of feeling will be purified and perfected as Ratnasambhava. Having transmuted one's earth-element into Lochana (Female Buddha-eye) and having obtained the inherent wisdom of all the superior qualities possessed by Ratnasambhava, one will act on behalf of all sentient beings.

From the secret-abode (genitals) bliss-sustaining chakra jealousy will be liberated into the all-accomplishing wisdom. The obscurations of afflictive emotions and cognition will be purified and one will obtain the superior qualities of the activities of all of the Buddhas. The aggregates of the mental formation/constitutive factors will be purified and completed as the Arhant Amoghasiddhi himself. Having purified one's wind-element in its own being as Samaya Tara and having accomplished the unobstructed activities of the Action-Buddha family, one will act on behalf of all sentient beings.

རྫོགས་ཆེན་འཁོར་འདས་རང་གྲོལ་གྱི་རྩ་བར་འདི་ལྟར་གསུངས་སྟེ།

“དེ་ལྟར་ངོ་འཕྲོད་པས་འཁོར་བ་མ་སྤྱངས་གནས་སུ་དག་ཅིང་། འདོད་ཆགས་ཞེ་སྡང་གཏི་མུག་ང་རྒྱལ་ཕྲག་དོག་ལ་སོགས་རང་སར་གྲོལ་ནས། ཡེ་ཤེས་ལྔ་ལ་སོགས་པར་གྱུར་པས་ཏེ། དེ་ཡང་རྣལ་འབྱོར་པ་ཡིད་ཀྱི་སྒྲིབ་པ་བྱང་། སངས་རྒྱས་ཐམས་ཅད་ཀྱི་ཐུགས་ཀྱི་ཡོན་ཏན་ཐོབ། གཟུགས་ཀྱི་ཕུང་པོ་བཅོམ་ལྡན་འདས་རྡོ་རྗེ་སེམས་དཔར་གྱུར། ཆུའི་ཁམས་མཱ་མ་ཀཱིའི་རང་བཞིན་དུ་གནས་དག ཞེ་སྡང་མེ་ལོང་ལྟ་བུའི་ཡེ་ཤེས་གྲོལ་ཏེ། སངས་རྒྱས་རྡོ་རྗེ་རིགས་ཀྱི་ཐུགས་འཁྲུལ་པ་མེད་པ་ཐོབ་ནས། འགྲོ་བ་སེམས་ཅན་གྱི་དོན་བྱེད་པར་འགྱུར་རོ།།

ངག་གི་སྒྲིབ་པ་དག་ནས་སངས་རྒྱས་ཐམས་ཅད་ཀྱི་གསུང་གི་ཡོན་ཏན་ཐོབ། འདུ་ཤེས་ཀྱི་ཕུང་པོ་བཅོན་ལྡན་འདས་སྣང་བ་མཐའ་ཡས་ཉིད་དུ་བྱང་ཆུབ། མེའི་ཁམས་གོས་དཀར་མོ་ཉིད་དུ་གནས་དག འདོད་ཆགས་སོ་སོར་རྟོག་པའི་ཡེ་ཤེས་སུ་གྲོལ་ཏེ། སངས་རྒྱས་པདྨ་རིགས་ཀྱི་གསུང་འགག་མེད་པ་ཆོས་ཀྱི་སྒྲ་དབྱངས་ཐོབ་ནས། འགྲོ་དོན་བྱེད་པར་འགྱུར་རོ། །

ལུས་ཀྱི་སྒྲིབ་པ་བྱང་ནས་སངས་རྒྱས་ཐམས་ཅད་སྐུའི་ཡོན་ཏན་ཐོབ། རྣམ་ཤེས་ཕུང་པོ་བཅོམ་ལྡན་འདས་སྐུ་འགྱུར་བ་མེད་པ་ཆོས་ཀྱི་སྐུ་ཐོབ་ནས་འགྲོ་དོན་བྱེད་པར་འགྱུར་རོ། ལ་ལའི་སྐབས་སུ་རྡོ་རྗེ་སེམས་དཔའི་སྐུ། རྣམ་སྣང་གི་སྐུ་ཐོབ་པའང་གསུང་། གནས་འགྱུར་གྱི་ཁྱད་པར་ཙམ་ལས་དོན་གྱི་དགོངས་པ་ལ་ཁྱད་པར་མེད།

In the root-text of the Great Perfection Self-Liberation of Samsara-Nirvana it is explained thoroughly as follows:

"Once one has been introduced in this way, and has purified Samsara in its basic state without rejecting it (i.e. has allowed it to rest in the perfection of its innate being), and once desire, hatred, ignorance, pride, and jealousy have been liberated in their own natures, and have been transformed into the five wisdoms, then the yogi will purify his mental obscurations and will obtain the superior qualities of the Mind of all the Buddhas.

The bodily aggregates will be transformed into the Victorious, Transcendent Vajrasattva, the water-element will be transmuted into its nature as Mamaki and hatred will be liberated into the mirror-like wisdom. Having obtained the undeluded Mind of the Vajra-Buddha family, one will act on behalf of all sentient beings.*

Having purified the obscurations of speech, one will obtain the superior qualities of the Speech of all the Buddhas. One will purify and perfect the perception aggregates as the Victorious, Transcendent Amitabha himself, one will transmute one's fire-element into its natural state of Pandaravasini and desire will be liberated into the wisdom that realizes things as they are. Having obtained the dharma-melodies of the unobstructed Speech of the Lotus-Buddha family, one will act on behalf of all sentient beings.

Having purified the obscurations of the body one will obtain the superior qualities of the Body of all the Buddhas. Having (transformed) the aggregates of consciousness and obtained the unchanging absolute-truth body of the Victorious, Transcendent one, one will act on behalf of all sentient beings.

**Sometimes some people talk about obtaining Vajrasattva's body in place of obtaining Vairocana's. Other than this (minor) differentiation in the transformation (description itself) there is no real difference in the ultimate meaning (of the process)."*

ལུས་ངག་ཡིད་གསུམ་གྱི་སྒྲིབ་པ་དག སངས་རྒྱས་ཐམས་ཅད་ཀྱི་ཡོན་ཏན་ཆེ་བའི་ཡོན་ཏན་ཐོབ། ཚོར་བའི་ཕུང་པོ་རིན་ཆེན་འབྱུང་ལྡན་དུ་བྱང་ཆུབ། སའི་ཁམས་སྤྱན་མར་གནས་དག ང་རྒྱལ་མཉམ་པ་ཉིད་ཡེ་ཤེས་སུ་གནས་གྲོལ་ཏེ། རིན་ཆེན་འབྱུང་ལྡན་གྱི་ཡོན་ཏན་ཐམས་ཅད་མཁྱེན་པ་ཉིད་ཐོབ་ནས་འགྲོ་དོན་བྱེད་པར་འགྱུར་རོ།

ཉོན་སྒྲིབ་དང་ཤེས་སྒྲིབ་དག སངས་རྒྱས་ཐམས་ཅད་ཀྱི་འཕྲིན་ལས་ཀྱི་ཡོན་ཏན་ཐོབ། འདུ་བྱེད་ཕུང་པོ་བཅོམ་ལྡན་དོན་ཡོད་གྲུབ་པ་ཉིད་དུ་བྱང་ཆུབ། རླུང་གི་ཁམས་དམ་ཚིག་སྒྲོལ་མར་གནས་དག ཕྲག་དོག་བྱ་གྲུབ་ཡེ་ཤེས་སུ་གྲོལ་ཏེ་སངས་རྒྱས་ལས་ཀྱི་རིགས་ཀྱི་ཕྲིན་ལས་ཐོགས་པ་མེད་པ་འགྲུབ་ནས་འགྲོ་དོན་བྱེད་པར་འགྲུབ་པར་རོ། །ཞེས་ཡང་དག་པར་གསུངས་སོ།། །།

ང། ཉམས་སུ་བླང་ཐབས།

ཉམས་སུ་བླངས་ཐབས་ལ་རྫོགས་རིམ་སྐབས་སུ་བསྟན་པ་དང་རྫོགས་ཆེན་སྐབས་སུ་བསྟན་པ་གཉིས་ལས།

དང་པོ། རྫོགས་རིམ་སྐབས་སུ་བསྟན་པ་ནི།

གཡུ་ཐོག་སྙིང་ཐིག་བླ་སྒྲུབ་ཀྱི་རྫོགས་རིམ་སྐུ་གསུམ་རང་ཤར་ལས། འོག་སྒོ་བདེ་ཆེན་ལམ་མམ་ཀཱ་སུ་ཏྲ་བསྟན་རྗེས་སྟེང་སྒོ་རྣམ་གྲོལ་ལམ་སྐྱེ་སྤྲོས་མེད་རྫོགས་རིམ་འཇམ་ཕྲུག་རྒྱ་ཆེ་པོའི་ཉམས་ལེན་ཏེ།

"The obscurations of body, speech and mind will all be purified and one will obtain the greater superior qualities of all the Buddhas. The aggregates of feeling will be perfected and purified as Ratnasambhava, the earth-element will be transmuted into Lochana and pride will be liberated in its own being as the wisdom of sameness. Having obtained the inherent wisdom of all the superior qualities of Ratnasambhava one will act on behalf of all sentient beings.

The obscurations of the afflictive emotions and cognition will be purified and one will obtain the superior qualities of the activies of all of the Buddhas. The aggregates of formation will be purified and perfected as the Arhant Amogasiddhi himself, the wind-element will be transmuted into Samaya Tara and jealousy will be liberated into the all-accomplishing wisdom. Having accomplished the unobstructed activities of the Action-Buddha family, one will act on behalf of all sentient beings."

4) The method of putting into practice

There are two teachings on the method of putting into practice, one which is taught in the context of the Completion Stage and one which is taught in the Great Perfection. Of these, the first is the teaching in the context of the Completion Stage.

a) The Yuthok Nyingthig Guru Sadhana's 'Completion Stage Self-Arising of the Three Bodies' text, after revealing instructions on the Path of the Great Bliss of the Lower Gates or Karmamudra, the practice of the Path of Complete Liberation of the Upper Gates, the unelaborated Completion Stage or Great Seal Mahamudra (is taught), which is the complete and authentic practice of 'Cutting Through Hardness':

“རྒྱན་པ་དང་། མ་ནིང་། ཙྪ་ཤིན་ཏུ་ངན་པ་དག་གིས་གྲོལ་ལམ་ལ་བརྟེན་པར་བྱ་སྟེ། དབང་ཐོབ་ཅིང་དམ་ཚིག་ལྡན། ཕྱི་ནང་གི་བསྙེན་སྒྲུབ་ཐེངས་པས། བདེ་བའི་སྟན་ལ་རྐང་པ་སྐྱིལ་ཀྲུང་། ལག་པ་གཉིས་མཉམ་བཞག སྙལ་ཚིགས་དྲང་པོར་བསྲང་། དཔུང་པ་ཕྱིར་དབྱེ། མགྲིན་པ་དགུག ལྕེ་མཆུ་རང་བབས་སུ་བཞག མིག་བར་སྣང་གི་དཀྱིལ་དུ་མིག་འབྲས་མི་འགུལ་བར་ཧྲིག་གེ་བལྟས་ལ། རྣམ་རྟོག་འདས་པའི་རྗེས་མི་དཔྱད། མ་འོངས་པའི་སྔུན་མི་བསུ། ད་ལྟ་བ་ལ་བཅོ་བགྲང་མི་བྱ་བར་རྣམ་རྟོག་གང་སྐྱེས་བཀག་ལ་བཞག ཐུན་མཚམས་སུ་བླ་མའི་རྣལ་འབྱོར་བསྒོམ། གསོལ་བ་ཕུར་ཚུགས་སྙིང་ནས་གདབ། ལྷ་བ་གཅིག

ལུས་གནས་བལྟ་སྟངས་སྔར་དང་འདྲ། རིག་པ་ལེགས་པར་སྒྲིམས། སྲང་དུ་གཟུར། མ་ཡེངས་པར་གཟུན་ཏེ། རྣམ་རྟོག་རྣམ་རྟོག་འདས་པའི་རྗེས་མི་དཔྱད། མ་འོངས་པའི་སྔུན་མི་བསུ། ད་ལྟ་བ་ལ་བཅོ་བགྲང་མི་བྱ། དགྲ་ལ་ཞེ་སྡང་། གཉེན་ལ་བརྩེ་དུང་སོགས་རྟོག་པ་ཅི་མང་སྤྱེལ། སེམས་སྐད་ཅིག་ཀྱང་གནས་སུ་མི་འཇུག་པ་ཡུན་དུ་བཙུག ཐུན་མཚམས་སུ་གསོལ་བ་གདབ། ལྷ་བ་གཅིག

དེ་ནས་ལུས་བལྟ་སྟངས་སྔར་དང་འདྲ་ལ། ཆེད་དུ་སྤྲོ་ཡང་མི་སྤྲོ། ཆེད་དུ་བསྡུ་ཡང་མི་བསྡུ། རྣམ་རྟོག་གང་སྐྱེས་ངོས་ཟིན་ཙམ། མ་ཡེངས་པ་ཙམ་ལ་ལྷོད་ཀྱིས་གློད། ཤིག་གིས་བཤིག ཅོག་གེ་བཞག ཙང་གིས་བསྐྱུར། ཐུན་མཚམས་སུ་གསོལ་བ་བཏབ།

"Old people, intersex individuals, and those with very bad channels should rely on this path of liberation. For those who have received empowerments and who hold tantric vows, and who have completed the required number of recitations of the outer and inner approach and accomplishment retreat sadhana practices (do as follows): adopt a comfortable position with one's legs crossed. Place your two hands in the mudra of meditative equipoise, and hold your spine upright. Open up your shoulders and draw in your neck, and let your tongue and lips rest naturally. Focus your gaze in the middle of space and stare wide-eyed without moving your eyeballs. Don't analyze past discursive thoughts, don't welcome thoughts of what is ahead in the future, and don't speculate about the present. Stop whatever discursive thoughts arise and cultivate guru yoga during the breaks in your practice. Pray one-pointedly from your heart. (Do this) for one month.*

With your posture and gaze like before, concentrate thoroughly on innate awareness (rigpa), and focus on it directly and exclusively. Apply yourself without distraction. Do not analyze past discursive thoughts, do not welcome thoughts of what` is ahead in the future. Do not make calculations about the present. However many conceptual thoughts proliferate, apply the remedy of love to the enemy of hatred. When your mind does not abide in stability for even an instant, let it wander freely. Pray during the gaps. (Do this for) one month.

Then, with one's posture and gaze as before, without deliberately projecting or not projecting, without deliberately condensing or not condensing thoughts, whatever discursive thoughts arise recognize them as merely that, simply let go and relax without distraction. Completely relax and unravel yourself, rest in stillness and quiet. Let go of everything. Pray (fervently) during the breaks."

*The Tibetan term used here is ma ning. Translated variously as 'neuter', 'eunuch' or 'hermaphrodite' ma ning has historically been used in both religious and medical Tibetan literature to refer to a broad range of bodies and individuals which commentators have labeled as falling between idealized norms of 'male' and 'female'. Here in the root-text, Yuthok cites ma ning as part of a list of practitioners for whom Mahamudra/Trekcho may be a preferable alternative to Karmamudra. Yuthok seems to be implying that due to anatomical/physiological factors, for some inter-sex individuals (just as for those whose libido or sexual function has decreased due to aging or damaged channels) heterosexual penetrative sexual intercourse as typically occurs in partnered Karmamudra may prove impossible or undesirable. This is not to say that all inter-sexual individuals are categorically disqualified from practicing Karmamudra.

ཟླ་གཅིག་དེ་ལྟར་ཉམས་སུ་བླངས་ཚེ། དེ་རྗེས་དམིགས་སྐོར་འདི་གསུམ་གྱི་དུས་སུ་སེམས་གནས་པ་དང་། སྤྲོ་བ་དང་། རང་སོར་བཞག་པ་གསུམ་གྱི་ངོ་བོ་བཟང་ངན། མཐོ་དམན། རིང་ཐུང་། ཆེ་ཆུང་། དཀར་ནག་སོགས་དབྱེ་བ་ཨེ་འདུག་ལེགས་པར་རྩད་བཅད། ཕྱི་རོལ་སྣོད་ཀྱི་འཇིག་རྟེན་འབྱུང་བ་ལྔ་ལས་གྲུབ་པ་དང་། ནང་བཅུད་ཀྱི་སེམས་ཅན་འབྱུང་བ་ལྔ་ཡིས་བསྐྱེད་པ་དང་། གསང་བ་སེམས་ཀྱི་ཆོ་འཕྲུལ་སྣ་ཚོགས་སུ་འཆར་བ་འདི་རྣམས་གཅིག་གམ་ཐ་དད། ཐ་དད་ན་སོ་སོར་འབྱེད་མཁན་དེ་སུ་ཞིག་ན་དུས་ནམ་གྱི་ཚེ་ཚུལ་ཇི་ལྟར། གཅིག་ཏུ་མཐོང་མཁན། དང་སྣམ་དུ་རྩད་ལེགས་པར་བཅད། རྩད་གཅོད་མཁན་དེའི་མཁན་པོ། དེའི་མཁན་པོ་སོགས་བརྒྱུད་མ་ནས་བརྒྱུད་མར་དྲག་ཏུ་དེད་ནས་བལྟས་པས། སྣང་སྲིད་འཁོར་འདས་ཀྱི་ཆོས་ཐམས་ཅད་རང་གི་སེམས་སུ་ཐག་བཅད། སེམས་ཀྱི་ངོ་བོ་ཡེ་གདོད་མ་ནས། སྐྱེ་འགག་གནས་བྲལ་མཐའ་དབུས་སྤྲོས་པའི་དྲི་མ་དང་བྲལ་བ། གཤིས་ཅིར་ཡང་མ་གྲུབ་པ། མདངས་སྣ་ཚོགས་སུ་འཆར་བ། འཆར་བཞིན་དུ་འཆར་མཁན་གཞི་རྩ་བྲལ་བ། བློ་བསམ་ཤེས་བརྗོད་བློ་ཡུལ། ཐམས་ཅད་ལས་འདས་པའི་རིག་པ་གཅེར་བུ་ལྷང་ངེ་བ། རྒྱུན་ཁྲོས་སེ་བ་ཞིག་ལ། སྣང་བ་ཕྱི་རུ་མ་ལུས། རིག་པ་ནང་དུ་མ་ལུས། ཡེ་ཤེས་ཟང་ཐལ་དུ་མ་ལུས། ཉོན་མོངས་དན་ཧྲི་ཕྱང་རྒྱུ་དང་སྤྱོད་མཁན་བྲལ་བ། ཡེ་ཛི་བཞིན་པའི་གནས་ལུགས་དེ་མཐོང་རྒྱུ་མེད་པའི་ཚུལ་གྱིས་གནས་ལུགས་དེ་མཐོང་། ཉམས་མྱོང་རིག་པའི་ཡེ་ཤེས་འགྱུར་མེད་བློའི་གཏིང་དུ་འཆར་བས། དེ་ཉིད་འགྲོ་འཆགས་ཉལ་འདུག་ལུས་ངག་ཡིད་སྤྱོད་ཀུན་དུ་སོ་མ། ལྷུག་པ། མ་བཅོས་པ། རང་མདངས་བཅོས་མེད་དུ་སྐྱོང་དེ། རྗེན་ཁྲོས་སེ་བའི་ངང་ལ་མ་ཡེངས་ཙམ་བསྐྱངས་པས། ཚེ་འདིར་ཀུན་བཟང་གི་དགོངས་པ་མངོན་དུ་འགྱུར་བ་ཐེ་ཚོམ་མེད་པ་སྟེ། ཡིད་ཆེས་སྐྱུར་འཆར་བའི་ཁྲིད་ཚར་རོ།།” ཞེས་པ་ནི་ཁྲིགས་ཆོད་ཉམས་ལེན་ཚད་དང་ལྡན་པ།

"When you've applied the practice in this way for one month, afterwards (do the following) round of contemplations: investigate thoroughly to (see if) there's any distinction between the three times or stages of mental stability, mental elaboration, and resting the mind as it is, between the three essences, between good and bad, high and low, long and short, big and small, black and white, and so on. Investigate whether the outer phenomenal world composed of the five elements, the inner sentient beings which are its inhabitants (which are likewise) composed of the five elements, and the secret appearances which are the manifold magical projections of mind are unitary or distinct. If they are distinct, analyze thoroughly: who is it that has made them so, how have they been differentiated in terms of time? If they appear as unitary, then thoroughly inspect the seer that sees them in this way. By vigorously tracking and observing, from moment to moment the one who analyzes, and the one who analyzes the analyzer, and the one who analyzes the analyzer of the analyzer, and so on, confirm that all dharmas or phenomena, all appearances and arisings of Samsara-Nirvana, are in your own mind.

(Perceive) the primordial mind-essence, which does not arise, cease, or abide, that is free of the stain of limiting conceptions, of mental elaborations of center and periphery. It is not composed of any essential nature at all - though it appears as diverse and radiant arisings, even as it arises it lacks anything that arises with either basis or root. Allow this naked and vividly present awareness which is beyond all and every mental reification, beyond speaking or imagining, which is inconceivable and ineffable, to freely unfold. It is completely relaxed and open, it is all outer appearances, all inner awareness without exception, it is utterly unobstructed wisdom, which has no need to reject the bad afflictive emotions usually meant to be rejected. Perceive this natural state (that appears) imperceptibly as the natural state of primordial is-ness, let the unchanging wisdom of experiential awareness arise deep in one's mind. Loosen up into the fresh and spontaneous presence of the sheer suchness of walking, moving around, lying down, and sitting, of body, speech, mind and all actions, into totally free, uncontrived, and natural self-radiance. Sustain a state of being that is merely undistracted, naked, and completely relaxed and open. Practicing like this, your own mind will be actually transformed into the mind of Samantabhadra, and its arising as the body of absolute-reality itself will be brought to completion."

བཅོག་བཞག་གསུམ་གྱི་གཞི་བཅའ་ནས། སེམས་གནས་པ་སྡེ་གནས་པ་སེམས་ཀྱི་རྒྱུན་ནམ་གནས་ས་གནོད་མའི་ངང་དུ་གནས་པ་དང་། སེམས་འཕྲོ་བ་སེམས་ཀྱི་རོལ་པའམ་ཡེ་ཤེས་ཀྱི་རོལ་པར་འཆར་བ། གཉིས་མེད་མཉམ་པའི་ངང་དུ་གནས་པ། སེམས་རང་སོར་བཞག་པ། རྣམ་རྟོག་རང་སར་ཞི་བའི་ཞི་གནས་དང་ཡིན་ལུགས་སྒྲིབ་མེད་དེ་ཉིད་ལྷག་ཏུ་མཐོང་བའི་མདོ་ལུགས་ཀྱི་ཞི་ལྷག་ཟུང་འབྲེལ་གྱི་གནད་ཚང་བས་མ་ཟད། ལམ་རྟགས་ནོར་བུའི་སྒྲོན་མེར། སྟེང་སྒོ་ལ་བརྟེན་པའི་གྲོལ་ལམ་ཉམས་སུ་བླངས་པས། བདེ་གསལ་མི་རྟོག་པའི་ཉམས་ལེན་སྐྱེ་བ་རྩེ་གཅིག དེའི་རྟོགས་པ་ཤར་བ་སྤྲོས་བྲལ། སྣ་ཚོགས་འདོད་ཐོག་ཏུ་བབས་པ་རོ་གཅིག བསྒོམ་བྱ་བསྒོམ་བྱེད་ཀྱི་འབད་རྩོལ་དང་བྲལ་བ་བསྒོམ་མེད། ཅེས་ཕྱག་རྒྱ་ཆེན་པོའི་རྣལ་འབྱོར་བཞིའི་ཉམས་ལེན་ཡང་ཆ་ཚང་ཡིན་པ་དང་། རིག་ངོ་བསྐྱུང་ནས་ཅིར་སྣང་རང་གྲོལ་འཛིན་མེད་ཀྱི་འོད་གསལ་རྫོགས་ཆེན་བཅས་མདོ་སྔགས་ལྷ་བསྒོམ་ཐམས་ཅད་ཀྱི་གནད་ཀུན་འདུས་སུ་བསྟན་པ་ནི་ཐུན་མིན་གྱི་མན་ངག་ལ་གོ་བར་བྱའོ།།

གཉིས་པ། རྫོགས་ཆེན་སྐབས་སུ་བསྟན་པ་ནི།

འཁོར་འདས་རོ་སྙོམས་ཆེན་མོ་ལས། ངོ་འཕྲོད་ནས་རང་གི་རྒྱུད་ཐོག་ཏུ་བཀལ་ཞིང་ཉམས་སུ་ལེན་ཐབས་བསྟན་པ་ནི། རྣལ་འབྱོར་བ་རབ་ལ་རབ་འབྲིང་ཐ་གསུམ་དང་། རྣལ་འབྱོར་བ་འབྲིང་ལ་རབ་འབྲིང་ཐ་གསུམ་དང་རྣལ་འབྱོར་ཐ་མལ་བ་རབ་འབྲིང་ཐ་གསུམ་ཞེས་རྣལ་འབྱོར་བ་རིགས་དགུ་སྟེ། རྣལ་འབྱོར་བ་རབ་ཀྱི་རབ། རབ་ཀྱི་འབྲིང་། རབ་ཀྱི་ཐ་བཅས་གསུམ་དང་། རྣལ་འབྱོར་བ་འབྲིང་གི་རབ། འབྲིང་གི་འབྲིང་། འབྲིང་གི་ཐ་བཅས་འབྲིང་ལ་གསུམ། རྣལ་འབྱོར་བ་ཐ་མའི་རབ། ཐ་མའི་འབྲིང་། ཐ་མའི་ཐ་བཅས་གསུམ་གསུམ་དགུས་ཉམས་ལེན་བྱ་སྟངས་རང་ཁམས་མཐུན་པའམ་གང་ལ་གང་འདོད་ཀྱི་ལུགས་གསུངས་སྟེ།

Having laid the foundation of the threefold 'freely resting's (i.e. the freely resting mountain, ocean, and awareness)*, stabilize one's mind by abiding in the primordial essence of the ornaments or abodes of the mind. Let the mind's elaborations or projections arise as the mind's own display, as the play of wisdom. Abiding in nondual equanimity, let the mind rest as it is. (This practice) not only encompasses all of the essential points of peaceful-abiding (shamatha), which pacifies discursive thought in its own ground or place (i.e. by leaving it as it is), and 'seeing-beyond' (vipashyana), which sees beyond to the unobscured such-ness of reality as it is, which are united in the Sutric system but as it says in the 'Lamp of the Jewel of the Signs on the Path':

"Having put into practice the path to liberation that relies on the upper gates, (one experiences) the unembellished dawning of the realization of the one-pointed arising of the practice of bliss, clarity, and non-conceptuality, one perceives all of one's manifold desires as 'one taste', the non-meditation that is devoid of striving after either meditator or meditation object."

This encompasses the whole of the practice of the four yogas of Mahamudra. We can (thus) understand the Clear Light Great Perfection – which is the sustaining of the essence of awareness and self-liberating without grasping of whatever arises - as an uncommon pith instruction, which condenses all of the essential points of the entirety of the View and Meditation of the Sutras and Tantras.

b) Regarding the teachings in the context of the Great Perfection,
According to the 'Great Pointing Out of Samsara-Nirvana':

*"When it comes to the teachings on recognizing (one's own nature) and taking it to heart, as well as the way to practice, there are said to be nine different kinds of yogic practitioner and nine ways to practice (three groups of three): the greater, average, and lesser great yogi; the greater, average, and lesser average yogi; and the greater, average, and lesser lesser yogi. This is taught as a way of practicing that accords with each person's disposition or as system (that fits with) with whatever they might want or require.**

*See Appendices D

རྣལ་འབྱོར་བ་རབ།

དེ་ཡང་འཁོར་འདས་རང་གྲོལ་གྱི་རྒྱ་བར་ "དེ་ལྟར་ངོ་སྤྲོད་ཅིང་འཕྲོད་པར་བྱའོ། ། ངོ་འཕྲོད་ནས་རང་གི་རྒྱུད་ཐོག་ཏུ་བཀལ་ཞིང་། ཉམས་སུ་ལེན་ཐབས་བསྟན་པ་ནི། རྣལ་འབྱོར་བ་རབ་ཀྱིས་རབ་ཡེ་གྲོལ་ཆེན་པོར་ཉམས་སུ་བླང་། རབ་ཀྱི་འབྲིང་གིས་རང་གྲོལ་ཆེན་པོར་ཉམས་སུ་བླང་། རབ་ཀྱི་ཐ་མས་ཡོངས་གྲོལ་ཆེན་པོར། ཞེས་གསུངས་པ་ལྟར། ཡེ་གྲོལ་དང་། རང་གྲོལ་དང་ཡོང་གྲོལ་གསུམ་ལས།

ཡེ་གྲོལ་ནི། རིག་པ་རང་ཤར་ལས། "ཡེ་གྲོལ་ཅོག་བཞག་དང་ལས་གཞན་མེད་པས།། རང་བྱུང་བརྡལ་བའི་སྐུ་དེ་གང་བདེར་གློད།།"

The Great Yogi

As it is further stated in the root-text of the Self-Liberation of Samsara-Nirvana:

"Thus should it be pointed out and recognized - once it's been recognized, the way that one should take it to heart and practice is taught as follows:

The greater great yogi will practice through the great primordial liberation (yetrol); the average great yogi will practice via the great self-liberation (rangtrol); the lesser great yogi will practice through the great total liberation (yongtrol).

Of the three categories of the primordial liberation, self-liberation and total liberation, the 'Self-Arising Awareness' states, regarding the primordial liberation: "The primordial liberation is none other than freely resting, (it is) letting go in whatever way is comfortable into the self-emerging, all-pervasive body."

རྒྱལ་དབང་ལྔ་པའི་རྫོགས་ཆེན་ཁྲིད་ཡིག་རིག་འཛིན་ཞལ་ལུང་ལས། དེའི་འགྲེལ་བར་འདི་ལྟར་གསུངས་སྟེ།

“དྲི་མ་ཐམས་ཅད་དང་བྲལ་བའི་ད་ལྟའི་རིག་པ་རང་གསལ་རང་གསལ་རྗེན་པ་འདི་ལ་ཅེར་གྱིས་བལྟས་ངོ་བོ་རང་བཞིན་ཐུགས་རྗེ་གསུམ་བརྡལ་བའི་ཆོས་སྐུ་ཐིག་ལེ་ཆེན་པོ་གྲ་ཟུར་མེད་ཅིང་ག་◌ཅིག་ཏུ་བཟླུམ་པ་གཙུག་མའི་གཤིས་ཀྱི་གནས་ལུགས་སྟོང་པ་རིག་པའི་སྙིང་པོ་ཅན། ཐུགས་རྗེ་ཡེ་ཤེས་ཀྱི་སྙིང་པོ་ཅན་འདི་ལ་རྟོག་པ་མ་འཕྲོ། རྩེ་གཅིག་ཏུ་མ་བཟུང་། སྣང་བླང་དང་རེ་དོགས་ཀྱི་མ་སླད། གཞིས་ཅིར་ཡང་མ་གྲུབ་པའི་སྟོང་བ་ལ་གདངས་གང་དུའང་མ་འགགས་པར་སྟོང་བས་གར་ཁྱབ་ལ་གསལ་པས་ཁྱབ་པས་གསལ་འཛིན་པ་མེད། དྭངས་ལ་ཕྱི་ནང་མེད། ཡངས་ལ་འཆལ་བར་མ་ཤོར། རང་གདངས་ལ་ངོས་བཟུང་མེད། གསལ་བས་གར་ཁྱབ་ལ་རིག་པས་ཁྱབ་པས་ཟང་ཐལ་ཆམ་བརྡལ་བའི་སྟོང་གསལ་རིག་གསུམ་དབྱེར་མེད་ཉག་གཅིག་མཁྱེན་ཆ་ནང་ནས་གསལ་ཞིང་རྟོག་པས་མ་བསླད་པ་ཡེ་ཤེ་སུམ་ལྡན་དེ་ཉིས་ཀྱི་གཤིས་རང་བབས་ཅོག་བཞག་རྒྱ་ཡན་ཆེན་པོར་བཞག་པས། སྣོད་བཅུད་ནམ་མཁའ་ལ་བརྟེན་ཀྱང་ནམ་མཁའ་ལ་སྣོད་བཅུད་ཀྱིས་མ་གོས་ཤིང་། ཉི་མའི་སྙིང་པོ་སྨུན་པ་ཐམས་ཅད་དང་གཏན་བྲལ་ཡིན་པ་ལྟར་ལ་ངེས་པ་སྐྱེད་ནས་རྒྱུན་བསྐྱང་ངོ།།

The Great Perfection instruction manual of the Great Fifth Dalai Lama, 'The Oral Transmissions of the Awareness-Holders' gives the following commentary:

"Having looked directly at the present primordial awareness devoid of all impurity, at this naked, innate lucidity, it has the essence of rigpa, of primordial awareness, which is the essential nature of the three compassions of the all-pervading body of absolute-reality, the great thigle or light-sphere of the basis of the singularly ('edge-less/corner-less) encompassing sphere of innate being, which is the ultimately empty natural state. This primordial awareness which is the quintessence of compassion and wisdom is uninterrupted by thought, is non-fixated, and unsullied by desire and aversion, hope and fear.

Since this emptiness is without any basis whatsoever, wherever its radiance shines forth it does so unobstructedly. Since this all-pervasive display is totally lucid and permeating, it is clear without grasping. Its limpidity is without inside or outside, its absolute spaciousness never lapses, its innate radiance is without recognizing or grasping (i.e. of any object, it is always and already present). Its lucid all-pervasive display unfolds via pervading awareness. It is totally clear and unsullied by conceptual thought, and comes from the unified and undifferentiated cognizing aspect of the all-pervasive, entirely unencumbered threefold emptiness-clarity-awareness. Resting freely and naturally in the great and vast space of no restraint that is the basic nature of suchness endowed with three wisdoms. (Perceive that) though the universe and its inhabitants emerge from space, space is nonetheless entirely unstained by the universe and its beings. Like the essence of sun that is cut off from all darkness, having truly found the primordial awareness, practice remaining in the natural state."

རྒྱས་པར་སྨྲོ་ན། སྙིང་ཏིག་ལས།

དྲི་མེད་དག་པའི་སངས་རྒྱས་ནི།། རང་རིག་ཆོས་སྐུ་འགྱུར་བ་མེད།། གསལ་ལེ་སིང་ངེ་ཁྲལ་ལེ་བ།། སྤྲིན་མེད་སྟོན་ཀའི་ནམ་མཁའ་བཞིན།། མི་འགྱུར་བརྟན་པ་རི་བོ་བཞིན་དུ་ཞོག། མི་གཡོ་དྭངས་པ་རྒྱ་མཚོ་བཞིན་དུ་ཞོག། ཡངས་དོག་བྲལ་བ་ནམ་མཁའ་བཞིན་དུ་ཞོག། གང་ལྟར་གནས་ཀྱང་རིག་པའི་ངང་ཡིན་ཞོག། གང་ལྟར་ཤར་ཡང་རིག་པའི་གདངས་ཡིན་ཞོག། འགྲོ་གནས་རང་རིག་དྭངས་སངས་ཕྱེད་པར་ཞོག།" ཅེས་གསུངས་པ་བཞིན་རིག་ངོ་བསྐྱང་རྒྱུ་དང་། སྣང་སྲིད་འཁོར་འདས་གདོད་མ་ནས་ཀ་དག་རྩོལ་མེད་དང་གཉེན་མེད་དུ་གྲོལ་བའི་བའི་རིག་པའི་ངང་དུ་འཇོག་པ་ཡིན་ཏེ། རྒྱལ་དབང་ལྔ་བའམ་སྟུགས་ཐན་གང་ཤར་རང་གྲོལ་གྱི་རྫོགས་ཆེན་ཁྲིད་ཡིག་རིག་འཛིན་ཞལ་ལུང་ལས། "གསུམ་པ་གཉིས་མེད་མཉམ་པའི་ངང་དུ་གནས་པ་ནི། འགྲོ་གནས་གཉིས་སུ་མེད་པ་སྟེ། གནས་བསྡོ་བའི་དུས་སུ་མིག་བསྒྲིལ་བ་འགྲོ་བ་རང་བབས་སུ་གནས་ལ། འགྲོ་བདོ་བའི་དུས་མིག་མི་འགུལ་བར་བར་ཆམ་བཞག་པས་གནས་ཏེ་འགྲོ་གནས་གཉིས་སུ་མེད་ཅིག་གཅིག་མི་གསལ་རྒྱ་མཚོའི་ངང་དུ་ཞི་བ་ལྟར་བཞག་གོ དེའང་གནས་མི་གསེང་། འགྲོ་བ་མི་དགག མཉམ་པ་མི་སྒྲུབ། གང་ཤར་ཡང་འཛིན་མེད་གླད་དོར་རེ་དོགས་དང་བྲལ་བའི་ཆོས་ཉིད་ཡེ་གྲོལ་རྫོགས་པ་ཆེན་པོར་ངོ་སྤྲོད་པ་ནི་གཞི་གོམས་དང་རྒྱུན་མིག་ལ་བརྟེན་པའོ།།" ཞེས་གསུངས་སོ།

To elaborate, it says in the Nyingthig:

"Concerning the stainless and pure Buddha(hood): Rest in the unchanging reality-body of ultimate self-awareness, radiant, clear, and vivid, like the cloudless autumn sky. Rest like the immovable, stable mountains, like the still and limpid sea. Rest like the limitless sky - whatever may abide, whatever may arise, rest in primordial awareness and its radiance. Rest in the radiance of the self-cognizing awareness clarified entirely of mental arising and abiding."

One should practice maintaining the essence or true face of awareness as described here, and should settle into the awareness which liberates without (the applying of any) antidotes, which is the primordial and original purity of all the arisings and appearances of Samsara-Nirvana, devoid of all striving. In the Great Perfection instruction manual of the Great Fifth Dalai Lama, The Oral Transmissions of the Awareness-Holders', (who in his role as a senior tantrika is also known as) Gangshar Rangdrol (Self-Liberating Whatever Arises') it says:

"Concerning the third (type of) abiding, the remaining in the equanimity of non-duality: (this means) remaining without either mental arising or abiding. When mental-abiding stagnates, one rolls one's eyes upwards and rests in the natural state of mental arising. During times of the stagnation of mental arising, one rests without moving one's eyes and stares in a relaxed way straight ahead. Devoid of both mental arising and abiding, one rests in a state of peace like an ocean, without saying a word. Don't try to refresh one's abiding, don't try to block one's mental arisings, don't try to achieve equanimity. Fix your gaze by virtue of having familiarized yourself with this foundation, this recognition of the Primordially Liberated Great Perfection that is the ultimate reality of existence (dharmata) which is without hope and fear, attachment and aversion, and which doesn't hold onto to anything that arises."

རང་གྲོལ་ནི། རྒྱལ་དབང་ལྔ་བའམ་སྔགས་རྒྱན་གང་ཤར་རང་གྲོལ་གྱི་རྫོགས་ཆེན་ཁྲིད་ཡིག་རིག་འཛིན་ཞལ་ལུང་ལས། "གཉིས་པ་འཕྲོ་བ་སེམས་ཀྱི་རོལ་བར་ཤར་བ་ནི། སྣ་ཚོགས་པའི་རྟོག་པ་སྤྱོད་ལ་དགག་སྒྲུབ་རེ་དོགས་མེད་པར་གང་ཤར་འཛིན་མེད་ཡན་དུ་བཙུག་པས་སྔ་ཕྱི་དྲན་བསམ་གྱི་མདུན་མདུད་པ་བོར་ནས་ད་ལྟའི་རིག་པ་ཐོལ་སྐྱེས་ཐོལ་ནུབ་ཏུ་འགྲོ་བ་གཞིས་ཀྱི་གནས་ལུགས་ཇི་ལྟར་འཕྱོད་ཀྱང་རྫིངས་ལ་གནས་པའི་བྱ་བཞིན་ཆོས་ཉིད་ཀྱི་རོལ་བ་ལས་མི་འདས་པ་རྒྱ་མཚོ་ལས་རླབས་པོ་ཆེ་ཤར་བ་ལྟར་རང་ཤར་རང་གྲོལ་ཐུགས་རྗེ་འགག་མེད་དུ་ངོ་སྤྲོད་དོ" ཞེས་རང་གྲོལ་གྱི་གནས་ལུགས་དང་། ཡང་དེ་ལས། "སྙིང་པོར་དྲིལ་ན་དྲན་འཛིན་རེ་དོགས་སྣང་དོར་ཐམས་ཅད་ནི་སེམས་ཀྱིས་བྱས་པའི་སྒྲིབ་རྐྱེན་ཡིན་ལ། འཛིན་མེད་རང་གྲོལ་དུ་བཞག་པས། རིག་པ་ཡེ་ཤེས་རྟོག་མ་དང་བྲལ་བའི་ཆུ་ལྟར་གྲོལ་ལོ།" ཞེས་གསུངས་པ་ནི་ཉམས་ལེན་ལ་གནད་དུ་ཆེ་བས་འཛིན་མེད་རང་གྲོལ་དུ་སེམས་འཛོག་པར་བྱ་ལ།

འཁོར་འདས་རང་གྲོལ་ཆེན་མོའི་རྒྱ་བར་ཡང་"མདོར་ན་སྣང་སྲིད་འཁོར་འདས་བདག་གཞན་པན་ཚུན། བཟང་ངན་རེ་དོགས་སྤང་བླང་ཉེ་རིང་བཏང་གཞག་སོགས་གཉིས་ཆོས་ཐམས་ཅད་ཀྱི་འདུན་པ་ཐྲལ་ལ། ཡེ་ཤེས་རོལ་པ་ཀུན་རྫོགས་འཁོར་འདས་རང་གྲོལ་ཆེན་པོར་ཉམས་སུ་བླང་ངོ་། །"ཞེས་གཡུ་ཐོག་ཆེན་པོ་གསུངས་སོ།

Regarding Self-Liberation, the Great Perfection instruction manual of the Great Fifth Dalai Lama 'The Oral Transmissions of the Awareness-Holders' states:

"Concerning the second, the dawning of mind's playful and emanative display: as diverse thoughts radiate outwards, by letting go (like an animal let free without an owner), without affirming or refuting, with neither hope nor fear, without holding onto anything that arises, untie and release whatever memories of the past or thoughts of the future are before you. Sinking into the suddenly-arising awareness of the present moment, you should encounter the basic reality like a bird that stays with or keeps pace with the boat, (in no way trying to) pass beyond the playful display of the ultimate nature. Like a great wave that arises from the ocean, you will recognize (this state) as self-arising and self-liberating unimpeded compassion."

And also:

"If you condense it to its essence, since all mental fixations, hopes and fears, attachments and aversions are obscurations and faults produced by the mind, by resting in the self-liberating state of non-fixation, primordial awareness and wisdom will be liberated like clear and still water."

The main, essential point for practice being that one should settle one's mind into a state of self-liberating non-grasping.

And as the Great Yuthok also says in the root-text of the 'Great Self-Liberation of Samsara-Nirvana':

"In summary, releasing yourself from all the appearances and arising of Samsara and Nirvana, of Self and Other, Hither and Thither, Good and Bad, Hope and Fear, Attachment and Aversion, Near and Far, Retaining and Letting Go, from a desire or inclination for all dualisitic phenomena, take as your practice the utterly perfected wisdom-display of Samsara-Nirvana's great Self-Liberation."

ཡོང་གྲོལ་ནི། རྫོགས་ཆེན་ལྟ་བ་མཁའ་ཀློང་གཡོག་བརླབ་ལས། "དུག་གསུམ་རྩ་བ་བྲལ་བའི་སེམས་ཉིད་འདི།། མ་བསྒོམ་མངོན་སུམ་སྣང་བ་བློ་རི་བདེ།། ཐོག་མ་ཐ་མ་རང་བཞིན་དག་པའི་ཆོས།། ཡེ་གྲོལ་ཡོངས་གྲོལ་འབད་རྩོལ་ཞིག་པ་མཚར།།" གནས་པ་སེམས་ཀྱི་རྒྱུན་དུ་ཤར་བ། ལུས་ངག་ཡིད་གསུམ་ཁོང་གློད་ལ་སོས་དལ་དུ་གནས་པའི་ངང་ནས་རྟོག་པ་སྣ་ཚོགས་འཕྲོར་བཅུག ཆམ་གྱིས་བཞག་ལ་ཅེར་གྱིས་བལྟས་པས་རྒྱ་མཚོ་ལ་རླབས་ཞི་བ་ལྟར་འཕྲོ་མཁན་དང་འཕྲོ་བྱ་མ་གྲུབ་པར་གཞི་མེད་རྩ་བྲལ་གྱི་རང་བཞིན་གཞིའི་ངང་དུ་གནས་པ་ནི་གདོད་མའི་ཀ་དག་གི་གནས་ལུགས་ཆོས་སྐུ་འཕོ་འགྱུར་མེད་པ་ཡིན་ཅིང་དེར་ངོ་སྤྲོད་དོ།། " ཅེས་གསུངས་པ་ནི་ཡོང་གྲོལ་གྱི་དོན་དུ་མཐོང་ངོ་།།

རྣལ་འབྱོར་བ་འབྲིང་།

འཁོར་འདས་རང་གྲོལ་དུ། "འབྲིང་གི་རབ་ཀྱིས་སྣང་སྲིད་འཁོར་འདས་ཀྱི་ཆོས་ཐམས་ཅད་དབྱེར་མེད་ཆེན་པོར། འབྲིང་གི་འབྲིང་གིས་ཀུན་རྫོབ་དོམ་དམ་ཟུང་འཇུག འབྲིང་གི་ཐ་མས་ཀུང་སྤྱང་བླང་མེད་པར།" ཞེས་གསུངས་པ་ལྟར།

འབྲིང་གི་རབ་ཀྱིས། དབྱེར་མེད་ནི་སྣང་སྟོང་དང་གསལ་སྟོང་དབྱེར་མེད་ལ་གོ་བས། སྣང་སྲིད་འཁོར་འདས་ཀྱི་ཆོས་ཐམས་ཅད་སྣང་སྟོང་དབྱེར་མེད། བདེ་སྟོང་དབྱེར་མེད། གསལ་སྟོང་དབྱེར་མེད་ཆེན་པོར་ཉམས་སུ་བླངས་པར་བྱའོ།།

Regarding the Total Liberation, the 'View of the Great Perfection, the Flight of the Garuda' states:

"How blissful is the mind's own nature, free of the root of the three poisons, the plainly manifest (state of) non-meditation! How wonderful are the qualities of purity of the (ultimate) nature of (all) beginnings and endings! How marvellous the primordial and total liberation that dissolves all effort!" Abiding in it dawns as mind's own ornament. Completely relaxing body, speech, and mind, resting leisurely and completely, totally giving up being drawn into all manner of discursive thoughts, having beheld directly, rest like a wave dissolving in the ocean. Recognize the reality of original and primordial purity, the body of absolute-reality that is unchanging and without transition – this is the resting in the basic nature, which is devoid of either conceptualizer or concept, and which contains neither root nor foundation."

This is seen as the meaning of 'Total Liberation'.

The Average Yogi

As it says in the Self-Liberation of Samsara-Nirvana:

"For the greater average yogi there's the great undifferentiation of all phenomena, of all appearances and arisings of Samsara-Nirvana. For the average average yogi; the (indivisibility) inter-penetration of ultimate and relative truths; and for the lesser average yogi the absence of either attachment or aversion."

The 'undifferentiation' of the greater average yogi refers to the undifferentiation of appearances and emptiness, and clarity and emptiness. The greater average yogi should take as his practice the non-differentiation of all phenomena appearing and arising in Samsara and Nirvana, the non-differentiation of bliss and emptiness, the great non-differentiation of clarity and emptiness.

འབྲིང་གི་འབྲིང་གིས། བདེན་གཉིས་ཟུང་འཇུག་སྟེ། ཀུན་རྫོབ་བདེན་པ་དང་དོན་དམ་བདེན་པ་ཟུང་འཇུག་གི་གནད་ཤེས་རབ་ཕ་རོལ་ཏུ་ཕྱིན་པའི་དོན་གོ་ནས་ཉམས་སུ་ལེན་པ་སྟེ། རྫོགས་ཆེན་ལྟ་བ་མཁའ་ལྡིང་གཤོག་བརྡབ་ལས། “ཕྱི་རོལ་ཀུན་རྫོབ་སྣང་གྲགས་ཆོས་རྣམས་ཀུན།། ཐམས་ཅད་སྟོང་པ་ཉིད་དུ་མ་རྟོགས་པར།། ལྟ་བ་བསྒོམ་ན་སྒོམ་ཡང་ཅི་ཞིག་བསྒོམ།། དེ་ཡི་ཕྱིར་ན་དང་པོ་འདི་ལྟར་དུ།། རེ་འགའ་བླ་མར་གསོལ་བ་འདེབས་ཀྱིན་ལྟོས།། རེ་འགའ་གློད་ཀྱིན་བསྒྲིམ་ཀྱིན་ལེགས་པར་ལྟོས།། དེ་ལྟར་བལྟས་ཚེ་སེམས་ལ་དགའ་བ་དང་།། ཐམས་ཅད་སྟོང་པ་ཉིད་དུ་ལམ་ལམ་དུ།། ཤར་ནས་ཕྱི་རོལ་སྣང་བའི་ཡུལ་རྣམས་ལ།། ལག་པས་རེག་ཅིང་འཛིན་རྒྱུ་མེད་སྙམ་དང་།། ལྟ་བ་འདི་ཉིད་ངེས་པར་ཡིན་པར་འདུག། སྙམ་པའི་ངེས་ཤེས་གཏིང་ཚུགས་སྐྱེ་བར་ངེས།། དེ་དུས་ལྟ་བའི་ངེས་ཤེས་སྐྱེད་པ་ཡིན།། འཛིན་པས་མ་བསླད་འཛིན་མེད་ངང་ལ་གློད།། རོ་སྙོད་ཐེབས་ནས་ཉམས་སུ་མ་ལོན་ཀྱང་།། འཆི་ཚེ་བར་དོར་འཇིགས་སྐྲག་ཅི་བྱུང་ཡང་།། ཐམས་ཅད་རང་སྣང་སྟོང་པའི་རང་གཟུགས་སུ།། ཤེས་ནས་ཀ་དག་གཞི་ལ་འཚང་རྒྱའོ།།” ཞེས་ཤིན་ཏུ་གསལ་བར་ཀུན་རྫོབ་བདེན་པ་དང་དོན་དམ་བདེན་དབྱེར་མེད་རྟོགས་པའི་ཤེས་རབ་ཕ་རོལ་ཏུ་ཕྱིན་དོན་གནད་མ་གསུངས་པ་བཞིན་སྟོང་ཉིད་ཀྱི་ལྟ་བ་རྟོགས་ཤིང་བསྒོམ་པར་བྱའོ།།

འབྲིང་གི་ཐ་མས། དྲན་པ་དང་འཛིན་པ་དང་། འཁོར་འདས་བཟང་ངན་དང་རེ་དོགས། རྟོག་ཚོགས་དང་། ཉོན་མོངས་དང་ཡེ་ཤེས་དབྱེ་འབྱེད་དང་བླང་དོར་ཐམས་ཅད་ནི་སེམས་ཀྱིས་བྱས་པའི་སྒྲིབ་རྐྱེན་ཡིན་པས་འཛིན་མེད་རང་གྲོལ་ལམ་སྤང་བླང་མེད་པར་ཉམས་སུ་ལེན་པར་བྱའོ།།

For the average average yogi, there's the indivisibility of the two truths, of relative and ultimate reality, which in its essence is understood to mean the transcendental wisdom ('the gone beyond' wisdom of the 'other shore'), and is what this kind of yogi practices. In the 'View of the Great Perfection, the Flight of Garuda' it says:

"If one thinks that one is 'meditating on the View', but one still hasn't realized that all phenomena, all the external sights and sounds of relative reality, are inherently empty, what kind of 'cultivation of the View' could one possibly be doing? This being so, first it's like this: sometimes one relies on praying to the lama, sometimes one relies thoroughly on relaxing while still staying alert all the while. By relying in this way one feels joy, and everything dawns vividly as innately empty. By thinking of all the objects of external appearances as intangible, ungraspable, this view becomes something absolutely certain. Conviction born of one's reflections arises with certainty as something deeply felt. Having found certainty in the view, at that point relax in a state of non-fixation uncorrupted by grasping. Once you've undergone some introduction (to the basic nature of being) then even if you haven't really practiced, regardless of what terrors might emerge at the point of death in the intermediary state, by comprehending all self-appearances as inherently empty of form, you will realize perfectly your own basic, primordially pure and enlightened nature."

As is stated so very clearly here, you should realize and cultivate the view of emptiness, the essential truth of the transcendent wisdom that realizes that relative and ultimate truths are inseparable."

Seeing as all mental recollections and fixations, every good and bad thing in Samsara-Nirvana, all hopes and fears, conceptual patterns, afflictive emotions, discriminating wisdoms, every attachment and aversion are obscurations and faults produced by the mind, the lesser average practitioner should take as his practice the path of non-grasping self-liberation which is devoid of either attachment or aversion.

རྣལ་འབྱོར་བ་ཐ་མ།

ཕྱ་བར་”ཐ་མའི་རབ་ཀྱིས་བསྐྱེད་རྫོགས་གཉིས་མེད་ཆེན་པོར་ཉམས་སུ། ཐ་མའི་འབྲིང་གིས་བསྐྱེད་རྫོགས་ཟུང་འཇུག་ཏུ། ཐ་མའི་ཐ་མས་བླང་དོར་གང་བདེར། ངོ་འཕྲོད་པའི་གནད་ཀྱིས་ཟིན་པར་བྱས་ལ་ཉམས་སུ་བླང་། “ཞེས།

རྣལ་འབྱོར་ཐ་མའི་རབ་ཀྱིས། སྐྱེ་བ་དང་ཐ་མལ་སྣང་ཞེན་སྦྱོང་བྱེད་ཀྱི་བསྐྱེད་རིམ་དང་། འཆི་བ་དང་ཕྱ་ཐིག་ལྷུང་གསུམ་སྦྱོང་བྱེད་ཀྱི་རྫོགས་རིམ་སྟེ་བསྐྱེད་རྫོགས་གཉིས་མེད་ཆེན་པོར་ཉམས་སུ་བླངས་ཐབས་སངས་རྒྱས་སྨན་གྱི་བླའི་བསྐྱེད་རྫོགས་ཟུང་འཇུག་གཡུ་ཐོག་བླ་སྒྲུབ་བླ་མ་ནད་སྒྲུབ་དགོས་འདོད་ཀུན་འབྱུང་ལྟ་བུ་དང་། དེ་ལས” བདེ་གསལ་མི་རྟོག་པའི་ངང་ལ་ཤེས་པ་ལྷོད་གློད་ལ་བཞག ཤིག་ཤིག་མེར་མེར་གཟུང་འཛིན་གྱི་རྟོག་པ་སྤྲངས་ལ་བཞག སེམས་འཕྲོ་ནའང་ཐོང་། གང་ཤར་ངོས་ཟིན་པ་ཀྱིས། སྟོད་ནའང་སྟོད། བྱིང་རྨུགས་སྟེང་པོར་མ་ཤོར་ཞིང་ཞན་པ་མ་བྱེད། སེམས་ཀྱི་ངོ་བོ་གང་ལ་ཡང་གཏད་བཟུང་མེད་པར། རྒྱུ་བཅད་རང་འཐག་བཞིན་ཅོམ་མེར་བཞག ལམ་དུ་བོར་བའི་རྡོ་བ་བཞིན་ཁྲོལ་ལེ་ཡིང་ངེ། བདག་ཏུ་མ་བཟུང་། དངོས་པོའི་མཚན་མེད་པར་ཁྲོལ་ལེ་ཞོག བསྒོམ་བྱ་བསྒོམ་བྱེད་མེད་པར་ཐུན་བཞིན་བྱའོ།།”ཞེས་སྤྲོས་མེད་རྫོགས་རིམ་རྫོགས་ཆེན་གྱི་ལུགས་ལྟར་གསུངས་སོ།།

The Lesser Yogi

In the root-text it says:

"The greater lesser yogi (takes) as her practice the great (practice) that is devoid of both the Creation and Completion stages; the average lesser practitioner (takes as his practice) the union of the Creation and Completion stages; and the lesser lesser practitioner has (the practice) of taking up and rejecting as feels comfortable. Having really grasped the vital point of recognizing (one's own nature), practice (in this way)."

The greater lesser yogi's method of practice is the great (approach) devoid of either Creation or Completion stages - of either the Creation stage that purifies attachments to birth and ordinary appearances, and the Completion stage that trains one for death and refines and purifies the channels, drops and winds. As it says in the inner guru sadhana of Yuthok, the Medicine Buddha who unites the Generation and Completion stages, 'The Coming-to-Pass of all one's desires':

"Realizing the bliss-clarity of non-conceptuality, stay completely and totally relaxed. Whatever thoughts might arise cast them aside, rest in a state of rejecting (insubstantial) wavering concepts of subject and object completely. Whatever arises, recognize it for what it is. Whatever remains, remain (along with it). Don't lose yourself in the midst of mental torpor and dullness, do nothing else. Remain free of doubts like a water-mill blocking a river, stay completely relaxed and free like a stone flung from a road. Don't hold onto the sense of self, rest completely open and relaxed in the absolute substancelessness of things - like this cultivate in the four sessions the meditation that is without either meditator or meditation object."

So is it taught in the unelaborated completion stage of the system of the Great Completion.

ཐ་མའི་འབྲིང་གིས། སངས་རྒྱས་སྨན་གྱི་བླའི་བསྐྱེད་རྫོགས་ཟུང་འཇུག་གཡུ་ཐོག་བླ་སྒྲུབ་བླ་མ་ནང་སྒྲུབ་དགོས་འདོད་ཀུན་འབྱུང་དང་གསང་སྒྲུབ་སྐལ་ལྡན་མྱུར་འདྲེན་ཉམས་སུ་ལེན་པ་དང་། ཡང་ན་བླ་སྒྲུབ་ཐོན་རྗེས་བསྐྱེད་རིམ་གྱི་རྨང་བརྟན་པའི་སྒྲོ་ནས་ཆོས་དྲུག་གཏུམ་མོ་དང་སྒྱུ་ལུས་རྣལ་འབྱོར་སོགས་རྫོགས་རིམ་མཐར་ཕྱིན་པ་བྱའོ།།

ཐ་མའི་ཐ་མས། རྡོ་རྗེ་ཐེག་པའི་སྔོན་འགྲོ་རྟགས་ཐོན་རྗེས་སུ། རྒྱལ་ཀུན་གསང་བ་རྩ་གསུམ་ཀུན་འདུས་སྐུ་གསུམ་ངོ་བོ་སྨན་རྒྱལ་གཡུ་ཐོག་པའི་བླ་སྒྲུབ་བཞིའམ་ཡང་ན་གང་རུང་། དེ་ནས་ཆོས་དྲུག་གང་རུང་ངམ་གང་ཐུབ་ཉམས་སུ་ལེན་རྒྱུ་ནི་རྣལ་འབྱོར་པ་སོ་སོའི་རྒྱུད་ཚོད་ལ་བརྟེན་པའི་གདམས་པ་ཁྱད་པར་ཅན་ཡིན་ནོ།།

The average lesser yogi will practice the inner guru sadhana of Yuthok, the Medicine Buddha who unites the Creation and Completion stages, 'The Coming-to-pass of All one's Needs and Wishes', as well as the secret sadhana 'Speedy Delivery of the Fortunate Ones', or alternatively, after having produced (results from) the guru sadhana, with the Creation stage as a foundation they will master the six Dharmas of Naropa - the yogas of inner-heat ('Fierce Lady' or Tummo) and the Illusory Body, and so on – of the Completion stage.

For the lesser lesser yogi, once they have experienced signs (of accomplishment) after practicing the Vajrayana preliminaries, they will practice the four guru sadhanas of the King of Medicine Yuthok, 'The Essence of the Three Kayas, the Assembly of All-Victorious Secret Three Roots', or whatever is appropriate. Then, they will practice the Six Dharmas in whatever way is appropriate or to whatever extent they are able.

These are the specific instructions that depend on each yogi or yogini's capacity or disposition.

གཡུ་ཐོག་རྫོགས་ཆེན་འཁོར་འདས་རང་གྲོལ་ཆེན་མོ་ལས། “དེའང་ཉམས་སུ་བླངས་ཞེས་བྱ་བ། རང་ལ་མེད་པ་ཞིག་གཞན་ནས་བཙལ་ཏེ་རྙེད་པ་དང་། དེ་ཉིད་འཆང་ཞིང་སྒྲི་ཡོག་བྱེད་པ་ལྟ་བུ་མ་ཡིན་ཏེ། འཁོར་ཞེས་པ་ཡེ་ཤེས་ལྔ་ལ་སོགས་པ་ཐམས་ཅད་གདོད་མ་ནས་རང་ལ་རང་ཆས་སུ་ཚང་བར་ཡོད་པ་ལ། སྔར་རང་ངོ་མ་ཤེས་པས་འཁྲུལ་འཁོར་དུ་འཁོར། ཞེས་བྱ་བ་ལས། འདས་ཞེས་བྱ་བ་འཁོར་བར་འཁོར་བ་ཉིད་ཀྱི་ཚེ་རང་གི་ངོ་ལ་བལྟས་པས། རྟག་ཆད། མཐའ་དབུས། ཡོད་མེད་བདེན་རྫུན་སོགས། མཐའ་བཞི་མཐའ་བརྒྱད་ཀྱི་སྤུ་མཐའ་སྨྲ་བསམ་ཤེས་བརྗོད་ཀྱི་ཡུལ་བློ་ཐམས་ཅད་ལས་འདས་པ་ཉིད་དོ། ། རང་ཞེས་བྱ་བ་ནི། དེང་ཕྱིན་ཆད་ཆོས་ཀྱི་སྐུ་རང་ལ་རང་ཆས་སུ་ཡོད་པ། གསལ་གཞག་མེད་པར་ངོ་ཤེས་བཞིན་གདེང་ཐོབ་པར་བྱེད་པ་ལས། ལོག་ཏུ་རྡུལ་ཕྲ་རབ་ཙམ་ཡང་ངོ་སྤྲད་དུ་མེད་པའོ། །གྲོལ་ཞེས་པ་འབྲས་བུ་ཡིད་སྨོན་གྱི་དུས་སུ་མ་ལུས་པར། གང་ཤར་ངོས་ཟིན་ཕན་ཆད། དེ་ཉིད་དུ་ཡེ་ཤེས་རང་སྣང་རོལ་པའི་རྩལ་གསུམ་གཞི་ཐོག་ཏུ་རྫོགས་པས། གཟུང་འཛིན་གྱི་འཆིང་བ་ཐམས་ཅད་རང་ཞི་རང་དག་རང་ཡལ་རང་གྲོལ་དུ་འགྱུར་བའོ།། ཆེན་པོ་ཞེས་པ་འདི་ལྟ་བུའི་གང་ནས་སྤྲད་རྒྱུ་ཡང་མེད། ཉམས་སུ་བླང་རྒྱུ་ཡང་མེད། ལྟ་བ་འཁོར་འདས་རང་གྲོལ་མཐོང་ཡུལ་ལས་འདས་པ། སྒོམ་པ་འཁོར་འདས་རང་གྲོལ་ཉམས་ལས་འདས་པ། སྤྱོད་པ་འཁོར་འདས་རང་གྲོལ་བྱ་བྱེད་ལས་འདས་པ། འབྲས་བུ་འཁོར་འདས་རང་གྲོལ་བླང་དོར་ལས་འདས་པ།”

ཞེས་གསུངས་པའི་དོན་ཅིག་བཞག་གསུམ་གྱིས་ཀ་དག་ཁྲེགས་ཆོད་ཀྱི་གནས་ལུགས་མངོན་དུ་གྱུར་བ་བྱ་དགོས་སྟེ།

ལུས་གནད་ལྷོད་འདུག་རི་བོ་ཅོག་བཞག མིག་གནད་མི་འགུལ རྒྱ་མཚོ་ཅོག་བཞག སེམས་གནད་མི་བཅོས་རིག་པ་ཅོག་བཞག་བཅས་གསུམ་གྱི་སྒོ་ནས་སྣང་སྲིད་འཁོར་འདས་བདག་གཞན་ཕན་ཚུན། བཟང་ངན་རེ་དོགས་སྤང་བླང་ཉེ་རིང་བཏང་བཞག་སོགས་གཉིས་ཆོས་ཅན་གྱི་འདུན་པ་བྲལ་ལ། ཡེ་ཤེས་རོལ་བ་ཀུན་རྫོགས་འཁོར་འདས་རང་གྲོལ་ཆེན་པོར་ཉམས་སུ་བླང་ངོ།།

In the 'Great Self-Liberation of Samsara-Nirvana' it says:

"Moreover, 'the putting into practice' means not rolling back and forth between holding onto the essence of things themselves and searching trying to find it outside oneself. 'Samsara' is defined as 'wandering in delusion on account of not having previously understood one's own essential nature - despite the fact that the five wisdoms and all such things exist intrinsically and primordially entirely within one's own being. 'Nirvana' is known as 'the very essence of going beyond all describable or imaginable limits of the four extremes and eight (conceptual) limitations - when one, in the very moment of wandering around and around in Samsara, by having seen one's own nature, goes beyond (dualistic) conceptual limitations of things either permanently existing or completely non-existing, as having either an edge or a center, as either being or non-being, being true or false, and so on.'

As for 'one's own nature', that is described as 'the fact of the dharmakaya of absolute reality being intrinsic to one's own being - in accordance with recognizing this, without trying to either push away the fact or hold onto it, one from this time on obtains such confidence that this recognition remains firm for even the subtlest of particles.'

Liberation is known as 'the fruition of one's wishes in every moment of wishing without exception – (it's when) once one has recognized whatever arises, from then on three-fold wisdom, self-manifestation and creative display are perfected in their basic ground of being as such-ness, and every bond of clinging and grasping thereby subsides and vanishes of its own accord, is purified and liberated in and of itself.'

'Great' is that for which there is nothing to be given (or introduced) at all, for which there is nothing to be practiced at all.

The View of the Self-Liberation of Samara-Nirvana transcends any object that can be seen, the Meditation of the Self-Liberation of Samsara-Nirvana transcends all experience, the Conduct of the Self-Liberation of Samsara-Nirvana goes beyond all activity, and the Fruit of the Self-Liberation of Samsara-Nirvana goes beyond all accepting or rejecting."

ཞེས་གསུངས་པའི་དོན་ཅིག་བཞག་གསུམ་གྱིས་ཀ་དག་ཁྲེགས་ཆོད་ཀྱི་གནས་ལུགས་མངོན་དུ་གྱུར་བ་བྱ་དགོས་སྟེ།

ལུས་གནད་ལྷོད་འདུག་རི་བོ་ཅོག་བཞག མིག་གནད་མི་འགུལ་རྒྱ་མཚོ་ཅོག་བཞག སེམས་གནད་མི་བཅོས་རིག་པ་ཅོག་བཞག་བཅས་གསུམ་གྱི་སྒོ་ནས་སྣང་སྲིད་འཁོར་འདས་བདག་གཞན་ཕན་ཚུན། བཟང་ངན་རེ་དོགས་སྤང་བླང་ཉེ་རིང་བཏང་བཞག་སོགས་གཉིས་ཆོས་ཅན་གྱི་འདུན་པ་བྲལ་ལ། ཡེ་ཤེས་རོལ་བ་ཀུན་རྫོགས་འཁོར་འདས་རང་གྲོལ་ཆེན་པོར་ཉམས་སུ་བླང་ངོ་།།

Thus by means of these stated meanings and the three 'restings' should one actualize the ultimate reality of the primordial purity and cutting through hardness:

Let your body rest, sitting as it is, relaxed, like a mountain

Let your gaze rest without moving, as it is, like the ocean

Let your mind rest as it is in its natural awareness

Through these three restings, and without any inclination for dualistic phenomena, for what appears or arises in Samsara or Nirvana - for self and other, here or there, good or bad, hopes or doubts, rejecting or accepting, near or far, sending out or retaining - take as your practice the all perfected display of wisdom, the Great Self-Liberation of Samsara-Nirvana.

མདོ་དོན།

སློབ་དཔོན་ཆེན་པོ་ཀ་དག་ཁྲེགས་ཆོད་ཀྱི་མདོ་ཕྱིལ་གྱིས་དྲིལ་བ་འདི་ལྟར་གསུངས་སྟེ།

"འདི་དོན་ཕྱིལ་གྱིས་དྲིལ་ན་ལྟ་སྒོམ་སྤྱོད་འབྲས་འཁྲུལ་གྲོལ་སོགས་སྣང་སྲིད་འཁོར་འདས་ཀྱིས་བསྡུས་པའི་ཆོས་ཐམས་ཅད་རང་གི་སེམས་སུ་འདུས་ལ། སེམས་ཁོ་རང་གི་གཤིས་ལ་ཁོ་རང་གིས་འཚོལ་རྟོགས་བྱས་པའི་ཚེ་ཡོད་མེད་བདེན་རྫུན་གཅིག་ཐ་དད་རྙེད་མ་རྙེད། སྟོས་ཆོས་སྤྲོས་པ་རྡུལ་ཙམ་ཡང་མི་རྙེད། བརྗོད་བྲལ་ཆེན་པོ་ཀུན་ཏུ་བཟང་པོ། ཐ་སྙད་ཀྱི་ཆོས་སུ་མ་གྲུབ་པ། ཆོས་ཐམས་ཅད་ཀྱི་ཤེས་རིག་རང་ཡོག་རང་གཤེད་ལ་ཕབ་ནས་བརྟགས་པས། བརྟགས་ཞེན་གྱི་གཞི་རྩ་ཡལ། བརྟག་བྱའི་ཡུལ་དོར། རྟོགས་བྱེད་ཀྱི་མཁན་པོ་བརླག གྲུབ་མཐའ་སྤྲོས་པའི་བློ་ལས་བརྒལ། དྲན་བསམ་ཐམས་ཅད་སྐད་ཅིག་ལ་ཡར་སངས། སྣང་དོར་ཨ་ལེ། ཤར་ཚོད་རིག་དོར་ཨ་ལེ་ཡལ། འཆར་གཞི་ཅི་ཡང་མེད་པས་དང་སང་ངེ་བ་ལ་དྲན་རིག་ཅི་ཡང་མ་འགགས་ཀུན་ཏུ་འཆར་བ། ཤར་ཡང་གཞི་མེད་དུ་རང་དག་པས་ཀ་དག བཙལ་རྒྱུ་མ་གྲུབ་སྟོང་ལོག་གིས་ཤེས་པ་དང་། འཚོལ་མཁན་མ་གྲུབ་སྟོང་ལོག་གིས་ཤེས་པ་དང་། འཚོལ་མཁན་ལྟ་བྱེད་ཀྱི་རིག་པ། རྟག་གེ་བ་དབྱེར་མེད་དེ། བརྗོད་བྲལ་སྐད་ཅིག་ལ་གཞི་མེད་དུ་རང་མདངས། ཤེས་བྱ་སེ་ལེ་བ་ལ། ཤེས་བྱེད་འཛིན་པ་དག་མེད་ཤེས་རང་ལོག་མི་ཡུལ་བྲལ་བས། ཁུངས་བྲལ་དོན་བཟུང་རྣམ་པར་ཅིར་ཡང་མ་མཐོང་། མ་མཐོང་སྣམ་པ་ཡང་མ་མཐོང་། གཞི་མེད་ཙམ་དུ་འཛིན་པའང་མ་རྙེད།

The Fundamental Meaning

The King of Medicine Yuthok taught his completely condensed summary of the Primordial Purity and Cutting Through Hardness as follows:

"If one condenses this meaning down in its entirety, the View, Meditation, Conduct, Fruit, Delusion, and Liberation, and so on, all phenomena comprising the appearances and arisings of Samsara-Nirvana, they are all within one's own mind.

If the mind, in its own basic nature, itself searches and tries to see whether it can discover its existence or non-existence, whether it's true or false, singular or differentiated, even at the level of the tiniest particle of conceptually elaborated dependent or conditioned phenomena, it won't find anything. The cognizant awareness of the thinker who thinks 'nothing has been found, there's nothing that can be found or expressed' reaches a point of refuting and undermining itself - having realized this, attachment to the basis of what has been realized disappears. The object of investigation is abandoned, the one who investigates is annihilated, one passes beyond the mind of philosophical tenets and conceptual elaborations entirely. All recollections and speculations, memories and thoughts are generally and wholly purified, appearances are clear and resplendent in their very essence, whatever arises dissolves into this clarity of the essence of awareness. All appears without any ground for appearing whatsoever, pure and clear, unobstructed by any mindful awareness. Being self-pure without any basis for arising at all, one realizes that one comes up empty-handed, that that which is sought after doesn't exist. One realizes that one comes up empty-handed too in trying to find anyone who searches, and that the awareness that observes this 'searcher' is wholly undifferentiated, without any individual parts at all. Manifesting ineffably in an instant, it is self-radiant without any basis whatsoever. The object of cognition is clear and vivid, the cognizer or knower, realizing that it is without any graspable self, turns back on itself and is without any 'home' or location. Thus, being without any origin, it has no recognizable characteristics that can be perceived, nor can even this thought of its imperceptibility be perceived in any way either. Not even the slightest basis to hold onto can be found at all."

མ་རྟེད་པ་འང་རྟེད་བཞིན་ཞ་ལེ་བ་བར་སྣང་དག་པའི་དབྱིངས་ལྟར་ངོས་གཟུང་མེད་པར་རང་མདངས་སུ་དང་གིས་གནས་པས། གང་དུ་ཡང་རྒྱ་མ་ཆད། ཕྱོགས་སུ་མ་ལྷུང་མཐའ་དབུས་གང་ཅིའི་ངོ་བོ་ཡང་མ་གྲུབ། རང་རིག་དྲན་པ་དངོས་མེད་དུ་རང་གྲོལ་དྲན་བརྟག་འགྲོ་འོང་གསལ་བ་བསམ་བརྟག་ཡིད་བྲལ། མ་བསྒོམས་དོན་དང་འདུ་འབྲལ་མེད་པས། མིང་ཚིག་གི་བསམ་བརྗོད་བློ་འདས་ཆེན་པོར་རྟོག་མེད་ཚུལ་དུ་རྟོགས་ན་འཕྲོད་པ་སྟེ། འཕྲོད་ནས་ཡེ་ཇི་བཞིན་པའི་ཞེས་ལུགས་ལ། ཡེ་ཇི་བཞིན་པར་བསྐྱངས་པས། ཡེ་ཇི་བཞིན་པར་མཐོང་བར་འགྱུར་བའོ། ། འདི་ལྟ་བུའི་གནད་མཚང་རིག་ན། གཉིས་སྣང་འགྱུར་བ་རྗེས་མེད་དང་། མཚན་སྣང་རྨི་ལམ་་བག་ཆགས་དྲན་པས་མ་ཟིན་ནས། མི་བདེན་པ་ལ་བདེན་ཆ་འཛིན་པའི་སློམས་རྟོག་ཕྲ་མོ་ལྡང་ཡང་། དྲན་པ་དང་། གཉིད་སད་རྗེས། གཞི་མེད་ཀྱི་གདེང་གིས་ཟིན་ན། རང་གྲོལ་དུ་འགྲོ་ཞིང་སྐྱོན་མེད་དོ། །” ཞེས་དང་།

"Remaining in a state of one's own innate self-radiance, not grasping at or identifying anything, this discovery of non-discovery is vivid and clear like the vast expanse of the pure heavens. It is not limited in scope in any way at all, it is unbiased, has not fallen into any particular view or perspective. No essential quality of either centre or periphery exists for it at all. It is the mindfulness of self-cognizing awareness that is liberated in and of itself into insubstantiality, undistracted by the derailing of mindfulness or the break-down of concentration from the coming, going, and clearing away of thoughts.

Since it is the essential meaning of non-meditation, devoid of coming together or coming apart, if one, in a state of non-conceptuality, realizes and then recognizes the great going beyond of the mind which thinks or expresses itself in words, by coming to know the way of this primordial is-ness and by maintaining it, you will come to (directly) perceive it. If one can understand these vital points in this way, then just as dualistic appearances transform from one thing to the next leaving no trace, and just as even night time dream appearances which one hasn't managed to catch mindfully (become lucid of) are flawlessly self-liberated upon waking, so it is with one's thoughts. When subtle discursive thoughts which one holds to be true but which really aren't arise, if one is mindful and possesses a sense of confidence in the baselessness of these, so too will such thoughts be self-liberated flawlessly."

མཐར་གཡུ་ཐོག་པའི་རང་ལུགས་ཀྱི་ཀ་དག་ཁྲེགས་ཆོད་འདི་ནི་ཉམས་ལེན་གཞན་ལས་ཁྱད་དུ་འཕགས་པའི་སྐོར་ཡང་རྫོགས་ཆེན་ངོ་སྤྲོད་འཁོར་འདས་རང་གྲོལ་དུ། “ སྙིང་ཐིག་བླ་མེད་གསང་ཆེན་འདི་ལྟ་བུ་དང་མ་མཇལ་ན། ཉན་རང་བྱང་སེམས་གསུམ་འཁོར་བ་བལྟས་པར་བྱེད། ཀྲི་ཡོག་སྡེ་གསུམ་བཟང་རྟོག་བལྟས་པར་བྱེད། བསྐྱེད་རྫོགས་གཉིས་ཀྱི་དོན་ལ་ཡིད་དཔྱོད་སྦྱོར། ཨ་ཏི་དང་ཕྱག་ཆེན་ཕལ་གྱིས་དོན་བློར་བཞག་ནས། གོ་ཡུལ་ལ་གཏོར་བྱས་པས་ཁ་འབྱམས། ངེས་དོན་སྙིའི་སྙན་བརྒྱུད་ཀུན་ནས། བདག་གིས་ཆོས་པར་བཤད་ཀྱང་། ཆོས་ཀྱིས་བདག་ཚུར་མ་རྟོགས་རྣམ་བཤད་ཁ་བསྡུས་སུ་སོང་། གལ་ཏེ་བདག་མེད་དུ་རྟོགས་ཀྱང་། རྟོགས་བྱེད་ཁོ་རང་ལྟ་བྱེད་ཚད་མ་ཆོད། གལ་ཏེ་མཁན་པོ་ཚད་ཆོད་ཀྱང་གཞི་ངོས་མ་ཟིན། གཞི་མེད་ཙམ་དུ་ཤེས་ཀྱང་ཡེ་ཤེས་རང་གཤིད་ལ་མ་ཕེབས། བརྗོད་བློའི་མཐར་ལྷུང་སྟེ། ཡོད་མེད་རྟག་ཆད་མཐའ་བྲལ། ཟུང་འཇུག་གང་རུང་ཞིག་ལ་ངེས་ཤེས་དང་། བཅས་པའི་འཛིན་པ་རང་གིས་མ་ཚོར་བར་འཇུག བརྗོད་རྒྱུ་རེ་ཆེད་པས་བརྗོད་བྲལ་གྱི་དོན་མ་མཐོང་། ཚད་མ་ཆོད། གཏིང་མ་རྟོགས་ཏེ། མ་ཚོར་ཡིད་བྱེད་ཀྱི་ངར་འཛིན་དུག་རོ་ཁོང་དུ་ལངས་པ་དང་འདྲ་བས། རོ་ལངས་བྱེད་ལྟ་སྒོམ་ལ་ཤི་ལོག་འོང་བས། བླ་མ་དམ་པའི་ཞལ་གྱི་བདུད་རྩི་ལ་ངོམས་པ་མེད་པའི་གུས་པས་གདུང་བར་བྱའོ། ། “ཞེས་གསུངས་སོ།། །།

Finally, in the 'Recognition of Great Perfection, the Self-Liberation of Samsara-Nirvana', the superiority of Yuthok's approach to Primordial Purity and Cutting through Hardness as compared to other practices is explained:

"If one does not encounter such an unparalleled Great Secret as the Nyingthig, one's perspective on samsara will be that of a shravaka, pratyeka-buddha or bodhisattva, one will look upon good thoughts from the perspective of the three lower classes of tantras, Kriya, Upa (Charya) and Yoga. One will make assumptions based on the meaning of the Creation and Completion stages. Having got into one's mind the common or vulgar meaning of the Great Perfection and Great Seal, one will put (such inferior) dogma first, and all it will amount to will be idle (and misleading) chatter. All the oral lineages (which possess) in general the definitive meaning agree in their commentaries that even if one preaches Dharma out there in the world to others that doesn't mean that one has realized Dharma inwardly from one's own side. Even if one has realized non-self, one still won't have investigated that which observes the knower (of non-self). Even if one has inspected this knower, one still won't have recognized its (true) basis. Even if one has understood that there really isn't any basis, one won't have arrived at the point where even this wisdom overcomes (and counter-acts) itself. Having lapsed into (the space of) expressible mind or thought, by not having certainty in the absolute indivisibility of mind, and by having failed to notice that one's mind is free from the extremes of either being or non-being, of eternalism or nihilism, and by still finding something to express, one will have failed to perceive the essential meaning, to cut to the root, to realize (the nature of mind) in its deepest sense. The unnoticed mental activity of grasping onto a 'self' rises up inside like the poison of a chronic sickness. This View and Meditation that returns the dead to life has brought you back from the (brink of) death - for that you should be overcome with inexhaustible reverence for the nectar of the holy lama's face."

བོགས་འདོན།

རྫོགས་ཆེན་གྱི་བོགས་དབྱུང་འདི་ནི་མེད་ཐབས་མེད་པ་ཞིག་ཡིན་པ་དང་། འདིར་གཡུ་ཐོག་སྙིང་ཐིག་རྫོགས་རིམ་སྐུ་གསུམ་རང་ཤར་དུ་བོགས་འདོན་རྒྱུན་འཁྱེར་ལུགས་སུ་བསྟན་པ་ནི། "སྣང་སྲིད་འཁོར་འདས་ཀྱི་ཆོས་ཐམས་ཅད་རང་གི་སེམས་སུ་ཐག་བཅད། སེམས་ཀྱི་ངོ་བོ་ཡེ་གདོད་མ་ནས། སྐྱེ་འགག་གནས་བྲལ་མཐའ་དབུས་སྤྲོས་པའི་དྲི་མ་དང་བྲལ་བ། གཞིས་ཅིར་ཡང་མ་གྲུབ་པ། མདངས་སྣ་ཚོགས་སུ་འཆར་བ། འཆར་བཞིན་དུ་འཆར་མཁན་གཞི་རྩ་བྲལ་བ། སྨྲ་བསམ་ཤེས་བརྗོད་བློ་ཡུལ། ཐམས་ཅད་ལས་འདས་པའི་རིག་པ་གཅེར་བུ་ལྷང་ངེ་བ། རྒྱུན་ཁྲོལ་སེ་བ་ཞིག་ལ། སྣང་བ་ཕྱི་རུ་མ་ལུས། རིག་པ་ནང་དུ་མ་ལུས། ཡེ་ཤེས་ཟང་ཐལ་དུ་མ་ལུས། ཉོན་མོངས་ངན་ཧེ་སྤང་རྒྱུ་དང་སྤྱོད་མཁན་བྲལ་བ། ཡེ་ཇི་བཞིན་པའི་གནས་ལུགས་དེ་མཐོང་རྒྱུ་མེད་པའི་ཚུལ་གྱིས་གནས་ལུགས་དེ་མཐོང་། ཉམས་མྱོང་རིག་པའི་ཡེ་ཤེས་འགྱུར་མེད་བློའི་གཏིང་དུ་འཆར་བས། དེ་ཉིད་འགྲོ་འཆགས་ཉལ་འདུག་ལུས་ངག་ཡིད་སྤྱོད་ཀུན་དུ་སོ་མ། ལྷུག་པ། མ་བཅོས་པ། རང་མདངས་བཅོས་མེད་དུ་ལྷོད་དེ། རྗེན་ཁྲོལ་སེ་བའི་ངང་ལ་མ་ཡེངས་ཙམ་བསྐྱངས་པས། ཚེ་འདིར་ཀུན་བཟང་གི་དགོངས་པ་མངོན་དུ་འགྱུར་པ་ཐེ་ཚོམ་མེད་པ་སྟེ།"

The Enhancement (for stabilizing awareness) Practices

This enhancing practice of the Great Perfection is indispensable, and is described here in the daily enhancement practice system of the Completion stage teachings of the Yuthok Nyingthig (called) the 'Spontaneous Arising of the Three Kayas':

"Having ascertained that all the phenomena, all the appearances and arisings of Samsara-Nirvana exist within your own mind, recognize the essence of one's mind as primordial - it does not arise, cease, or abide, it is free of either center or periphery, of the stain of (spatial) elaboration. Devoid of any basic characteristics whatsoever, it appears as a manifold display of radiance (of light and colour), and yet even in appearing it is devoid of any fundamental basis of an 'appear-er'. Beyond expression and thought, inconceivable, ineffable, the naked primordial awareness is clear and bright, totally relaxed and open. It is all external appearances without exception, it is all internal awareness without exception. It is wholly unobstructed wisdom. It is beyond the need for rejecting afflictive emotions and bad actions, and is free of any 'rejecter'. Perceive, without perceiving any 'thing', the natural state of this primordial is-ness. With this changeless wisdom of experiential awareness appearing in the depths of one's mind, relax into the freshness of this suchness, the immediacy (that pervades) the four activities of walking, moving, lying down and sitting, of body, speech and mind, every activity. Let go into relaxed and uncontrived presence, relax into your own uncontrived spontaneously manifesting self-radiance. Maintaining this awareness in its bare and open state without any distraction whatsoever, your own mind will undoubtedly be transformed into that of Samantabhadra within this very life."

ཞེས་རིག་རྔོ་འཕྲོད་ཚར་ནས། འགྲོ་བའི་དུས། འཆགས་པའི་གནས་དུས་དང་། ཉལ་བའི་དུས་དང་འདུག་པའི་གནས་དུས། ལུས་ཀྱི་ལས་ཀ་སོགས་ཀྱི་སྤྱོད་ལམ་དང་། ངག་གིས་གཏམ་འདྲ་མིན་བཤད་པ་དང་གོ་བའི་སྤྱོད་ལམ། ཡིད་ཀྱི་རྣམ་རྟོག་དུག་ལྔ་དང་ཚོར་བ་བཟང་ངན་དང་སེམས་བདེ་མི་བདེ་བ་གང་བྱུང་ན་ཡང་རིག་པས་ཟིན་དགོས་པ་ནི་རྫོགས་ཆེན་པོགས་འདོན་ཁྱད་པར་ཅན་ཡིན་པ་དང་།

དེ་ཡང་ཉུང་བསྡུས་ཙམ་རྒྱལ་དབང་ལྔ་བའམ་སྟག་རྒན་གང་ཤར་རང་གྲོལ་གྱི་རིག་འཛིན་ཞལ་ལུང་གི་པོགས་དབྱུང་ལ། "པོགས་དབྱུང་བ་ལ། དུག་ལྔ་རང་གྲོལ། སྒོ་ལྔ་རང་གྲོལ། ཚོགས་དྲུག་རང་གྲོལ་གསུམ་ལས། དང་པོ་དུག་ལྔ་རང་གྲོལ་ནི། ཕྱི་ནང་གི་འདོད་ཆགས། ཞེ་སྡང་། གཏི་མུག ང་རྒྱལ། ཕྲག་དོག་བསྟུན་མི་བཟོད་པ་སྐྱེས་པའི་ངོ་བོ་ལ་ཅེར་གྱིས་བལྟས་ནས་ཆམ་གྱིས་བཞག་པས་དང་པོ་ལ་བདེ་སྟོང་གཉིས་མེད།། གཉིས་པ་ལ་གསལ་སྟོང་གཉིས་མེད། གསུམ་པ་ལ་ཆོས་སྐུ་གཞི་བྲལ། བཞི་བ་དང་ལྔ་པ་ལ་གཙུག་མ་ལྷན་གཅིག་སྐྱེས་པའི་ཡེ་ཤེས་སུ་རང་གྲོལ་ལོ་ཞེས་འདོད་ཆགས་སྐྱེ་པའི་སྐབས་སུ་འདོད་ཆགས་ཀྱི་པོར་བལྟས་ན་བདེ་སྟོང་གཉིས་མེད་དུ་གྲོལ་བ་དང་། ཞེ་སྡང་གི་ངོ་བོར་བལྟས་ན་གསལ་སྟོང་གཉིས་མེད། གཏི་མུག་གི་ངོ་ལ་བལྟས་ནས་བཞག་ན་ཆོས་སྐུ་གཞི་བྲལ་དང་། ང་རྒྱལ་དང་ཕྲག་དོག་གི་ངོ་ལ་བལྟས་ན་ལྷན་ཅིག་སྐྱེས་པའི་ཡེ་ཤེས་སུ་རང་གྲོལ་དུ་འགྱུར་བས། དུས་རྒྱུན་ཉོན་མོངས་གང་ཐུང་སྐྱེ་བའི་དུས་སུ་དྲན་ཤེས་ཀྱིས་ཟིན་རྒྱུ་ཤིན་ཏུ་གལ་ཆེའོ།།

This then is the special, Great Perfection enhancing practice: once one has succeeded in recognizing the true face or essence of awareness, all and any circumstances or activities must be encompassed by awareness - while walking, during times and situations of moving, lying down (sleeping), and sitting, in one's daily physical activity, in the conduct of one's body, while making and listening to various speech-utterances, and when whatever discursive thoughts of the five poisons, good or bad sensations, as well as happy or unhappy states of the mind arise.

This is elaborated a little further in the enhancing practices (section) of the 'Oral Transmissions of the Awareness-Holders' of the Great Fifth or the old ngakpa Gangshar Rangdrol:

"With the enhancing practices there's the self-liberation of the five poisons, the five gates, and the six collections (i.e. aggregates of consciousness). Of these three, regarding the first, the self-liberation of the five poisons: when inner and outer desire, anger, ignorance, pride, and jealousy arise intolerably, having looked squarely at their essence, one lets go completely. The first (poison) will be self-liberated into non-dual blissful-emptiness, the second into non-dual clear-emptiness, the third, into the groundless dharmakaya, and the fourth and fifth will be self-liberated into the instantaneously arising wisdom of the ultimate nature.

When desire arises, having gazed upon the essence of this desire, it will be liberated into non-dual bliss-emptiness; having looked at the essence of anger, (it will be liberated into) nondual clarity-emptiness; if one looks upon the essence of confusion and lets go, it will be liberated into the groundless dharmakaya; looking upon the essence of pride and jealousy these will be self-liberated into instantaneously arising wisdom. Accordingly, it's very important to grasp any regularly-occurring afflictive emotions with mindfulness, the moment that they arise."

གཉིས་པ་སྒྲོ་ལྔ་རང་གྲོལ་ནི།

མིག རྣ་བ། སྣ། ལྕེ་དང་ལུས་རྣམས་ཀྱི་འཛིན་པ་གང་སྐྱེས་དེའི་ངོ་བོ་ལ་ཅེར་གྱིས་བལྟས་ལ་ཆམ་གྱིས་བཞག་པས་ཆོས་སྐུ་ཀ་དག་ཆེན་མོར་རང་གྲོལ་ལོ། ཞེས་པ་ནི་མིག་གཟུགས་ལ་འཛུག་དུས་ཆོས་ཐམས་ཅད་མེ་ལོང་དུ་ཤར་བ་བཞིན་དུ་གསལ་ལ་འཛིན་པས་མ་སླད་པ། རྣ་ཡིས་སྒྲ་གོ་དུས་བྲག་ཆ་ལྟ་བུའམ་སྤུགས་དང་ཆོས་སྒྲ་ལས་སྒྲ་ལ་ཆགས་ཞེན་དང་སྤང་བླང་མེད་པ། སྣ་ཡིས་དྲི་ཚོར་དུས་རྫི་ལམ་གྱི་དྲི་བཞིན་དྲི་ཞིམ་མི་ཞིམ་གྱི་ཚོར་བ་ལས་འདས་པ། ལྕེ་ཡིས་རོ་མྱོང་བའང་རྫི་ལམ་གྱི་རོ་ལྟ་བུ་ཆགས་ཞེན་དང་སྤང་བླང་མེད་པ། ལུས་ཀྱི་རེག་བྱ་ལའང་བདེ་སྟོང་གི་ངོ་བོ་ལས་བདེ་སྡུག་གི་བདེན་འཛིན་ལས་གྲོལ་བ་སྟེ། གུ་རུ་རིན་པོ་ཆེས། བཟུང་བའི་ཆོས་ཀྱིས་མ་སླད་ཅིང་།། འཛིན་པའི་ཆོས་ཀྱིས་མ་གོས་པ།།

ཞེས་གསུངས་པ་བཞིན་རིག་ངོ་བསྐྱང་པར་བྱའོ།།

གསུམ་པ་ཚོགས་དྲུག་རང་གྲོལ་ནི།

གཟུགས་སྒྲ། དྲི། རོ། རེག་བྱ། ཡིད་ཀྱི་བྱུང་ཚོར་དྲན་རིག་གི་དགག་སྒྲུབ། ཆགས་སྡང་སྐྱེས་པ་དེའི་ངོ་བོ་ལ་ཅེར་གྱིས་བལྟས་ལ་ཆམ་གྱི་བཞག་བཞག་པས་ཡེ་སྟོང་རྩ་བྲལ་ཆེན་པོའི་ངང་དུ་ལ་ཟློས་ཏེ། གནས་ལུགས་སྟོང་གསལ་མཉམ་པ་ཆེན་པོར་ལྷུན་གྱིས་གྲུབ་བོ།། དེས་ནི་གང་ཤར་བླང་དོར་རེ་དོགས་ལས་འདས་པ་མ་བསྒོམ་ཡེ་ཤེས་ལྷུག་པ་རང་བཞིན་དུ་ཁྲིགས་ཆོས་པས།

"Secondly, when it comes to the self-liberation of the five gates: by looking squarely at the essence of whatever might arise that has been apprehended by the eyes, ears, nose, tongue, and body and by letting go completely, it will be self-liberated into the great primordial purity of the dharma-body of absolute reality.

This refers to apprehending all phenomena clearly as untainted, where they (are seen like objects) appearing in a mirror from the moment when they enter (into consciousness) as visual forms. When sounds are heard by the ears they are (experienced) as being entirely free of desire or attachment, of clinging or aversion, as nothing other than echoes off a cliff, or (beautiful) mantras and dharma-sounds. When the nose experiences smells, (these are treated) like fragrances in a dream, that go beyond all perceptions of being delicious or not delicious. Tastes of the tongue too, are like tastes in a dream, devoid of desire and longing, attachment or aversion. Bodily or tactile sensation, as well, (are experienced as) nothing more than the essence of bliss-emptiness that have been freed from all apprehension as either pleasurable or painful, as inherently real. As Guru Rinpoche said, "unadulterated by apprehended phenomena, untainted by grasped-onto phenomena." So should the essence of awareness be maintained.

Thirdly, regarding the self-liberation of the six collections - the affirming and negating mindfulness (conscious awareness) and mentally-arising perceptions of sights and sounds, smells, tastes, tactile sensations - by observing directly the essence of these desirous appearances and arisings, and by completely letting go, one passes beyond into the great state of rootless, primordial emptiness, and the great equivalence of the emptiness-clarity of the natural state is realized spontaneously. Thus, cut through hardness to the natural state of totally awake relaxation, to the wisdom of non-meditation that goes beyond attachment and aversion, hope and fear, regardless of whatever arises."

ཀློང་གསལ་ལས། དེ་ལྟར་རྒྱུན་དུ་ཉམས་སུ་བླངས་པས་ནམ་ཞིག་ན་སྣང་སེམས་འདྲེས་ཏེ་དགེ་སྦྱོར་ལ་ཆོད་འཛིན་མེད་ཀྱང་བྱ་རོག་གཟིངས་ལ་འཕོར། གཉེན་པོའི་བྱ་ར་མི་དགོས་ཉམས་སྐྱོང་ཟད།། ཅེས་གསུངས་པ་སོགས་ཀྱིས་ཤེས་སོ།། ཞེས་པ་ནི་རྫོགས་ཆེན་ལུགས་ཀྱི་ཉོན་མོངས་ལམ་ཁྱེར་ཐུན་མོང་མ་ཡིན་པ་ཡིན་ནོ།།

རྫོགས་ཆེན་གྱི་གནས་ལུགས་ལོག་པར་རྟོག་ན་ལྟ་སྤྱོད་ཡ་བྲལ་དུ་འགྲོ་ཉེན་ཆེ་བས།
གུ་རུ་རིན་པོ་ཆེས་ལྟ་བ་ནམ་མཁའ་ལས་མཐོ་ཡང་།། ལས་འབྲས་བག་ཕྱེ་ལྟར་བཞིབ།།
གསུངས་པ་ལྟར་ལྟ་བའི་རྗེས་སུ་སྤྱོད་པ་མ་ཤོར་བ་དགོས་ཏེ།
ཁྱད་པར་སྙིང་རྗེ་ཆེན་པོའམ་བྱང་ཆུབ་སེམས་ཀྱི་ཐུགས་རྒྱུད་ཟིན་རྒྱུ་གལ་ཏ་ཅང་ཆེ་སྟེ།

རྫོགས་ཆེན་ལྟ་བ་མཁའ་ལྡིང་གཤོག་བརླབ་ལས། "དེ་ལྟར་མ་རྟོགས་འཁོར་འཁྱམས་འགྲོ་ཀུན་ལ།།
མ་ཡིས་བུ་གཅིག་དག་ལ་བརྩེ་བ་ལྟར།། བཅོས་མིན་སྙིང་རྗེ་སྐྱེ་བ་རྫོགས་ཆེན་གྱི།། ལྟ་བའི་ཁྱད་ཆོས་ཡིན་པའང་ཤེས་པར་གྱིས།།
ཐམས་ཅད་སྟོང་པ་ཉིད་དུ་ཐག་བཅད་ནས།། དགེ་སྤྱངས་སྡིག་ལ་འཛེམས་མེད་སྤྱོད་གྱུར་ན།།
ནག་པོ་ཁ་འབྱམས་བདུད་ཀྱི་ལྟ་བ་སྟེ།། དེ་འདྲའི་བདུད་ལྟའི་དབང་དུ་མ་ཤོར་གཅེས།།
ཞེས་རྫོགས་ཆེན་ངོ་སྤྲོད་སྐབས་སུ་གསུངས་པ་འདི་གནས་སྐབས་ཀུན་ལ་ཐུགས་ལ་ངེས་རྒྱུ་གལ་ཆེའོ།།

In the 'Clear Expanse' it says:

"Having regularly practiced like this, when mind and appearances become mixed up, without even trying to re-calibrate or exert control in your spiritual practice, (just be like) a crow circling a ship (which will eventually have to return to it). The experience will exhaust itself without you having to remedy it."

By this you will realize (the practice).

This is the uncommon practice for bringing afflictive emotions 'onto the path' (i.e. using daily experiences as they arise as opportunities for practice).

There is a great danger that if one misunderstands the ultimate nature of the Great Perfection one's view and conduct can become separated from each other. Thus - as Guru Rinpoche stated "My view is higher than the sky, yet my conduct is as fine as flour" - one's conduct must not go astray from one's view. In particular, it's very important for one to retain great compassion, or a mind-stream (governed by) bodhichitta. The 'Flight of the Garuda' describes the View of the Great Completion as follows:

"Thus, one loves each and every unrealized being wandering in Samsara like a mother loves her only child. One must realize that the generating of uncontrived compassion is the special characteristic of the View of the Great Perfection. If, having ascertained that everything is essentially empty, one indulges unreservedly in grave sin, then (this amounts to) the view of demons who prattle on (about how goodness and moral conduct are empty). It's imperative that one doesn't fall under the influence of such a demonic view as this."

It's important that one keeps in mind this teaching, which (appears) in the context of the Introduction to the Great Perfection, in all circumstances.

དེ་བཞིན་ཁྲེགས་ཆོད་ལུགས་ཀྱི་ལྟ་བསྒོམ་སྤྱོད་འབྲས་བཞི་སྨན་རྒྱལ་གཡུ་ཐོག་སྙིང་མ་ཡོན་ཏན་མགོན་པོས་རྣམ་ཐར་དུ”དེ་ཡང་རྣལ་འབྱོར་མ་རྟོག་པའི་རང་གྲོལ་མས་གཡུ་ཐོག་ལ་ཉམས་རྟོགས་ལུགས་ཤིག་གསུངས་དང་གསུངས་བྱུང་བས། གཡུ་ཐོག་ཆེན་པོས་ཉམས་དབྱངས་ཀྱི་མགུར་འདི་གསུངས་སོ།

Milarepa (1040-1123) Meditating in a Mountain. Tibet, 18th century. Tibets's Secret Temple Exhibition, Collection of the Newark Museum.

The four-fold View, Meditation, Conduct, and Fruit of the Cutting through Hardness system are taught in the spiritual biography of the King of Medicine Yuthok Yonten Gonpo the Elder as follows:

Moreover, the yogini 'The Self-Liberation of Conceptuality' (Tokpai Rangdrolma) taught a system of experiential realization to Yuthok, and once it was transmitted the Great Yuthok sang this short and easy-to-understand song of experience or realization:

ན་མོ་གུ་རུ། ཀུན་ཁྱབ་ཆོས་སྐུར་ཤར།། དག་སྣང་ཕྱོགས་མེད་སྐྱེས།།
སོས་གུས་ལ་འགྱུར་བ་མེད།། རང་སེམས་ལ་དད་པ་ཐོབ་པ་འདི།།
ཆོས་མེད་སྨྱོན་པ་ངའི་གསོལ་འདེབས་ཡིན།།

ཕྱོགས་འཛིན་གྱི་འཁྲུལ་པ་སངས།། ཕྱོགས་མེད་མཐའ་བྲལ་དུ་ཤར།།
ཟུང་འཇུག་བློ་འདས་སུ་རྟོགས་པ་འདི།། ཆོས་མེད་སྨྱོན་པ་ངའི་ལྟ་བ་ཡིན།།

བློ་སྒོམ་གྱི་འཛིན་པ་ཞིག། ཡེ་སྒོམ་ལ་འབྲལ་མེད་གནས།།
མཉམ་བཞག་རྗེས་ཐོབ་འདྲེས་པ་འདི།། ཆོས་མེད་སྨྱོན་པ་ངའི་སྒོམ་པ་ཡིན།།

ཁྲི་ཚུལ་འཆོས་ཀྱི་སྤྲིག་ཆོས་ཞིག། སྒོ་གསུམ་འདི་རང་གྲོལ་དུ་སོང་།།
གཏད་མེད་ཤུགས་སུ་འབྱུང་བ་འདི།། ཆོས་མེད་སྨྱོན་པ་ངའི་སྤྱོད་པ་ཡིན།།

རེ་དོགས་ཀྱི་མཚན་མ་ཡལ།། འཁོར་འདས་འདི་གཅིག་ཏུ་འདྲེས།།
སྐུ་གསུམ་རང་ལ་སྨིན་པ་འདི།། ཆོས་མེད་སྨྱོན་པ་ངའི་འབྲས་བུ་ཡིན།། “ ཞེས་གོ་སླ་ཚིག་ཙང་དུ་གསུངས་སོ།།

"Praise to the Guru!

That mind will dawn as the all-pervading Dharma-body of Absolute Reality, that it will arise as impartial undivided Pure Vision, that unchanging devotion and faith in the nature of one's own mind will be obtained - this is my Prayer, I, a madman without Dharma!

The purification of the delusion of partiality, mind shining forth without bias or limits, the realization of the transcendent union beyond the intellect - this is my View, I a madman without Dharma!

The grasping of analytic meditation, the undivided abiding of the meditation on primordial (wisdom), the attainments that come after resting in meditative equipoise – the merging of all of these is my Meditation, I, a madman without Dharma!

While outwardly appearing to conduct myself in a calculating, hypocritical manner, (all perceptions of) the three gates have been self-liberated. Such spontaneous emergence with no specific target, this is my Conduct, I, a madman without Dharma!

The attributes of either hope or fear having disappeared, this Samsara-Nirvana having merged as one, this ripening of the three bodies in my own being - this is my Result, I, a madman without Dharma!"

ATI YOGA SPONTANEOUS SONG

by Nida Chenagtsang

Ati Yoga Spontaneous Song

སྔགས་མང་ལ་རྫོགས་ཆེན་བསྒོམ་པར་སྐུལ་བའི་མགུར་གླུ་གང་ཤར་མ།

A spontaneously arisen song of realization for encouraging the ngakpa community to contemplate the Great Perfection:

རང་བྱུང་སངས་རྒྱས་པད་མ་འབྱུང་གནས་དང་དབྱེར་མ་མཆིས་པའི་སྨན་རྒྱལ་གཡུ་ཐོག་ཡོན་ཏན་མགོན་པོ་
ལ་ཕྱག་འཚལ་ལོ། མཆོད་དོ། སྐྱབས་སུ་མཆིའོ།། གདོད་མའི་མགོན་པོ་སྤྲོས་པ་དྲི་མ་མེད།།
ཁ་སྦྱོར་ཡན་ལག་བདེ་ཆེན་ཀློང་དུ་གྲོལ།། འཇའ་ལུས་རྡོ་རྗེའི་བདག་ཉིད་སྤྲུལ་བའི་སྐུ།།
ཀུན་བཟང་བླ་མས་དུས་རྟག་བྱིན་གྱིས་རློབས།།

I prostrate, make offerings, and go for refuge to the self-arisen Lotus-Born Buddha and the King of Medicine Yuthok Yönten Gonpo, who are inseparable from one another!

Primordial protector, unelaborated and stainless, may the qualities of union be liberated into the vast expanse of Great Bliss,

O Guru Samantabhadra, emanation body of the very essence of the vajra rainbow-body, grant your blessings at all times!

མཆོག་གསུམ་དབྱེར་མེད་གུ་རུ་རིན་པོ་ཆེ།། སྐུ་གསུམ་བདག་ཉིད་རྩ་བའི་བླ་མ་དང་།།
རྩ་གསུམ་དབྱེར་མེད་བརྒྱུད་པའི་བླ་མའི་ཚོགས།། བསླུ་མེད་སྐྱབས་གནས་ཡིན་ནོ་སྔགས་པ་ཚོ།།

The Precious Guru who is inseparable from the Three Jewels, the Root-Lama who is the personification of the Three Bodies, the Assembly of the Guru of the lineage that is inseparable from the Three Roots - these, o ngakpas, are the unfailing refuge!

ཐུན་མོང་བློ་ལྡོག་རྣམ་བཞིས་བློ་སྦྱོང་ལ།། ཐུན་མིན་སྔོན་འགྲོ་རྩ་གསུམ་མཐར་ཕྱིན་བསྙེན།།
རྩ་རླུང་ཐིག་ལེའི་རྩལ་དང་བོགས་ཐོན་ནས།། འོད་གསལ་རྫོགས་ཆེན་ཞུས་ཤིག་སྔགས་པ་ཚོ།།

Train your mind via the four common contemplations that steer one away from Samsara, complete the recitations of the uncommon preliminaries of the three roots, master and enhance the practices of the channel-wind-and-drops practices, then, having done all this, o ngakpas, request the teachings of the Clear Light Great Perfection!

ཆོས་རྣམས་སེམས་ལ་འདུས་པའི་སེམས་ཀྱི་སྡེ།། སྣང་སྲིད་ཆོས་ཉིད་ཀློང་འདུས་ཀློང་སྡེ་དང་།།
འཁོར་འདས་དབྱེར་མེད་རང་གྲོལ་མན་ངག་སྡེ།། རྫོགས་ཆེན་སྡེ་གསུམ་ཡིན་ནོ་སྔགས་པ་ཚོ།།

The mind-category of all phenomena which are contained within the mind, the expanse-category of all appearances and arisings contained within the expanse of ultimate reality, the pith instruction-category of the self-liberation of indivisible Samsara-Nirvana, these, o ngakpas, are the three divisions of the Great Perfection!

ཞེ་སྡང་གཉེན་པོར་མ་ཧཱ་ཡོ་ག་བསྟན།། འདོད་ཆགས་གཉེན་པོ་ཨ་ནུ་ཡོ་ག་ཡིན།།
གཏི་མུག་རང་སངས་ཨ་ཏི་ཡོ་ག་སྟེ།། རྒྱུད་མཐུན་ཉམས་སུ་ལོངས་ཤིག་སྔགས་པ་ཚོ།།

The teachings of Maha yoga that are the antidote for hatred, Anu yoga which is the antidote for desire, Ati yoga which spontaneously dissolves the darkness of confusion - practice these, o ngakpas, in accordance with your mental capacity!

སྔོན་བསགས་ལས་མེད་བསྟན་པ་འདིར་མི་མཇལ།། རིག་ངོ་འཕྲོད་ནས་བསྐྱང་ན་མི་གྲོལ་མེད།།
འཇིག་རྟེན་འཁོར་བར་བྲེལ་བ་ཆེ་བའི་དུས།། རྫོགས་ཆེན་ངོ་སྤྲོད་དགོས་སོ་སྔགས་པ་ཚོ།།

You won't encounter this teaching save through previously accumulated karma, if you recognize the true face of awareness and sustain it, you cannot not be liberated. When worldly life is busy and distracting that's when, o ngakpas, you need the pointing out instructions of the Great Perfection!

མཐོང་ན་ཞིང་པ་འབྲོག་པ་གྲོལ་བར་འགྱུར།། མ་མཐོང་བླ་ཆེན་སྤྲུལ་སྐུ་འཁྲུལ་བར་འགྱུར།།
རྟོགས་གྲོལ་ཅིག་ཅར་ཡེ་ཤེས་རྗེན་པ་འདི།། མ་འཁྲུལ་སྐྱོང་ཤིག་ལས་ཅན་སྔགས་པ་ཚོ།།

If it's perceived, even farmers and nomads will be liberated, if it's not perceived, even people acting like great gurus and holding the titles of reincarnate lamas will remain deluded. So nurture without delusion, o lucky ngakpas, this naked wisdom that grants realization and liberation simultaneously!

འཇིག་རྟེན་འཁོར་བ་བྲེལ་འཚུབ་ཆེ་བའི་དུས།། ཉོན་མོངས་མང་ལ་རྩོད་ཉོག་དར་བའི་དུས།།
སྣང་རིག་ཟང་ཐལ་ཅན་གྱི་རྫོགས་ཆེན་བསྒོམས།། འདི་ཕྱི་གཉིས་ཀ་སྐྱིད་དོ་སྔགས་པ་ཚོ།།

When worldly life is busy and frantic, when afflictive emotions proliferate and controversies unfold, o ngakpas, cultivate the all-penetrating and completely transparent visionary awareness of the Great Perfection, and be happy and carefree in both this life and the next.

སྐྱེས་སྟོབས་ཤེས་རབ་མེད་ན་མེད་དུ་ཆུག། སྦྱངས་པའི་ཡོན་ཏན་དམིགས་བསལ་དགོས་མ་ཡིན།།
ཞི་ལྷག་བསྐྱེད་རྫོགས་མང་པོ་མི་ཤེས་ཀྱང་།། རྫོགས་ཆེན་རིག་ངོ་འཕྲོད་དགོས་སྔགས་པ་ཚོ།།

If you don't have in-born wisdom, then let it be so. Specially trained spiritual qualities aren't necessary. Even if you don't understand Peaceful Abiding, Direct Insight (Shamatha and Vipashyana), and Creation and Completion stage meditation practices very much, you should still recognize, o ngakpas, the true face of awareness of the Great Perfection!

རྫོགས་ཆེན་བླ་མ་བཤད་ལ་མཁས་མི་དགོས།། རྫོགས་ཆེན་བླ་མར་མང་པོའི་ལུང་མི་དགོས།།
རྫོགས་ཆེན་བླ་མར་རྒྱུད་པའི་བྱིན་བརླབ་དང་།། རིག་ངོའི་ཉམས་མྱོང་དགོས་སོ་སྔགས་པ་ཚོ།།

You don't have to be an expert in the explanations of the Great Perfection guru, nor do you need a lot of reading transmissions. All you need, o ngakpas, is the blessing of the Great Perfection guru's lineage and to experience the true face of awareness!

ཁ་བདེ་ལྷེ་བདེས་རྫོགས་ཆེན་སྟོན་མི་ཐུབ།། འཆད་རྩོད་རྩོམ་པས་རྫོགས་ཆེན་གཞལ་མི་ཐུབ།།
སྟོན་ལས་རྟོགས་ལྡན་བླ་མ་ཁོ་ན་ལས།། བརྗོད་མེད་དོན་དེ་རྟོགས་ཡོང་སྔགས་པ་ཚོ།།

A silver tongue cannot reveal the Great Perfection, nor can it be measured through lecturing, debating or writing. It is only from your karmic meeting with a realized guru, o ngakpas, that you will come to realize the ineffable essential meaning!

ཟང་ཐལ་རྗེན་པའི་རིག་པ་མ་མྱོང་ན།། དབང་ལུང་ཁྲིད་ཀྱི་གྲངས་ཀས་ག་ལ་གྲོལ།།
དཔེ་མང་ལྷ་མང་རྗེས་སུ་མ་རྒྱུག་པར།། རིག་ངོའི་བླ་མ་བསྟེན་ཅིག་སྔགས་པ་ཚོ།།

If you haven't ever experienced unobstructed naked awareness, even with scores of empowerments, reading transmissions and oral instructions, how can you ever be liberated? So rely soley, o ngakpas, on the essence of awareness of the guru, without chasing after scores of deities or books!

ཚུལ་འཆོས་འཛུམ་གྱིས་གྲོལ་བར་མི་འགྱུར་ལ།། ཁ་མཁས་བཤད་དང་རྩོད་པས་ག་ལ་གྲོལ།།
སྔགས་དང་རིམ་གྲོ་སོགས་ཀྱིས་མི་གྲོལ་བ།། རིག་ངོ་ཁོ་ནས་གྲོལ་ལོ་སྔགས་པ་ཚོ།།

You won't be liberated through outward displays of smiling hypocrisy - how can eloquent discourse or debate (about the dharma) ever liberate you? Things like mantras and standard rituals won't liberate you either - o ngakpas, only the essence of awareness can do that!

ཁ་དོག་དཀར་དམར་ཡིན་དང་མ་ཡིན་དང་།། འཁོར་འདས་ཡོད་དང་མེད་སོགས་རྩོད་མི་དགོས།།
ཡིད་དཔྱོད་སྤྲོས་བཅས་དམིགས་པ་འཛིན་མེད་དུ།། གནས་ལུགས་ལྷུན་གྲུབ་སྐྱོངས་ཤིག་སྔགས་པ་ཚོ།།

You don't have to debate whether something is or isn't red or white, whether Samsara and Nirvana exist or not, on and on. Without focusing on any object of mental activity or fabrication, maintain, o ngakpas, the spontaneously present and effortlessly realized natural state!

དགའ་རབ་རྡོ་རྗེས་ཚིག་གསུམ་གནད་བརྡེག་བསྟན།། དེང་དུས་འགྲེལ་པ་སུམ་བརྒྱས་འཁྲུལ་དུ་བཅུག།
ཆེ་ཆེ་མཐོ་མཐོའི་ཚིག་མང་མི་དགོས་པས།། ཉམས་ལྡན་བླ་མ་བསྟེན་ཞིག་སྔགས་པ་ཚོ།།

Nowadays, 'The Three Statements that Strike the Vital Points' taught by Garab Dorje have been distorted through three hundred commentaries. O ngakpas, you don't need lots of big and lofty words - just rely on the experienced guru.

བཤད་རྒྱུའི་ཚིག་གིས་བརྗོད་མེད་དོན་དེ་གབ།། བཟང་ངན་སྤང་བླང་བློ་ཡིས་བློ་འདས་ཤོར།།
གཅིག་ཤེས་ཀུན་གྲོལ་རིག་པ་ཟང་ཀ་མ།། རྟོགས་ལྡན་བླ་མར་ཞུས་ཤིག་སྔགས་པ་ཚོ།།

The essential, ineffable meaning is hidden by spoken words, transcendent mind is lost through thoughts of good and bad and moral prescriptions. Request from the realized guru then, o ngakpas, that single awareness, which being realized, liberates all things in and of itself!

ཞེ་སྡང་ཆེ་ཡང་རྫོགས་པ་ཆེན་པོས་གྲོལ།། འདོད་ཆགས་ཅན་ཡང་རྫོགས་པ་ཆེན་པོས་གྲོལ།།
གཏི་མུག་རང་གྲོལ་རྫོགས་པ་ཆེན་པོ་ནི།། མཐར་ཐུག་གྲོལ་ལམ་ཡིན་ནོ་སྔགས་པ་ཚོ།།

Even great hatred is liberated by the Great Perfection, even those filled with desire are freed. O ngakpas, this Great Perfection which self-liberates the fog of ignorance is the ultimate path of liberation!

འཛིན་མེད་ཟང་ཀ་མ་དེ་རྩོལ་མེད་སྐྱོང་།། སྔགས་པ་སྔགས་མ་སུ་ཡང་ངེས་པར་གྲོལ།།
དུག་ལྔ་རང་ཤིག་ཚོགས་དྲུག་རང་ཤར་ནི།། གེགས་མེད་ལམ་འཁྱེར་ཡིན་ནོ་སྔགས་པ་ཚོ།།

Any ngakpa or ngakma who effortlessly maintains awareness devoid of grasping just as it is will truly be liberated. The five poisons spontaneously obliterating themselves, the six collections of consciousness dawning of their own accord - this, o ngakpas, is the bringing onto the path that is devoid of obstacles!

ཟང་ཐལ་རྗེན་པའི་རིག་པ་མ་མཐོང་ན།། ཆེ་ཆེ་མང་མང་ཚིག་གིས་ཅི་ཞིག་བྱ།།
རྣམ་རྟོག་ལྷ་དང་རྩོལ་བཅས་རྫོགས་རིམ་སོགས།། རྫོགས་ཆེན་གོལ་སར་བསྟན་ནོ་སྔགས་པ་ཚོ།།

If you haven't perceived the unobstructed and naked awareness, what's the use of a whole lot of big words? All the concepts, deities, and effort of the Completion stage practices, and so on - may the Great Perfection reveal these, o ngakpas, as so many potential pitfalls!

ཟང་ཐལ་སོ་མའི་རིག་པ་བསྐྱང་ཐུབ་ན།། རྣམ་རྟོག་རྩོལ་བཅས་ཆོས་གཞན་དགོས་མ་ཡིན།།
འབུམ་བསྙེན་ཁྲི་བསྒོམ་མི་ཚེ་བསྐྱལ་ན་ཡང་།། རིག་ངོ་མ་མཐོང་མི་གྲོལ་སྔགས་པ་ཚོ།།

If you're able to maintain the unobstructed freshness of awareness, there's no need for any other teaching, for any other concepts or efforts. Even if you carry out 100,000 sadhana-accumulations and 10 000 (sessions of) meditation in your lifetime, if you don't perceive the true face of awareness, you will not be liberated, o ngakpas!

ཞབས་དཀར་དྲིན་གྱི་རིག་པའི་གསེར་ཐུར་གྱིས།། མ་རིག་བདག་འཛིན་སྐྱ་འགྲིབ་ཡོངས་སུ་ཕྱིས།།
གཉིས་འཛིན་ལས་དང་ཉོན་མོངས་ལས་གྲོལ་ན།། ཀ་དག་ཁྲེགས་ཆོད་ཡིན་ནོ་སྔགས་པ་ཚོ།།

As kind Shabkar's 'Golden Stick of Awareness' says, having completely cleared away the cataracts of non-awareness and self-grasping, when you are liberated from duality and afflictive emotion, this, o ngakpas, is the Primordial Purity Cutting Through Hardness!

ཞབས་དཀར་དྲིན་གྱི་བདུད་རྩི་བུམ་བཟང་གིས།། སྒྲོན་བཞི་སྣང་བཞིའི་དྲི་མ་ཡོངས་སུ་དག།
སྣང་སྟོང་འོད་གསལ་གཞོན་ནུ་བུམ་སྐུ་འགྲུབ།། ལྷུན་གྲུབ་ཐོད་རྒལ་ཡིན་ནོ་སྔགས་པ་ཚོ།།

As kind Shabkar's 'Most Excellent Vase of Nectar' says, having completely purified the imperfections of the four lamps and visions, you will attain the youthful vase-body of manifesting clear-light emptiness. This, o ngakpas, is the Spontaneously-Realized Direct Crossing!

ཅོག་བཞག་གསུམ་གྱི་གནད་ཀྱིས་བསྒོམ་ན་ཡང་།། ལྟ་སྟངས་གསུམ་གྱི་གནད་ཀྱིས་གཟིགས་ན་ཡང་།།
རྩ་རླུང་འཕྲུལ་གྱི་འཁོར་ལོ་བསྐོར་ན་ཡང་།། རིག་ངོ་ཞི་གནས་མ་ནོར་སྔགས་པ་ཚོ།།

Even while you meditate via the vital-points of the three 'restings as is', even as you train your gaze through the vital-points of the three gazes, even while you work through the cycles of 'magical movements' of the channels and winds, abide peacefully and unerringly, o ngakpas, in the essence of awareness.

གཉིས་སྣང་བདག་འཛིན་ཉོན་མོངས་མཐུག་པོ་ནི།། ལས་སྒྲིབ་མཁྲེག་གམ་ཁྲེགས་པོ་ཡིན་པས་ན།།
ཤེས་རབ་སྟོང་ཉིད་མེད་གཅིག་ཕྱལ་ལྷུན་གྱིས།། གཉིས་འཛིན་རྩ་མེད་ཆོད་ཅིག་སྔགས་པ་ཚོ།།

Dualistic appearances, self-grasping and afflictive emotions are dense, karmic obscurations are hard and unyielding, so sever duality utterly, o ngakpas, through the spontaneous realization of the uniformly void wisdom-emptiness!

རིག་པའི་རྩལ་དབང་བཞུགས་དང་གཟིགས་སྟངས་གནད།། སྒོ་ཡུལ་རིག་གནད་སྒྲོན་བཞིའི་ངོ་འཕྲོད་ལ།།
དཀར་ནག་ཁྲ་གསུམ་སྣང་བཞིའི་ཐོད་རྒལ་ནི།། མཐར་ཐུག་འཇའ་ལུས་ཡིན་ནོ་སྔགས་པ་ཚོ།།

The vital points of the body postures and gazes of the expression and empowerment of awareness, recognizing the four lamps of the points of awareness of the objects of the three gates, the four visions of the three colours, white, black, and many-hued of the Direct Crossing - this, o ngakpas, is the ultimate (attainment of the) rainbow body!

གྲུ་བཟུར་ཉམས་མེད་ཐིག་ལེ་ཆེན་པོའི་ཀློང་།། སྣང་སྟོང་འཁོར་འདས་ཁྱབ་རྒྱབ་ཕྱལ་ལེ་བ།།
བསྒོམ་དང་བསྒོམ་མཁན་བྲལ་བའི་རིག་པའི་ཀློང་།། མཇལ་མེད་ངང་དུ་མཇལ་ཞིག་སྔགས་པ་ཚོ།།

The vast expanse of the great light sphere which is free of corners, edges and all decline, the all-encompassing, all-perfected uniformity of Appearance-Emptiness, Samsara-Nirvana, the expanse of primordial awareness that is free from either meditation or meditator - encounter this, o ngakpas, without having to encounter anything at all!

རྩེ་གཅིག་སྤྲོས་བྲལ་རོ་གཅིག་བསྒོམ་མེད་ཀྱི།། ལྷན་སྐྱེས་ཡེ་ཤེས་བདེ་ཆེན་ཕྱག་རྒྱ་ཆེ།།
གནས་པ་དབྱིངས་དང་འགྱུ་བ་རིག་པའི་རྩལ།། ཕྱག་རྫོགས་དབྱེར་མེད་སྐྱོང་ཤིག་སྔགས་པ་ཚོ།།

The co-emergent Wisdom and Great Bliss of the Great Seal Mahamudra of the 'one taste' devoid of meditation, which is one-pointed and free of conceptual elaboration, the basic space of abiding and the proliferating creative display of awareness – o ngakpas, maintain the Great Seal Mahamudra and Great Perfection Dzogchen together inseparably!

དབེན་གསུམ་དང་དུ་འོད་གསལ་སྒྱུ་ལུས་ཤར།། ཟུང་འཇུག་ལྷན་སྐྱེས་བདེ་ཆེན་རྒྱུན་ཆད་མེད།།
བླ་མེད་རྒྱུད་ཀྱི་གསང་བའི་སྙིང་པོ་དང་།། རྫོགས་ཆེན་དབྱེར་མེད་བསྒོམ་ཞིག་སྔགས་པ་ཚོ།།

The dawning of the illusory clear-light body through the three isolations, the inter-penetrating, inborn, ever-flowing Great Bliss, the essence of the secret of the Highest Yoga Tantras, cultivate these and the Great Perfection inseparably, o ngakpas!

ཤེས་རབ་ཡུམ་ཆེན་རྣམ་ཀུན་རྡོ་རྗེའི་དབྱིངས།། སྣང་སྟོང་དབྱེར་མེད་ཟབ་ཞི་སྤྲོས་པ་བྲལ།།
རྟེན་འབྲེལ་སྙིང་པོ་དབུ་མ་ཐལ་འགྱུར་དང་།། ཁྲེགས་ཆོད་དབྱེར་བསྒོམ་ཞིག་སྔགས་པ་ཚོ།།

The Great Mother of Wisdom who is the non-dual vajra-space of all attributes, the profundity, peace, and simplicity of indivisible appearance-emptiness, the Consequentialist school of the Prasangika Madhyamika that is the essence of interdependence, cultivate these and Cutting Through Hardness inseparably, o ngakpas!

ཕྱི་ནང་གཞན་གསུམ་སོར་སྡུད་བསམ་གཏན་དང་།། སྲོག་རྩོལ་འཛིན་པ་རྗེས་དྲན་ཏིང་འཛིན་གྱི།།
མཆོག་གི་སྟོང་གཟུགས་བདེ་ཆེན་དུས་འཁོར་དང་།། རང་རིག་དབྱེར་མེད་བསྒོམ་ཞིག་སྔགས་པ་ཚོ།།

The self-absorption of mental stability of the three outer, inner, and other natures, the meditative concentration of the recollecting and holding of the yogic 'life-force exerting' practices (which come from the teachings of) the Kalachakra supreme empty-form Great Bliss, the indivisible self-cognizing awareness - cultivate all these inseparably from the self-cognizing awareness, o ngakpas!

མདོར་ན་མ་རྒྱུད་འོད་གསལ་སྙིང་པོ་དང༌།། ཕ་རྒྱུད་དག་པའི་སྒྱུ་ལུས་མཐར་ཐུག་པ།།
གཉིས་མེད་ཟུང་འཇུག་རྡོར་འཆང་གསང་ཚིག་དང༌།། ཁྲེགས་ཐོད་དབྱེར་མེད་བསྒོམ་ཞིག་སྔགས་པ་ཚོ།།

In sum, the clear-light essence of the Mother Tantra, the consummation of the illusory-body of purity of the Father Tantra, the unified non-dual secret words of the Vajra-Holder, the inseparable Cutting Through Hardness and Direct Crossing - cultivate all these inseparably from Trekcho and Togal, o ngakpas!

རྫོགས་ཆེན་ལྟ་བ་མཐོང་ན་ཀུན་མཁྱེན་ཡིན།། དབྱིངས་རིག་ཀློང་ཆེན་མཇལ་ན་རྫོགས་ཆེན་ཡིན།།
འཁོར་འདས་ཟང་ཐལ་རབ་འབྱམས་ཡེ་ཤེས་འདི།། རྩོལ་མེད་སྐྱོང་ཤིག་སྔགས་པ་སྔགས་མ་ཚོ།།

If you see things from the View of the Great Perfection, it's omniscience. If you see the great expanse of the unity of basic space and awareness, it's the Great Perfection. O ngakpas and ngakmas, maintain without effort this wisdom of the unimpeded vastness of Samsara-Nirvana!

སད་དང་གསོན་དུས་དུག་ལྔ་རང་གྲོལ་དགོས། གཉིད་དང་འཆི་སྐབས་འོད་གསལ་རྟོགས་པ་དགོས།
མཉམ་རྗེས་གཉིས་མེད་གདིང་ཆེན་ཐོབ་གྱུར་ན།། དོན་གྱི་སྔགས་འཆང་ཡིན་ནོ་སྔགས་པ་ཚོ།།

The five poisons must be self-liberated while awake and alive, the clear-light must be realized during sleep and at the moment of death. If you can achieve great confidence (that lasts) beyond either the meditation session or the period after it - this, o ngakpas, is the fundamental meaning of being a mantra-holder!

རྫོགས་ཆེན་ཀློང་ལ་མ་འདུས་ཆོས་གཞན་མེད།། རྫོགས་ཆེན་མ་རྟོགས་གཞན་གྱིས་གྲོལ་མི་འགྱུར།།
བླ་མའི་དྲིན་ལས་རིག་པ་སྐད་ཅིག་མ།། ཡེངས་མེད་རྩོལ་མེད་སྐྱོངས་ཤིག་སྔགས་པ་ཚོ།།

All other dharmas are included within the vast expanse of the Great Perfection, without realizing the Great Perfection, no other means will liberate you. The instantaneous awareness that comes from the kindness of the guru - maintain this effortlessly and unwaveringly, o ngakpas!

བརྗོད་མེད་རང་རིག་ཡེ་ཤེས་མཐོང་བའི་ཚོ།། འཛིན་མེད་ལྟ་བ་ཕྱོགས་མེད་ཕྱལ་བར་ཐོངས།།
ལྷ་སྔགས་ཏིང་འཛིན་འོད་གསལ་དེ་ལ་འདུས།། སྐུ་གསུམ་རང་རིག་ཡིན་ནོ་སྔགས་པ་ཚོ།།

Upon seeing the inexpressible primordial wisdom of self-cognizing awareness, cast aside all grasping and partiality in exchange for the limitless View. The deities, mantras, meditative absorption, the clear-light are all encompassed by it - this, o ngakpas, is the self-cognizing awareness of the three bodies!

རྡུལ་ཙམ་མ་གྲུབ་ངོ་བོ་སྟོང་ནས་སྟོང་།། འགག་མེད་རང་བཞིན་གསལ་ལ་དྲི་མ་བྲལ།།
བྱང་སེམས་ཐུགས་རྗེ་ཕྱོགས་མེད་ཀུན་ལ་ཁྱབ།། སྐུ་གསུམ་རང་སེམས་ཡིན་ནོ་སྔགས་པ་ཚོ།།

Its essence is utterly empty, not even the tiniest particle of substance exists in it. Its clear and unobstructed nature is stainless, its bodhichitta and compassion pervade everywhere without bias - this, o ngakpas, is the nature of the mind of the three kayas!

འཇིག་རྟེན་ཆོས་བརྒྱད་སྒྱུ་མའི་དཔེ་བརྒྱད་ཡིན།། ཉོན་མོངས་དུག་ལྔ་ཡེ་ཤེས་རིགས་ལྔ་ཡིན།།
འཁོར་འདས་རང་གྲོལ་མ་བསྒོམ་སངས་རྒྱས་ཡིན།། བསྒོམ་གྱི་ལམ་འཁྱེར་མ་བརྗེད་སྔགས་པ་ཚོ།།

The worldly concerns and examples of illusoriness are eight-fold, the poisons of the afflictive emotions and wisdom-families are both five in number. The Self-Liberation of Samsara-Nirvana is the Buddhahood Without Meditation - don't forget, o ngakpas, to bring (all worldly experiences) onto the path of meditation!

འདོད་ཆགས་ཐ་མལ་མ་འཛོག་བདེ་སྟོང་བསྒོམ།། ཁོང་ཁྲོ་ཐ་མལ་མ་འཛོག་གསལ་སྟོང་བསྒོམ།།
གཏི་མུག་ཐ་མལ་མ་འཛོག་རིག་སྟོང་བསྒོམ།། ངེས་དོན་བསྒོམ་ཆེན་ཡིན་ནོ་སྔགས་པ་ཚོ།།

Meditate on the bliss-emptiness which prohibits ordinary desire. Meditate on the clarity-emptiness which prohibits ordinary anger. Meditate on the awareness-emptiness which prohibits ordinary confusion and ignorance - this, o ngakpas, is the Great Meditation on the Essential Meaning!

འདོད་ཆགས་རང་གྲོལ་བདེ་སྟོང་དང་དུ་འབྱམས།། ཞེ་སྡང་རང་ཞི་གསལ་སྟོང་ཀློང་དུ་ཡལ།།
གཏི་མུག་རང་སངས་རིག་སྟོང་དབྱིངས་སུ་ཤར།། བཟང་ངན་སྤང་བླང་མེད་དོ་སྔགས་པ་ཚོ།།

Let desire self-liberate and spread out into empty bliss. Let hatred be pacified of its own accord and open up into empty clarity. Let ignorance and confusion evaporate spontaneously and shine forth as the basic space of empty awareness - this, o ngakpas, is (the practice) devoid of either taking up good actions or rejecting bad ones!

ལྟ་བ་མཐོ་ཞིང་བསྒོམ་གྱི་རྩལ་རྫོགས་ཀྱང་།། བསླུ་མེད་རྟེན་འབྲེལ་ལས་འབྲས་གནད་ཤེས་ལ།།
འཁོར་བ་དོང་སྤྲུགས་རིགས་དྲུག་སྒྲོལ་བའི་ཕྱིར།། དམིགས་མེད་བྱང་སེམས་མ་བརྗེད་སྔགས་པ་ཚོ།།

Even if you have attained the highest View and have mastered the powers of meditation, though you may understand the essential points of the unerring truth of interdependence and cause and effect, so as to dredge up and liberate all beings of the six realms of Samsara, don't forget, o ngakpas, unconditional bodhichitta, without any specific object!!

ཚོགས་དྲུག་རང་གྲོལ་བྱིན་བརླབ་སྙིང་ལ་ཞུགས།། གཡུ་ཐོག་འཁོར་འདས་རང་གྲོལ་རང་ངོ་འཕྲོད།།
འོད་གསལ་རྫོགས་པ་ཆེན་པོའི་མགུར་གླུ་འདི།། འཛིན་མེད་བླངས་པ་ཡིན་ནོ་སྔགས་པ་ཚོ།། །།

I received the blessings of Tsokdruk Rangdrol (Shabkar) into my heart, I recognized the essential nature of Yuthok's Self-Liberation of Samsara-Nirvana. This song of the Clear-Light Great Perfection, O ngakpas, I received without grasping!

ཆོས་དབྱིངས་མཛོད་དང་ཡེ་ཤེས་བླ་མ་དང་།། ཁྱད་པར་ཚོགས་དྲུག་རང་གྲོལ་གསུངས་ཆོས་དག།
ཡང་ཡང་མཇལ་ནས་ལྟ་བ་ཐག་གཅོད་པ།། བོགས་འདོན་མེད་ཐབས་མེད་ཡིན་སྔགས་པ་ཚོ།།

The Treasury of Dharmadhatu (Choying Dzod) and the Wisdom of the Guru (Yeshe Lama), the teachings of (Shabkar) Tsokdruk Rangdrol in particular, having encountered these again and again and having decided upon the View - this, o ngakpas, is the indispensable enhancing practice!

རལ་པ་བཅིངས་དུས་བླ་མའི་རྣལ་འབྱོར་བསྒོམ།། གཟན་དཀར་གྱོན་དུས་དྲི་མེད་ཡེ་ཤེས་དྲན།།
བགྲང་ཕྲེང་འཛིན་དུས་ཐུགས་རྗེས་འགྲོ་བ་འདྲེན།། དྲན་པ་ཤེས་བཞིན་སྐྱོངས་ཤིག་སྔགས་པ་ཚོ།།

When you tie up your dreadlocks cultivate Guru Yoga. When you put on your white shawl remember stainless wisdom. When you thumb your prayer-beads, guide beings with compassion. Maintain, o ngakpas, mindfulness and vigilance!

ལྷ་སྒྲུབ་གཞན་ལ་མ་རྩོད་དག་སྣང་སྦྱོང་།། མདོ་སྔགས་དབྱེན་སྦྱོར་མ་བྱེད་ཟུང་འཇུག་བསྒོམ།།
ཆབ་སྲིད་འཇིག་རྟེན་ཆོས་ལ་མ་ཞེན་པར།། རིག་ངོ་སྐྱོངས་ཤིག་སྔགས་པ་སྔགས་མ་ཚོ།།

Train in pure vision that exerts itself with no other deity-sadhanas. Cultivate the unification which provokes no discord between Sutra and Tantra. Without being attached to worldly affairs or politics, maintain the essence of awareness, o ngakpas and ngakmas!

ཁྱིམ་ཚང་ཁྱིམ་མཚེས་སྙིང་རྗེ་བརྩེ་བས་སྐྱོངས།། ཁྱིམ་ལས་ཞིང་ལས་རྨི་ལམ་ལྟ་བུར་ལྟོས།།
ཚེས་བཅུའི་ཚོགས་དང་རྒྱུན་གྱི་རྣལ་འབྱོར་བསྒོམ།། རིག་པ་སོ་མ་སྐྱོངས་ཤིག་སྔགས་མ་ཚོ།།

Care for members of your household and your neighbours compassionately and tenderly, yet look upon house and farm work as a dream. Gather on Guru Rinpoche day, the tenth of the month, and cultivate regular yoga practice. (Acting thus,) o ngakmas, maintain the natural freshness of awareness!

སྟོང་ཉིད་སྙིང་རྗེ་དབྱེར་མེད་རྣལ་འབྱོར་མ།། བདེ་སྟོང་ཟུང་འཇུག་བདེ་ཆེན་ངོ་བོར་ལྟོས།།
སྤྲོས་པའི་མཐའ་བརྒྱད་བྲལ་བའི་ཡེ་ཤེས་ཀྱི།། གནས་ལུགས་རང་སོར་སྐྱོངས་ཤིག་སྔགས་མ་ཚོ།།

O yogini who is the inseparability of Emptiness and Compassion, look upon the essence of Great Bliss that is the inter-penetration of Bliss and Emptiness. Maintain, just as it is, o ngakmas, the natural state of reality of the wisdom devoid of the eight conceptual limitations!

ཡེ་ཤེས་མཚོ་རྒྱལ་ཇོ་མོ་སྨན་མོ་སོགས།། འཇའ་ལུས་མཁའ་སྤྱོད་སྔགས་མ་མཁའ་འགྲོའི་ཚོགས།།
འོད་གསལ་རྫོགས་པ་ཆེན་པོས་རང་གྲོལ་བྱུང་།། རྗེས་སུ་སྒྲུབ་དང་གྲོལ་ལོ་སྔགས་མ་ཚོ།།

Yeshe Tsogyel, Jomo Menmo, and others, the assembly of rainbow-body sky-goer ngakma dakinis who have been self-liberated through the Clear-Light Great Perfection – follow after their example, o ngakmas, and be liberated!

ཡུམ་ཆེན་ཤེར་ཕྱིན་དབྱངས་ཅན་ངག་གི་དཔལ།། སྒྲོལ་མའི་འཕྲིན་ལས་སེང་གདོང་དྲག་མོའི་ཤུགས།།
རྡོ་རྗེ་རྣལ་འབྱོར་མ་ཡི་བདེ་སྟོང་སྐུ།། རང་བྱུང་རིག་པར་བཞུགས་སོ་སྔགས་མ་ཚོ།།

The Great Mother Prajnaparamita of the Perfection of Wisdom, the Glorious Speech of the Melodious one Saraswati, the spiritual activity of Tara, the strength of the Wrathful Lion-faced one, the empty bliss body of Vajrayogini - dwell, o ngakmas, in their spontaneously arisen awareness!

རྣལ་འབྱོར་ཕོ་མོའི་ལུས་ལ་ཁྱད་པར་མེད།། རིག་པ་སུས་མཐོང་དེ་ནི་གྲོལ་པར་འགྱུར།།
ཐིག་ལེ་དཀར་དམར་བདེ་དྲོད་རང་འབར་ལ།། བུད་མེད་ཁྱད་དུ་འཕགས་སོ་སྔགས་མ་ཚོ།།

There is no difference between the bodies of either yogis or yoginis - whosoever sees the primordial awareness will be liberated. The white and red drops blaze of their own accord with blissful heat - o ngakmas, women are especially noble!

འགྲོ་བ་ཐམས་ཅད་དྲིན་ཅན་མ་ལ་བསྒོམ།། དམིགས་མེད་བརྩེ་བས་བཏང་སྙོམས་འགྲོ་ཀུན་སྐྱོང་།།
རང་མགོ་ཐོན་ནས་གཞན་དོན་ལ་འབད་ཅིང་།། ཐེག་ཆེན་བྱང་སེམས་བསྒོམ་ཤིག་སྔགས་མ་ཚོ།།

Meditate on the kindness of all mother sentient beings, care lovingly for all beings impartially and with no specific object. Having accomplished your own goals independently, strive for the well-being of others and cultivate, o ngakmas the bodhichitta of the Greater Vehicle!

གཏེར་སྟོན་གྲྭ་སྟོའི་མགོ་སྐོར་མ་ཐེབས་པར།། རྟོགས་ལྡན་བླ་མར་མཐར་ཐུག་སེམས་ངོ་ཞུས།།
གསོན་དུས་མི་འགྱོད་འཆི་དུས་མི་སྐྲག་པའི།། ནང་གི་རྟོགས་པ་དགོས་སོ་སྔགས་མ་ཚོ།།

Without being deceived by fake gurus and lamas, request the consummate (teaching) of mind's own essence from a realized guru. O ngakmas, what's needed is the inner realization of neither feeling regret during life nor fear during death!

དགོན་བཞུགས་བཙུན་མ་ཁྱིམ་གནས་སྔགས་མ་དང་།། དཔའ་བོའི་ཚེ་གྲོགས་སྲུ་གུའི་ཨ་ཡུམ་རྣམས།།
འབྲོག་མོ་ལས་བྱེད་མ་སོགས་གང་ཡིན་ཡང་།། ཀ་དག་རིག་ངོས་གྲོལ་ལོ་སྔགས་མ་ཚོ།།

Nuns who stay in nunneries, ngakmas who remain in the household, life-companions of tantric 'heroes' (male practitioners) and mothers of their children, female nomads and labourers, whoever you may be - be liberated, o ngakmas, through the essence of awareness of Primordial Purity!

ཕ་མའི་དྲིན་གྱིས་རིན་ཆེན་མི་ལུས་ཐོབ།། བསོད་ནམས་དྲིན་གྱིས་རྡོ་རྗེ་ཐེག་པ་མཇལ།།
བླ་མའི་དྲིན་གྱིས་རང་གྲོལ་ལྟ་བ་མཐོང་།། འགྲོ་ཕན་སྨོན་ལམ་ཐོབས་ཤིག་སྔགས་"མ་ཚོ།།

Having obtained a precious human body through the kindness of your parents, having encountered the Vajrayana thanks to your merit, having discerned the View of the Self-Liberation through the kindness of the guru - pray, o ngakmas, for the benefit of beings!

སྔགས་འཆང་རྟོགས་པ་སྐྱེ་བའི་བཀྲ་ཤིས་ཤོག། སྔགས་མའི་སེམས་ངོ་འཕྲོད་པའི་བཀྲ་ཤིས་ཤོག།
སྔགས་ཕྲུག་མང་དུ་འཕེལ་བའི་བཀྲ་ཤིས་ཤོག། སྔགས་མང་བསྟན་པ་རྒྱས་པའི་བཀྲ་ཤིས་ཤོག།

May conditions be auspicious for the birth of realized mantra-holders!
May conditions be auspicious for ngakmas to recognize the essence of mind!
My conditions be auspicious for the proliferation of child-ngakpas!
May conditions be auspicious for the spreading of the teachings of the tantrika community!

ཅེས་ངེས་དོན་རྫོགས་པ་ཆེན་པོའི་འཇའ་ལུས་བླ་མ་གཡུ་ཐོག་ཡོན་ཏན་མགོན་པོའི་གསུངས་རྫོགས་ཆེན་འཁོར་འདས་ངོ་སྤྲོད་ཆེན་མོའི་འགྲེལ་བ་དང་ལྷན་ཐབས་ཤིག་སྒྲིག་སྐབས་སུ། སྔར་བྱོན་གྱི་རྟོགས་ལྡན་མ་ཡེ་ཤེས་མཚོ་རྒྱལ་དང་། སྐྱེས་ཆེན་རྒྱལ་བ་ཀློང་ཆེན་རབ་འབྱམས་དང་། རྒྱལ་དབང་ལྔ་པ་སྔགས་རྒན་གང་ཤར་རང་གྲོལ་དང་། རྗེ་བཙུན་མ་མི་འགྱུར་དཔལ་སྒྲོན་དང་གཏེར་ཆེན་མ་སེ་ར་མཁའ་འགྲོ། ངེས་དོན་སྔགས་འཆང་ཞབས་དཀར་ཚོགས་དྲུག་རང་གྲོལ་རྣམ་པའི་སྐུ་དྲིན་རྗེས་སུ་དྲན་བཞིན་སྔགས་པ་ཧེ་རུ་ཀའམ་སྨན་པ་ཉི་ཟླས་རང་ལ་རང་གིས་ཁེར་ལབ་བྱས་པ་ཡིན་ནོ།། སྤྱི་ལོ་༢༠༡༦ ཟླ་གསུམ་པའི་ཚེས་ཉེར་བཞི་ཉིན་འཇར་མན་ནས་པོ་ལན་དུ་འཕུར་བའི་གནམ་གྲུའི་ནང་རྫོགས་པར་སྦྱར་བ་ཡིན་ལ་འདིས་ཀྱང་སྔགས་ཕྲུག་འགའ་རེ་ལ་ཕན་པའི་སྨོན་ལམ་དང་བཅས་སོ།། །།

Ngakpa Heruka, otherwise known as Dr Nida came up with this song spontaneously and sang it to himself while preparing commentary and supplementary instructions on the Great Pointing Out of the Great Perfection of Samsara-Nirvana, by Yuthok Yonten Gonpo who achieved the rainbow-body which is the definitive meaning of (the teaching of) the Great Perfection, and while remembering the kindness of past masters, the realized one Yeshe Tsogyel, the great and victorious being Longchen Rabjam, the victorious Great Fifth (Dalai Lama in his guise as) the old ngakpa Gangshar Rangdrol, the Venerable Lady Mingyur Paldron, the female treasure-revealer Sera Khandro, and that very definition of a mantra-holder Shabkar Tsokdruk Rangdrol. He finished composing it on the 24th of March 2016 while flying in a plane from Germany to Poland, with the hope that it would benefit some young ngakpas and ngakmas.

Dr Nida, after giving Atī Yoga instruction to the ngagpa and ngagma community for whom he composed this song' - Rigdzin Rabpel Ling in Amdo, Tibet, August 2016.

Short Practice of Medicine Protector Shanglon

Shanglon Dorje Duddul.
The special protector of the Tibetan Medical Tradition.

Visualize yourself as Vajrapani or Hayagriva. Then invite Shanglon; he emerges from his image in front of you to fulfill your wishes. Recite the prayer and mantra. At the end, Shanglon dissolves back into his image.

Short Shanglon Prayer

རཾ་ཡཾ་ཁཾ། ཨོཾ་ཨཱཿཧཱུྃ། ཧ་ཧོ་ཧྲཱིཿ

RAM YAM KHAM, OM A HUNG, HA HO HRI *(3x)*

སྨན་བསྲུང་ཞང་བློན་འཁོར་ལྔ་སྡེ་དགུ་ལ།།

Men sung zhang lön khor nga de gu la

Medicine Protector Shanglon and his retinue,

གསོལ་བསྟོད་མཆོད་མགྲོན་རེ་བསྐོ་ཐུགས་དམ་བསྐང་།།

Söl tö chö drön re ngo tuk dam kang

With praise and offerings, we invite you, may your heart be fulfilled.

ཕྱི་ནང་གསང་བའི་བར་ཆད་བཟློག་པ་དང་།།

Chi nang sangwe bar che 'dok' pa dang

Eliminate all inner, outer and secret obstacles.

ལས་བཞི་ལྷུན་འགྲུབ་མཆོག་ཐུན་དངོས་གྲུབ་སྩོལ།།

Le zhi lhün drup chok tün ngö drup tsöl

Spontaneously accomplish the four actions and transmit the common and uncommon siddhis. *(21x)*

Mantra of Wrathful Shanglon

ཨོཾ་མ་ཧཱ་ཀཱ་ལ་ཡཀྵ་བཛྲ་ཙིཏྟ་ཧཱུྃ་ཕཊ་རཏྣ་སིདྡྷི་ཧཱུྃ།

OM MAHAKALA YAKSHA BAZAR TSITA HUNG PHET
RATNA SIDDHI HUNG *(108x)*

Mantra of Peaceful Shanglon

ཨོཾ་བཛྲ་རཏྣ་ཙིཏྟ་རཱ་ག་རཱ་གེ་ཧཱུྃ་ཕཊ་སྭཱ་ཧཱ༔

OM BAZAR RATNA TSITA RAGA RAGE HUNG PHET SOHA *(108x)*

VI

APPENDICES:

A: Yuthok Nyingthig Tree
B: Ngöndro (Preliminary Practices)
C: 75 Identifyers
D: Nine Levels of Practitioners

GLOSSARY
BIBLIOGRAPHY

A. Yuthok Nyingthig Tree

Clear Light
Yoga
Illusory
Body Yoga
Concise
Guru Yoga
Bardo Yoga
Secret
Guru Yoga
Dream Yoga
P'howa
Mahamudra
Tummo
Yoga
Karmamudra
Inner
Guru Yoga
ATI YOGA
CREATION
STAGE
(Kyerim)
COMPLETION
STAGE
(Dzogrim)
DZOGCHEN
Outer
Guru Yoga
YUTHOK NYINGTHIG
Ngöndro
Common
Ngöndro
Routine
Ngöndro
Uncommon
Ngöndro

B. Ngöndro (preliminary practices)

General Vajrayana Ngöndro

I - Common Ngöndro

(Four Thoughts that Turn the Mind)

1. Precious Human Birth
2. Impermanence
3. Cause and Effect
4. Suffering of Samsara

[5. Benefits of Liberation]

II - Uncommon Ngöndro

1. Refuge
2. Bodhichitta (and the Four Immeasurables)
3. Prostrations
4. Mandala Offering
5. Circumambulations
6. Vajrasattva
7. Kusali (chod)

III - Routine Ngöndro

1. Veneration of the community of practitioners, the cherished spiritual guides and elders (Altruistic activities)
2. Giving of material offerings to the poor
3. Dispensing of medicines to the sick
4. Giving of spiritual teachings to those who lack them
5. Saving sick people and animals from death
6. Restoring Buddhist temples and monasteries, and so on
7. Improving dangerous roads and paths
8. Expounding the teachings of the Buddha and organizing group practice celebrations, etc

Ati Yoga Ngöndro

1 - Special Preliminaries

a) Outer Rushen
- Distinguishing Samsara from Nirvana
  (Acting out the suffering of the six realms with body, speech and mind)

b) Inner Rushen
- Purifying the six locations with the six syllables
- Vajra Recitation (OM AH HUNG) to burn up the seeds of the six realms, purify obscurations of body, speech, and mind, and eliminate attachment

2 - Actual Preliminaries

a) Striking the Essential Points by Resting the Three Gates
1. Body: Lie down like a corpse
2. Speech: Relax your voice like a silent lute whose strings have been cut
3. Mind: Let your mind rest without thinking

b) Three Gazes
1. Shravaka gaze: Gaze at tip of nose (For one's own self-perfection)
2. Bodhisattva gaze: Gaze straight ahead into space
   (For the spontaneous realization of benefit for others)
3. Wrathful gaze: Gaze up into space and shout
   HA HA HI HI HUNG HUNG PHET PHET
   (For liberation from samsara)

c) Three Gates
1. Body: Vajra Posture
2. Speech: HUNG
3. Mind - Analytical meditation - search for mind

C. 75 Identifyers

	OUTER	INNER	SECRET
FIVE BODIES	1 Vairocana	6 Wheel of Body	11 Dharmakaya
	2 Amitabha	7 Lotus of Speech	12 Sambhogakaya
	3 Vajrasattva	8 Vajra of Mind	13 Nirmanakaya
	4 Ratnasambhava	9 Jewel of Qualities/ Knowedge	14 Bodhikaya
	5 Amogasiddhi	10 Double Vajra of Activities	15 Vajrakaya
FIVE WISDOMS	16 Wisdom of the dharmadhatu	21 Condensed cognition wisdom	26 Wisdom of the essence of primordial purity
	17 Mirror-like Wisdom	22 Wisdom that sees things as they really are	27 Wisdom of the spontaneously present nature
	18 Wisdom of Equality	23 Wisdom that knows all that exists	28 Wisdom of all-pervading compassion
	19 Discriminating Wisdom	24 Elaborated wisdom	29 Wisdom that apprehends the attributes
	20 All-Accomplishing Wisdom	25 Wisdom of perfect activity	30 Directly perceived, self-manifesting wisdom
FIVE AGGREGATES	31 Form	36 Eyes	41 Seeing
	32 Sound	37 Ears	42 Hearing
	33 Smell	38 Nose	43 Smelling
	34 Taste	39 Tongue	44 Tasting
	35 Touch	40 Skin	45 Touching
FIVE ELEMENTS	46 Space	51 Mental Space	56 Empty space of mind's essence
	47 Wind	52 Breath	57 Mind in its unobstructed aspect
	48 Fire	53 Body heat/temperature	58 Clear and radiant feeling
	49 Water	54 Blood	59 All-pervading produced moisture
	50 Earth	55 Flesh and Bone	60 Mind's undefiled nature (ground)
FIVE LIGHTS/ SYMBOLS	61 White	66 White of Bones, etc.	71 White transference of discursive thoughts into bliss
	62 Blue	67 Blue marks of body and head hair	72 Blue of differentiating between characteristics to be adopted and rejected
	63 Yellow	68 Yellow of bile	73 Yellow of abiding deeply without wavering
	64 Red	69 Red of flesh and blood	74 Red perception of desire and lust
	65 Green	70 Green of vital winds	75 Green of assembling of subtle and gross discursive thought without measure

D. Nine Levels of Practitioners

Level of Yogi		Method of Practice
Great Yogi: རྣལ་འབྱོར་པ་རབ་ (naljor wa rab)	1) Greater Great	Primordial liberation ཡེ་གྲོལ་ (yetrol)
	2) Average Great	Self-liberation རང་གྲོལ་ (rangtrol)
	3) Lesser Great	Total liberation ཡོངས་གྲོལ་ (yongtrol)
Average Yogi: རྣལ་འབྱོར་པ་འབྲིང་ (naljor wa tring)	4) Greater Average	Undifferentiation of all Phenomena
	5) Average Average	Indivisibility of the two truths
	6) Lesser Average	Absence of attachment and aversion
Lesser Yogi: རྣལ་འབྱོར་པ་ཐ་མ་ (naljor wa thama)	7) Greater Lesser	Practice devoid of Creation and Completion stages
	8) Average Lesser	Union of Creation and Completion stages
	9) Lesser Lesser	Taking up and rejecting as feels comfortable

Glossary

Amitabha (Tib.Nangwa Thaye) – The Buddha of Infinite Light. In Vajrayana, he is typically red and heads the Lotus Buddha Families, along with his consort Pandaravasini (Gö Karmo). In Yuthok's Ati Yoga system he is associated with fire, the West, the Buddhas' Speech, the transmutation of the afflictive emotion of desire, and the throat chakra. He presides over the pure-land Dewachen or Sukhavati and is invoked in practices for extending longevity and for liberating beings after death (See Five Buddha Families).

Amogasiddhi (Tib. Döndrub) – The Buddha of Accomplishment. He heads the Karma Buddha Family, and is typically shown as green in color. He is associated with the North, with the wind element, with transmuting the afflictive emotion of jealousy, and the sexual organ chakra. His consort is Tara (Tib. Drolma) (See Five Buddha Families).

Anu Yoga – The 'Further' yoga, the middle of the three top-most 'Inner Yogas' in the nine-fold list of vehicles in the Nyingma school of Tibetan Buddhism. Directly preceding Ati Yoga, this vehicle emphasizes practices of the Completion Stage of Highest Yoga Tantra, and focuses on the manipulation of the Channels, Winds, and Drops to produce an 'Illusory Body' of a Buddha. The successful practice of Anu Yoga is said to guarantee Buddhahood in this life and this body, and often overlaps with Karmamudra practices (See Channels-Winds-Drops; Completion Stage; Karmamudra).

Ati Yoga – The 'ultimate' or 'supreme' yoga, the highest of the three Inner Yogas in the Nyingma system. Synonymous with the Great Perfection, this vehicle focuses on the practitioner's already-perfected Buddha nature, and the methods for spontaneously and naturally realizing and abiding in it (See Dzogchen).

Bardo – An intermediate, transitional or 'in-between' state of awareness or existence. The word is typically used to describe the liminal forms of awareness associated with dying, the after-death state, meditation, and dreaming.

Bardo Yoga – One of the Six Yogas. Describes practices for training in how to consciously recognize and navigate the bewildering after-death state in between incarnation (See Bardo; Six Yogas/Dharmas).

Bodhichitta (phonetic spelling) – The mind which aspires to Buddhahood for the sake of all sentient beings, one of the quintessential features of a Bodhisattva, and of Mahayana/ Vajrayana Buddhism (See Bodhisattva; Mahayana; Vajrayana).

Bodhisattva – A realized being who has transcended the round of death, rebirth, sickness, aging and death (Samsara), who chooses to continue to be reborn and manifest in existence to help liberate beings. A Buddha 'for others'.

Chagpori – 'The Iron Mountain'. Refers both to a hill or small mountain in Lhasa, Central Tibet and the Tibetan traditional medical college which was founded on top of it by the Regent Sangye Gyatso in 1696 (See Sangye Gyatso).

Clear Light Yoga (Tib. Osel Naljor) – One of the Six Yogas of Naropa/Niguma, in which the practitioner trains to remain aware during the state of deep, dream-less sleep, so as to perceive the innate luminosity of mind. This luminosity is similar to that experienced at death.

Completion Stage (Tib. Dzogrim) – Refers to advanced tantric yoga practices in which practitioners actually experience themselves as the meditational deity (Yidam), and thereby strongly familiarize themselves with their own enlightened nature. Typically follows after Creation Stage procedures, and involves complex manipulations of the channels, winds, and drops, where the winds are directed into the central channel and dissolve at the heart, causing the mind of Clear Light to manifest (See Channels-Winds-Drops; Creation Stage; Yidam).

Chakra (Tib. Khorlo or Tsakhor, 'Channel-Wheel') – A point or 'wheel' in the Vajra Body where the channels and energies meet. A location in the subtle body concentrated on by the yogi/ini as part of yogic practice, in which creative, vital energy is focused and transformed, lights and forms are visualized and so on.

Channels — Winds — Drops (Tib. Tsa-Lung-Thigle) – Three core features of the subtle anatomy of the Vajra Body of tantric physiology. Different kinds of wind (Sanskrit, Prana) or vital force flow through the channels (Sanskrit, Nadi) and influence the mind, body, and emotions. In this triad, 'Drops' refer to the condensed points of blissful energy located at various points in the Vajra Body (see Thigle; Tsa Lung)

Creation Stage (Tib. Kyerim) – The phase of tantric meditation or yoga in which practitioners visualize themselves and all appearances as the meditational deity and their Mandala, retinues etc. The practice involves meditating on the emptiness of phenomena and promotes the realization of the innate purity of all perceptions (See Mandala; Yidam).

Dakini (Tib. Khandro/Khandroma, 'Sky-Goer') – A tantric goddess. At times beautiful and at times hideous or terrifying, she appears in both 'wordly' and 'wisdom' forms. Worldly Dakinis can refer to either unenlightened disembodied goddesses and embodied human yoginis or female spiritual consorts, whereas wisdom Dakinis can point to non-physical, enlightened goddesses and female Buddhas, as well as to a particular quality or activity of enlightened awareness, to the dynamic, creative, playful, revelatory, and metaphorically feminine dimensions of innate wisdom-consciousness. Human women given this title are understood to be physical embodiments or equivalents of spiritual Dakinis and their qualities. Although 'Khandro' or 'Khandroma' as a label may be given to celibate female religious practitioners who have attained great spiritual power through tantric Buddhist mastery, the paradigmatic Khandro more often than not appears in non-celibate form. The wives of male tantric specialists or Ngakpa are thus honorifically referred to as 'Khandro' since they are considered by default to be the spiritual and sexual consorts of their husbands. That being said, Dakinis should not be thought of merely as spiritual helpers to men, and are full-fledged practitioners in their own right. In addition, for the tantric practitioner with purified perception, all women are Dakinis (See Ngakpa).

Dharmadhatu – As principally used in this book, the expanse or 'basic space' of absolute reality.

Dharmakaya – In the context of the 'Three Bodies' doctrine of Mahayana and Vajrayana Buddhism refers to the cosmic 'truth body' of the Buddha. The ultimate, non-dual, omniscient and wholly pure and liberated reality from which all Buddhas and Buddha-activities ultimately emerge, the source of both Sambhogakaya and Nirmanakaya Buddha forms (See Nirmanakaya; Sambhogakhaya).

Dream Yoga (Tib. Milam Naljor) – A set of meditative techniques through which the practitioner recognizes the subtle dreaming-state and uses this to train the mind. Through body postures, focused intention, contemplation, mantras and visualization dream yogi/inis learn to wake up while dreaming and to manipulate and transform their dream-worlds and experiences. In this way they gain profound insight into the nature of their minds and energy, and realize the equally dream-like quality of both dreaming and waking phenomena.

Dakini Palden Treng – 'The Glorious Garland/Rosary', the goddess who revealed the Yuthok Nyingthig to Yuthok Yonten Gonpo the Younger (See Yuthok; Yuthok Nyingthig).

Dzogchen – An alternative name for Ati Yoga. An abbreviation of the term Dzogpa Chenpo in Tibetan which means the 'Great Perfection' or 'Completion', and points to the fact that all beings are perfect as they are, lacking nothing. Since all beings' basic nature is Buddha-nature, pure and good, they are always and already complete, and there is nothing intrinsic to the ground of their being that can be added or taken away (See Ati Yoga).

Empowerment (Tib. Wang) – A special initiation ceremony in Vajrayana Buddhism through which individuals are 'empowered' to practice more advanced tantric sadhanas typically involving deity visualization. During the empowerment ritual, a teacher with experience in and mastery of the practice transforms into specific deities and Buddhas, and blesses would-be practitioners to 'enter the deity's Mandala' as the very embodiment of these beings. This unlocks the sadhana practice and ripens practitioners' minds, authorizing them to receive specific esoteric instructions and formulas and permitting them to actualize results in their practice. Forms part of an essential triad for practice with Lung (reading transmission of the sadhana text) and Tri (oral instruction in the practice) (See Mandala; Sadhana; Yidam).

Five Aggregates – The five psycho-physical constituents of beings. These are: materiality or form; sensation or feeling; perception or discrimination; conditioning factors or formations; and consciousness. Only the first of these is physical. While these aggregates or 'heaps' conspire together to create the illusion of an enduring and intrinsic self, no such self can be found upon investigation. The Buddha taught that attachment to this contingent, fabricated self is the root cause of all suffering.

Five Bodies (Kayas) A five-fold system of Buddha bodies or forms used in the Yuthok Nyingthig Ati Yoga teachings. In addition to the common triad of Dharmakaya, Sambhogakaya, and Nirmanakaya, Yuthok also discusses 'the body of the direct (perception) of a Bodhisattiva' (Bodhikaya) and 'the unchanging Vajra-body' (Vajrakaya), which is the ultimate non-dual, abiding nature of reality (see Dharmakaya, Nirmanakaya, Sambhogakaya).

Five Buddha Families – The five Buddha families or lineages in tantric Buddhism: the Tathagata family headed by Buddha Vairocana; the Vajra family headed by Buddha Aksobhya, the Padma (Lotus) family headed by Buddha Amitabha; the Ratna (Jewel) family headed by Buddha Ratnasambhava; and the Karma(n, Action) family headed by Buddha Amoghasiddhi, Given that a mandala can be divided according to its center and four main cardinal points, the five family scheme is an important cosmological and symbolic organizing principle in Vajrayana. Each family corresponds with a range of other important five-fold divisions in Buddhism (See individual Five Family entries).

Five Chakras – These are located at the crown of the head; the throat; the heart-center; the navel; and at the sex organs (see Chakra).

Five Elements – The five basic forces or principles which compose all things in existence: Space, Fire, Water, Earth, Wind. These five elements are referred to as the inner elements as opposed to the seasonal elements (Wood, Fire, Earth, Metal, Water).

Five Lights/ Symbols – The five colored lights – which are also called the 'five symbols' - are the dark blue, white, yellow, red, and green luminosities which are the most fundamental and rarified building blocks or expressions of existence. These lights appear in various modes and at various moments when practitioners access especially subtle states of consciousness, such as during Togal meditation darkness retreat or at the point of death (See Togal).

Five Poisons – These refer to the five primary afflictive emotions in Vajrayana tradition: ignorance or confusion; desire or attachment; aversion, hatred or anger; pride; and jealousy. These five afflictive emotions are transmuted through tantric practices or self-liberated through Ati Yoga and are transformed into the Five Wisdoms (See Ati Yoga).

Five Wisdoms – The five forms of primordial and transcendent consciousness that characterize Buddha-mind: the wisdom of Dharmadatu; the expanse of absolute reality; the mirror-like wisdom; the wisdom of equality or sameness; the discriminating wisdom; and the all-accomplishing wisdom.

Garab Dorje – The first human lineage-holder of Ati Yoga teachings in the Nyingma system. After receiving visionary Ati Yoga transmissions from Vajrasattva by way of the primordial Buddha Samantabhadra, Garab Dorje, 'The Exceedingly Joyful Vajra' passed these teachings onto Manjushrimitra and Shrisimha, who passed them onto the Tibetan translator Vairocana around 800 CE.

Guru Yoga – The practice of devotion to one's guru or spiritual teacher and guide, in which one trains in seeing one's teacher as a Buddha. Practitioners recite the guru's mantra, receive the guru's blessing, and ultimately unite their own minds with the guru's enlightened being. While sometimes misrepresented as the worship of fallible humans, Guru Yoga is at heart training in pure perception, and a mechanism for realizing one's own intrinsic 'guru' or Buddha-nature. Although Guru Yoga typically forms part of Ngöndro, the Yuthok Nyingthig system has outer, inner, secret and condensed Guru Yoga procedures which are frequently practiced after the completion of the Yuthok Ngöndro (See Ngöndro; Yuthok Nyingthig).

Gyushi, or Four Medical Tantras – The foundational textbooks of Sowa Rigpa, or Traditional Tibetan Medicine. According to tradition, the contents of the Gyushi were originally taught by the Medicine Buddha in his pure-realm of Tanaduk. These were then assembled as a Treasure text by Padmasambhava, who transmitted it to Vairocana/Vairotsana. Vairotsana then passed the teachings on to the Tibetan king Trisong Detsen, who hid them in Tibet's first Buddhist monastery Samye. These texts were later revealed to Drawa Ngonshe in the eleventh century and eventually found their way into the hands of Yuthok the Younger in the twelfth century (See Padmasambhava; Sowa Rigpa; Vairocana; Yuthok).

Hayagriva (Tib. Tamdrin) – The 'Horse-Necked' or headed deity. Existing in both Hinduism and Tantric Buddhism, Hayagriva is an important Yidam or meditational deity in Tibetan Buddhism, associated with healing, potency, and protection against harmful, demonic forces. He is especially important in some of the more advanced tantric yoga sadhanas of the Yuthok Nyingthig (See Sadhana; Yidam; Yuthok Nyingthig)

Highest Yoga Tantra – Called Anuttaratantrayoga in Sanskrit, refers to those tantric texts which contain advanced techniques for reaching extremely rarified levels of consciousness through the manipulation and transformation of the anatomy of the subtle body. In the four-fold classification of tantras popular in the New Translation school of Tibetan Buddhism, Highest Yoga Tantra is the fourth and most refined grouping of tantras. It includes as a category both Creation and Completion Stages, and encompasses Maha, Anu, and Ati Yogas as presented in the alternative system of the 'nine vehicles' used in the Old Translation or Nyingma school. (See Anu Yoga; Ati Yoga; Completion Stage; Creation Stage; Father Tantras; Kriya-Upa-Yoga Tantras; Mother Tantras).

Hinayana: 'The Lesser Vehicle'. Traditions of Buddhism which focus on the earlier Pali sutras and do not accept later Mahayana sutras as authentic scripture. While roughly equivalent to the Shravaka and Pratyeka mainstream schools of Theravada Buddhism that are dominant today in places like Sri Lanka, Thailand, Vietnam, Cambodia and Burma, the term is technically a pejorative one coined by Mahayana practitioners and is not used or particularly appreciated by Theravada practitioners themselves (See Mahayana; Pratyekabuddha; Shravaka).

Illusory Body Yoga (Tib. Gyü-lü Naljor) – Meditative procedures in which the yogi or yogini trains to see all thoughts and experiences as illusory and insubstantial. Illusory Body Yoga often involves contemplating one's reflection in a mirror and alternatively directing praise and blame towards it. These practices resolve neuroses and ego fixations, and loosen one's attachment to one's body. The term 'Illusion'/ 'Illusory Body' also appears in the context of Anu Yoga/Highest Yoga Tantra Dzogrim practices, where it refers to a special subtle body created through yogic practice with which the practitioner sustains Clear Light Mind consciousness and attains Buddhahood (See Anu Yoga; Completion Stage).

Inestimable Celestial Mansions – A name for the palaces or abodes of various divinities and transcendent beings in Buddhist cosmology. Seeing as they do not conform to conventional limitations of time-and-space, they are 'inestimable' or 'immeasurable'. In Yuthok's Ati Yoga, practitioners are able to purify their vision and perceive the mundane or external world as inestimable celestial mansions.

Kadak – A term used especially in Ati Yoga to refer to the 'primordial' or 'original' purity of the mind. The teachings in this book are focused on 'Kadak Trekcho' – methods for revealing the basic purity of the mind unadulterated by binary thinking via 'cutting through' (cho) the 'hardness' (trek) of dualistic appearances and our firm and stubborn attachment to the misperception of things and thoughts as having innate substance.

Kalachakra – A cycle of advanced esoteric teachings that arrived fairly late in Tibet from India in the eleventh century. The teachings of the Kalachakra (often translated as 'Wheel/ Cycles of Time' or 'Time Machine') include unique yogic practices, as well as distinct approaches to cosmology, astrology, embryology, medicine, and alchemy, all of which allow practitioners to transcend time and realize infinite bliss through transforming into the 'empty form' of a Buddha. The Kalachakra teachings influenced the Tibetan calendar and are millennial in quality, linked as they are with prophecies involving the fabled, much misunderstood kingdom of Shambala and its inhabitants.

Karmamudra – The 'Action' Seal or Symbol. Karmamudra can refer both to the practices of sexual yoga with a physical, human consort as taught in the context of Anu Yoga and Highest Yoga Tantra, and to the actual consort with whom one engages in this practice. While Karmamudra is often treated as synonymous with a female partner, it is important to note that yoginis can have yogi 'action seal' consorts as well. The physical Karmamudra contrasts with the Jnanamudra or 'Wisdom Seal', who is a visualized or mentally perceived, non-physical spirit consort (See Dakini; Mahamudra; Ngakpa).

Kriya and Yoga Tantras - Two of the four traditional categories of tantric texts and practices. The four categories, in order from least to most refined, are: Kriya Tantra ('Action Tantra'); Charya Tantra ('Performance' or 'Conduct Tantra'); Yoga Tantra ('Yoga' or 'Union Tantra'); and Anuttarayoga Tantra ('Highest Yoga Tantra'). Kriya tantras are usually said to focus almost exclusively on external ritual practices, on the proper arrangement of altars, making of offerings, and so on. Both Charya and Yoga tantras by contrast focus more on internal practices and thought processes, although descriptions about exactly how these two differ are not always consistent. Dr Nida has explained this division in terms of four sisters sharing a home: "The first sister, Kriya Tantra, is the one who says, 'Oh, it's important to clean your room, to have a nice house and so on. Then the second sister, Charya Tantra says, 'No! How you think and you feel internally is what's important!' Then the third sister, Yoga Tantra, says, 'Hey, they're both equally important! It's 50/50 - you focus half your energy on internal dynamics and half on external procedures.' Each sister is becoming smarter and smarter - the first one says, 'Clean your house!' the second one says, 'No, no, no clean your head! And the third says, 'Clean both of them!'" These three lower tantras are classed as 'outer tantras' in the nine vehicles system of the Nyingma tradition. Anuttarayoga Tantra, the highest of the four, is the most mature, or 'rock-star' sister in Dr Nida's version of things - Highest Yoga Tantra texts are the only ones out of the group of four to focus on meditational deities or Yidam in sexual union. By emphasizing the non-duality of the Clear Light Mind and the bliss of the indivisible union of the Father-and-Mother Yidams, this oldest sister thus goes beyond the inner-outer distinctions around which the younger sisters' arguments revolve. In Tibetan tradition, only the practices of the Highest Yoga Tantra class of texts can produce complete Buddhahood in a single human body and lifetime (See Anu Yoga; Ati Yoga; Highest Yoga Tantra; Maha Yoga).

Kusali - The name for a condensed and simple form of Chöd ('Cutting') practice, especially suited for daily use. Chöd is a meditative, ritual procedure involving singing, dancing and drumming in which practitioners, having called up Buddhas, Bodhisattvas, deities and harmful, worldly spirits, dissociate from their own body and transform this into an inexhaustible 'body offering' or 'feast' to satisfy and pacify these invoked beings. The practice not only serves the practical ritual function of subduing demons - themselves ultimately expressions of mind's own nature like all phenomena - but also powerfully severs or 'cuts' practitioners' own ego grasping or sense of self-importance, thus allowing them to develop profound generosity, compassion and fearlessness, as well as direct insight into the nature of reality. In the Yuthok Nyingthig Ngöndro, practitioners finish each Ngöndro session with recitations of a short Kusali liturgy written by the famous tantric prophet Jigme Lingpa (1730-1798) Unlike some more elaborate Chöd practices, this Kusali is quick and does not require the use of a bell, double-headed drum or human-thigh bone trumpet.

Magic Wheel (Tib. Trulkhor) – Various, typically sequential yogic exercises involving postures, movement, and breath-manipulation which prepare the physical and energetic bodies (the channels, chakras, and winds etc.) for more advanced tantric yoga practice. The 'Wheel' in question can be understood both as the cycle of movements that manipulate subtle flows and forces, and as the magical 'device' of the human body itself, with all of its transformative and miraculous potential. Trulkor exercises can serve as warm-ups for other meditative procedures or can be adapted as stand-alone exercises for improving health, energetic balance and mental clarity and stability.

Mahamudra (Tib. Chakchen/Chakgya Chenpo) – The so-called 'Great Seal' or Symbol. Mahamudra refers to the profound awareness in which everyday appearances and ultimate emptiness are inseparably united through resting in the basic uncontrived nature of mind. While all Tibetan traditions recognize Mahamudra, it is especially revered and important in Kagyu lineages, where it is represented as the highest possible teaching and experience. Different interpretations exist for the name - some commentators have emphasized how Mahamudra is the fundamental awareness that 'stamps' or 'seals' itself on all perceptible existence, while others have explained that it is the ultimate symbol beyond all referrents. Dr Nida suggests an alternative, punny gloss, where Mahamudra is the 'Great Hand' or 'slap' that jolts the meditator into un-fixated, unembellished basic awareness of the nature of consciousness. Mahamudra is sometimes paired with Karmamudra, as an alternative kind of 'Seal', and it has also been linked with Dzogchen/Ati Yoga by many masters. As in Yuthok's system, Karmamudra is often taught as the 'Path of Bliss' of the 'Lower Gate' (the sexual chakra/organs/desire etc.) while Mahamudra is called the 'Path of Complete Liberation' of the 'Upper Gate'. In Yuthok's system, a condensed form of Mahamudra instruction is taught on its own, as cognate with the Trekcho aspect of Ati Yoga, as both a parallel and as an alternative to Yuthok's teachings on Karmamudra (See Ati Yoga; Dzogchen; Kadak; Karmamudra).

Mahayana: 'The Greater Vehicle', the form of Buddhism that spread throughout China, Japan, Korea, and Tibet. A self-designation for developments in the history of Buddhism that consciously contrasted themselves with earlier forms of Buddhism, which they designated as Hinayana or 'Lesser Vehicle'. The Greater Vehicle gives pride of place to the Bodhisattva and Bodhisattva aspiration, and reveres later sutras (texts said to be the word of the Buddha) taught by various celestial Buddhas in a range of transcendent realms or pure-lands (See Bodhichitta; Bodhisattva; Hinayana; Sambhogakhaya; Vajrayana)

Maha Yoga – The lowest of the three 'inner yogas' in the Nyingma Nine Vehicles system. Roughly corresponds with the Creation Stage of Highest Yoga Tantra, in which practitioners visualize themselves as the Yidam and train to perceive their surroundings as the deity's Mandala (See Highest Yoga Tantra; Mandala; Yidam).

Mandala – A circular design which represents the idealized or enlightened cosmos and/or mind. Recalling a sovereign in their fortress or kingdom, the Mandala typically features a principal deity with or without consort in its center, surrounded by various retinues of gods, goddesses, and other spirits. As a picture of reality it portrays enlightened nature as something both transcendent and immanent, where realized awareness, energy and activity saturate every level of being and expresses themselves equally yet distinctly in every manifesting form.

Mantra – A Sanskrit word meaning 'to protect the mind', Mantra refers to a spoken or mentally intoned esoteric formula in the form of one or more syllables in Sanskrit or some other sacred language. As 'words of truth' revealed by great realized sages and adepts, mantras generate beneficial powers and qualities, focus the mind, and protect it from samsaric distractions. Mantras also operate as visual and sonic embodiments of the presence and power of particular deities or Buddhas.

Medicine Buddha (Tib. Sangye Menla) – The Buddha of Healing and Medicine. He is usually depicted as dark blue in color, with two arms, one face, and in a seated position. He is often shown holding an Arura or Myrobalan plant and is associated with rich blue or lapis-lazuli healing light. He is said to be the original author of the Gyushi (See Gyushi).

Mother Tantras - Father Tantras – A traditional way of distinguishing tantric texts of the Anuttaratantrayoga class. Mother tantras, also sometimes called 'Dakini' tantras, are Highest Yoga Tantra texts which are said to emphasize Wisdom over Method/Means when it comes to the advanced processes for achieving Buddhahood in one human body and lifetime that Highest Yoga Tantra texts describe. This emphasis on Wisdom is expressed through a focus on the Clear Light Mind. Female deities and Buddhas also typically predominate in the Mandalas of Mother tantras. Father tantras, by contrast, emphasize Method or Means over Wisdom, in this case in the form of the Illusory Body as an essential fulcrum for complete enlightenment. A third category of 'Non-Dual' texts is also often added to this gendered pair (See Anu Yoga; Highest Yoga Tantra).

Ngakpa, Ngakma, Ngakmang – Literally a 'mantra user' or 'practitioner of tantra'. Refers to a member of the alternative, non-monastic community of long-haired non-celibate tantric ritual specialists and yogis. Ngakpa (male) and Ngakma (female), like monks and nuns, are professional Buddhist renouncers who have taken formal vows to devote their lives to religious attainment, yet unlike their monastic counterparts they can engage in activities forbidden to the monastic community. While monastics are the 'yellow' (ser) clothed community and lay people are 'grey' householders (mi skya) clothed in no particular religious uniform, ngakpa, with their long hair and white and red shawls and robes are known as the gö kar janglo de, 'the white-robe, dreadlock (wearing) community'. Able to marry, have families, and pursue worldly work, Ngakpa nonetheless spend much of their time in study, meditative retreat or working as ritual specialists for hire (Ngakpa often specialize in particularly direct and wrathful methods for dealing with misfortune and for exorcising and controlling negative and natural forces like demons and the weather). Historically, Ngakpa lineages have been decentralized, and have frequently (but not exclusively) been hereditary. Although they have often operated outside of large-scale political and religious institutions, Ngakpa/ma have nonetheless built, supported and maintained relationships with institutions, and today Ngakpa/ma can still be found organized into community collectives of non-celibate tantric practitioners known as Ngakmang (See Dakini; Siddha).

Ngöndro – Preliminary contemplative, devotional and purifying practices undertaken as required preparation before one engages with more advanced tantric yoga sadhanas. The Common Preliminaries typically refer to contemplations on the 'Four Thoughts that Turn the Mind (i.e. away from Samsara)' meant to instill renunciation or 'definitive emergence' (Tib. Ngejung) from or disillusionment with Samsara. The Uncommon Preliminaries, which is what people usually mean when they say Ngöndro involve accumulating a certain number of repetitions of practices (usually 10, 000) aimed at purifying obscurations and removing obstacles. These practices include: Recitations of Refuge and Bodhichitta formulas; Prostrations; Mandala Offerings; Vajrasattva mantra and visualization practice; and Guru Yoga. The Yuthok Nyingthig adds to the Common and Uncommon preliminaries a third category of daily or Routine Ngöndro, which encompasses various forms of everyday social engagement and compassionate action (See Guru Yoga, Mandala, Sadhana, Vajrasattva).

Nirmanakaya – The 'emanation' or 'transformation' body, the body magically projected by a Buddha in order to interact with and help beings. One of the 'Three Bodies' or dimensions of existence in Mahayana/Vajrayana Buddhism. The Three Bodies doctrine provided a way to account for the Buddha's manifestation within an (apparently) perishable body 'inside' the conditioned time of Samsara. Nirmanakaya thus serves to explain the relationship between the person of the historical Buddha or Guru, the timeless ultimate nature of reality and enlightened mind, and the host of a- or trans-historical celestial Buddhas and Bodhisattvas which are all an important part of Mahayana Buddhism. Emanation is thus a process of mediation through which transcendent beings can communicate with and act for the benefit of deluded beings who are differently orientated in consciousness to them. Over time, the Tibetan translation for Nirmanakaya ('Tulku') came to refer more specifically to the figure of the (intentionally) reincarnated tantric Guru (See Dharmakaya; Phowa Yoga; Sambhogakaya).

Nirvana – Literally 'extinction', the unconditioned reality beyond all conditioned and impermanent phenomena of Samsara. The ultimate goal of the Buddhist path, where 'extinction; refers to the final cessation of afflictive emotions and the actions, effects and pain generated by these. While Nirvana is often described as a final escape from suffering, karma and the endless round of rebirth, it is important to remember that Samsara and Nirvana are exactly alike in their absolute lack of any inherent substance or existence. Samsara-Nirvana (Khor-De) thus appear as an indivisible pair in Yuthok's Ati Yoga teachings – all of Samsara AND Nirvana are wholly encompassed by the yogic practitioner's own awareness and being (See Five Poisons; Samsara).

Jamgon Kongtrul Lodro Rinpoche (a.k.a. Kongtrul Yonten Gyatso, 1813-1899) - A Tibetan master famous for helping found the Rime or non-sectarian religious revitalization movement that began in Eastern Tibet in the 19th century as a reaction to the persecution and suppression of the teachings of other lineages by some Gelukpa authorities. Born in the traditional Tibetan province of Kham, he was a prolific preserver, compiler, revealer, and writer of texts, who taught on a range of subjects, including medicine.

Padmasambhava - Also called Guru Rinpoche or the 'Precious Guru', the great realized tantric master or Ngakpa from Oddiyana in India/Pakistan who is thought of by Tibetans as a 'Second Buddha'. He is credited with firmly establishing Buddhism in Tibet in the 8th century by calling forth and taming all of the indigenous pre-Buddhist land-spirits of Tibet, and redirecting their energies towards the flourishing of the Dharma. Guru Rinpoche is also the originator of the Terma or 'Treasure' tradition, where teachings and blessings in the form of physical objects and texts, as well as more immaterial transmissions were hidden in the sky, under the earth, in rocks and caves, and in the mind-streams of Guru Rinpoche's closest disciples so as to be uncovered and disseminated by future incarnations in later lifetimes. Guru Rinpoche's activities ensured that Buddhist teachings and blessings could not only flourish in Tibet, but were now literally contained in the landscape of the country itself, and indelibly printed on the mind-streams of Tibetans. The core textbook of Sowa Rigpa, the Gyushi, is a treasure text which was transmitted by Padmasambhava (See Gyushi, Sowa Rigpa, Yuthok).

Phowa Yoga - The yoga of 'Transference', one of the Six Yogas of Naropa. Phowa refers to procedures for the controlled ejection of the consciousness from the body from the 'aperture of Brahma', the energy point at the top of the skull. These methods are geared especially towards the moment of death - once versed in Phowa, practitioners are able to intentionally direct their and others' transmigrating consciousness towards some better rebirth, most commonly the pure-realm of Buddha Amitabha, known as Sukhavati or 'Great Bliss'.Trongjuk, a subset of Phowa, is when practitioners project their consciousness into a dying or recently deceased person's body. Phowa Yoga has particular importance in Tibet, in no small part because the institution of succession through reincarnation is based on the premise that spiritually qualified gurus can fully control how, when and where they will be reborn. One sign of accomplishment in Phowa Yoga is the development of a small hole in the skull at the point of the aperture of Brahman.

Pratyekabuddha - A practitioner who achieves Buddhahood 'alone', through individual effort, without the help of a teacher in the final incarnation. Pratyekabuddhas do not usually teach others. Aside from the vast amount of merit they have accumulated in previous incarnations, they are also said to achieve realization specifically through contemplating dependent origination. Traditionally, there are two types of Pratyekabuddhas: the individual realizer who is 'like a rhinoceros' who lives and meditates alone in the forest, and the Pratyekabuddha who congregates with others (See Hinayana).

Rainbow Body (Tib. Jalü) – As a result of practicing Dzogchen/Ati Yoga, and Togal in particular, advanced practitioners may achieve the so-called 'rainbow body' in which all or most of their physical body dissolves into multi-colored light.when they die. Degrees of rainbow body exist – adepts may completely dissolve leaving no material trace behind, may leave nothing but fingernails and hair, or may exhibit a 'lesser transference rainbow body' in which their physical form dramatically and progressively shrinks over the course of about one week until it is the size of a small child. When this happens the meditator's head remains its adult size (See Ati Yoga; Great Perfection; Togal).

Ratnasambhava (Tib. Rinchen Jungne) – The Buddha who heads the Jewel Family in Vajrayana Buddhism. He is yellow or gold in color, associated with earth, the South, and transmutes the poison of pride into the wisdom of equality, equanimity or sameness. I.n Yuthok's system his consort is described as Chenma or Lochana, 'The (Buddha) Eye' (See Five Buddha Families).

Rigpa – Often translated as 'awareness' Rigpa refers to the basic nature of mind as it is, mind's wholly uncontrived wisdom or intelligence. It is the source of all Samsara-Nirvana. As the typically unrecognized basis of all experience, Rigpa contrasts with the Clear Light Mind in that it is not only accessible through induced states of extremely subtle consciousness, but is an all pervasive background reality, an already perfect, uncreated, spontaneous and natural awareness that can potentially be pointed out, recognized and stabilized at any moment.

Rushen – A special practice, unique to Ati Yoga teachings, which translates to something like 'Distinguishing the Gap (between Samsara and Nirvana)'. Outer Rushen in particular involves the strategic inducing and cycling through of extreme emotional states as a method for subsequently recognizing and stabilizing Rigpa (See Nirvana; Rigpa; Samsara).

Sadhana – Meaning 'method' or 'technique' in Sanskrit, this refers to a tantric ritual (both the text and the practice), typically one which involves the summoning, visualizing, making of offerings to and requesting of blessings from deities and Buddhas. In some Sadhanas the beings come before the practitioner, in others practitioners themselves transform into these beings. Sadhanas follow set patterns and can be more or less elaborate (See Vajrayana).

Samantabhadra (Tib, Kuntuzangpo) – The primordial Buddha, the 'All-Good/Beneficent One', the ultimate source of Ati Yoga teachings. He is depicted as dark blue, the color of deep, infinite space, and is naked and without adornments. He is shown in union with his similarly naked consort Samantabhadri. He points to the basic, unembellished foundation of bare natural awareness, already complete, perfect in itself, pure and free consciousness, the timeless union of awareness and emptiness.

Samaya (Tib. Damtsik) – A 'binding' or 'pure' pledge, the term used to denote a tantric vow or ritual commitment. In Vajrayana there are fourteen root tantric vows and eight 'thick' actions or secondary vows (although additional vows exist), which are presented in the form of behavior that the tantric practitioner ought to refrain from. The breaking of Samaya can have deleterious effects, and various amendatory and purifying procedures are performed in the event of this happening. Samaya vows are designed to create the perfect context for the practice of Guru Yoga and Highest Yoga Tantra, and are said to endure and to connect gurus and disciples across lifetimes (See Guru Yoga; Highest Yoga Tantra; Vajrayana).

Samsara – Literally 'Wandering/Circling around and around'. The state of conditioned existence, of continual rebirth and suffering (See Nirvana).

Sambhogakaya – The 'enjoyment', 'abundance' or 'pleasure' body of a Buddha according to the 'Three Bodies' doctrine of Mahayana and Vajrayana Buddhist philosophy. Representing a kind of middle zone between a Buddha's perishable, illusory Nirmanakaya form and the ultimate reality of Dharmakaya, the enjoyment body is the celestial, spiritually accomplished body of a Bodhisattva which is directly visible only to beings of equivalent attainment and perception. Such beings 'enjoy' the attainments of Buddhahood for themselves and others. The iconography of regal Bodhisattvas and realized Buddhist deities is thus an approximation of these beings' Sambhogakaya forms.

Sangye Gyatso (1653 -1705) – The Desi or Regent of the Great Fifth Dalai Lama. An accomplished doctor and keen political strategist, he designed and commissioned the first ever complete set of medical tapestries or Tangkas to serve as a visual complement to the written teachings of the Gyushi. He also founded Chagpori medical college and wrote the Blue Beryl, an important history of Tibetan medicine. He was killed following his defeat at the hands of Khoshut Mongol leader Lhazang Khan (See Chagpori; Gyushi).

Shravaka – A 'listener' or 'disciple', one who achieves Buddhahood through relying on a teacher and the teachings of the Buddha. The path of the Shravaka, along with that of the Pratyekabuddha encapsulates what according to adherents of Mahayana Buddhism is the 'Lesser Vehicle' of Hinayana Buddhism (See Hinayana; Pratyekhabuddha).

Siddha: An 'accomplished one'. A term used to refer to a realized tantric yogi/ini or saint, especially a non-celibate practitioner who has attained mastery in Highest Yoga Tantra and who can manipulate phenomenal appearances and perform miracles for the benefit of beings (See Dakini; Highest Yoga Tantra; Ngakpa; Vidyadhara).

Six Realms (of Samsara) – The six primary dimensions in which transmigrating beings may take rebirth in Samsara according to Buddhist cosmology. These are divided into three lower and three higher realms: the hell realm(s); the hungry ghost realm(s), and animal realm(s); and the human realm(s); demi-god realms, and god realms. While strictly speaking there are many billions of world-systems in Buddhism, this six-fold scheme is most commonly used to represent the scope of possible incarnations. The six realms have been variously described as actual dimensions of existence (specific cosmological 'places') and as a set of mental dispositions which shape the world of perception and possibility beings find themselves living in (See Samsara).

Six Yogas or Dharmas — A traditional collection of tantric meditative practices, the six Yogas are: Tummo or 'Inner Heat' Yoga; Illusory Body Yoga; Dream Yoga; Clear Light Yoga; Bardo or 'Intermediary State' Yoga; and Phowa or 'Transference' Yoga. Most commonly associated with the great eleventh century Indian tantric saint Naropa and his lineages of Tibetan disciples, but parallel yet distinct transmissions from Niguma, Naropa's sister/wife also exist. All six Yogas are taught comprehensively in the Yuthok Nyingthig. The Six Yogas comprise (in the order presented above) two day-time yogas, two night-time yogas, and two yogas for dying. As such, they are predicated on a kind of tantric humanism - taking the here-and-now conditions of human consciousness and embodied experience as their launching off point, they provide focused methods for transmuting all aspects of ordinary, deluded waking-sleeping-and-dying existence into pure, realized activity (See individual entries).

Shabkar Tsokdruk Rangdrol (1781-1851) - 'He of the White Feet, Self-Liberation of the Six Collections'. A prominent Ati Yoga master, Ngakpa, and celebrated poet who was born in Amdo, Eastern Tibet. He wrote a number of highly influential commentaries on Ati Yoga, perhaps the most famous of which is his 'Flight of the Garuda'. He lived for many years as an itinerant yogi-meditator and contributed significantly to the preservation and development of the Ngakpa tradition.

Shamatha (Tib.Shinay) - Translated as 'Peaceful Abiding' in Tibetan, Shamata refers to Buddhist methods for the cultivation of mental peace, concentration and stability. Shamatha together with Vipashyana, forms the backbone of Buddhist contemplative practice (See Vipashyana).

Shanglon - Also known by his fuller title Mensoong Shanglon Dorje Duddul ('The Medical Protector, the [Spirit] Minister from Shang, the Vajra-Demon-Tamer'), Shanglon is the chief spirit-protector of the Tibetan medical tradition. He is a Great Yaksha who appears in a variety of wrathful and semi-wrathful forms (Yaksha are powerful spirits associated with the earth, trees and treasures hidden within these). He is typically depicted surrounded by a retinue of four, or eight other protectors. His consort is Kundrubma, who is usually shown seated to his side, feeding him morsels of food with her fingers. She is said to be of the same mind-stream as Palden Lhamo. Shanglon is also said to have helped transmit the Gyushi to the treasure-revealer Drawa Ngonshe in the eleventh century (See Gyushi; Sowa Ripa).

Sowa Rigpa - 'The Science of Healing,' the system of Traditional Tibetan Medicine. Alternately can be translated as 'The Nourishment of Awareness' referring to the Yuthok Nyingthig tradition (See Yuthok Nyingthig).

Sugata - A title for Buddhas, which can be translated as 'wholly gone', well gone' or 'passed beyond to bliss'.

Sumton Yeshe (twelth century) - The heart-son disciple of Yuthok Yonten Gonpo the Younger. Like his master, he was great doctor and Ngakpa, and was the first editor of the Yuthok Nyingthig He also wrote a biography of Yuthok the Younger (See Ngakpa; Yuthok; Yuthok Nyingthig).

Thiglé - The Tibetan term for the tantric concept of 'bindu', often translated as 'seminal', 'essential', or 'energetic' drop in English. Drops form part of the subtle anatomy of the Vajra-body in tantric yogic systems. In this context, two main drops are described: a white 'lunar' or 'mercurial' drop at the top of the head, at the apex of the central channel, and a red 'solar' one at the bottom end of the channel around the perineum. While the word Thigle is used in a more exoteric and colloquial sense to refer to semen, the white and red drops correlate in a more esoteric or ultimate sense with the most refined of 'male' and 'female' essences in the body, derived from one's parents. When manipulated through the control of breath and vital energies or winds (Lung) as part of practices like Karmamudra, the Drops generate bliss. Thigle as a 'Great Sphere' can also refer in a more abstract way to the most essential, primordial and blissful basis of all phenomena and awareness. In Ati Yoga, and the teachings of Togal in particular, instead of being used to describe 'drops' inside the tantric body, Thigle can refer to nominally external, colorful circles of light which are perceived by meditators as they come to experience the luminous display of reality more and more directly (See Karmamudra, Togal).

Three Gates — An alternative designation for the three conduits for activity, namely, Body, Speech, Mind.

Three Gazes — The Shravaka, Bodhisattva, and Wrathful gazes, three body postures and methods of focusing one's gaze used in Ati Yoga Trekcho teachings so as to help hone the mind and recognize and stabilize Rigpa (See Ati Yoga; Rigpa; Trekcho).

Three Humors — Lung, Tripa and Beken in traditional Tibetan medicine, the three humors or vital forces or fluids which circulate through the human body and are deeply implicated in both sickness and health. These humors are referred to in Tibetan as Nyepa Sum, or literally, 'The Three Faults' or 'Transgressions', in reference to the fact that constitutive elements of the human body ultimately derive from karmic processes fueled by the Three Poisons of Ignorance, Hatred/Anger and Desire. While the three humors are usually respectively translated as wind, bile and phlegm in English, these terms have migrated very far from their earlier humoral connotations, and are quite misleading when it comes to rendering complex cosmological-cum-medical-cum-moral-and-religious Tibetan concepts such as these.

Three Roots — Refers to the trinity (in Tibetan) of 'Lama, Yidam, and Khandro' or 'Guru, Deva, Dakini' in Sanskrit. These are the three inner sources of Refuge (The outer are The Buddha, Dharma and Sangha, and the Secret are the Channels, Winds, and Drops). The

Lama is regarded as the source of blessings, the Yidam as the source of spiritual powers or accomplishments and the Khandro as the source of realized activity (See Dakini; Guru Yoga; Yidam).

Togal – 'Crossing', 'Leaping', or 'Skipping Over', also sometimes translated as 'Traversing the Skull'. The name given to advanced, highly esoteric Ati Yoga practices which involve inducing intense visionary experiences as part of recognizing the luminous nature of all perceived phenomena. Togal procedures are connected with the eyes, visual perception, and special subtle light channels, and form a complement to Trekcho. While Togal works with the 'appearance' or 'form' aspect of awareness, Trekcho emphasizes its emptiness quality. Togal is also a key practice involved in the attainment of the Rainbow Body (see Ati Yoga; Rainbow Body; Trekcho).

Tra (Pra) – Used to describe both a class of spirits/spirit vision, as well as the divinatory procedures used to call these forth. Tra diviners use special polished surfaces, like brass ritual mirrors, sword blades, or finger nails, to see visions that are produced by spirits known as Tra. Practitioners obtain such spirits and hone their capacities to see them clairvoyantly by engaging in special mantra recitation and visualization retreats, through which different meditational goddesses (Yidam) are petitioned to bestow Tra from their retinues. There are diverse kinds of Tra associated with different deities, natural spheres and elements. Tra divination procedures also sometimes make use of a pre-pubescent child-seer who talks with and describes the forms shown by the Tra, who is called down by an older ritualist who is not capable of seeing the spirit (that said, many Tra diviners are both seers and summoners) (See Mantra; Yidam).

Trekcho – See Kadak; Togal.

Tsa Lung – Literally, 'Channels-and-Winds'. Used as a shorthand to describe various traditional systems of yogic training, which involve working with and purifying the channels and winds of tantric physiology (See Channels-Winds-Drops).

Tummo Yoga – The Yoga of Inner heat, generated through special physical exercises and the manipulation of the breath and subtle energy. Named Tummo (literally 'Fierce Goddess') due to its use of visualizations of the wrathful Yidam Vajrayogini, one sign of accomplishment in this Yoga is that practitioners can dramatically raise their body temperature at will. Tummo has been subjected to much more scientific scrutiny than the other Six Yogas, and experiments have confirmed this ability. Traditionally, Tummo trainees are required to sit outside through the night virtually naked in sub-zero temperatures, covered in a soaked sheet. If they have gained mastery in Tummo the body heat they generate should keep them comfortable/alive and should be able to evaporate the moisture from the sheet until it is completely dry (See Six Yogas; Vajravarahi)

Two Truths – A key concept in Buddhist philosophy, the two truths are known in Tibetan as Kundzob Denpa, and Damden Denpa, 'Relative', 'Conventional' or 'Obscured'

Truth and 'Pristine' or 'Ultimate' Truth. Relative Truth refers to all ordinary conditioned or dependent phenomena which are falsely perceived by unenlightened beings. In the Madhyamaka school only the view of emptiness, of the total lack of intrinsic or independent enduring existence in all things, is Ultimate Truth. In the non-dual philosophy of Vajrayana, these two levels of reality are ultimately inseparable.

Vairocana – The Buddha at the center of the Five Buddha Families Mandala. He is white, heads the Buddha family, and transforms the poison of ignorance. Unlike some of the other Five Family Buddhas, his worship as a primordial Buddha connected with the transcendent Dharmakaya Body of the historical Buddha has been quite strongly elaborated over the centuries (Vairocana should not be confused with Vairocana/ Vairotsana, the 8th century Tibetan translator influential in spreading Dzogchen in Tibet) (See Dharmakaya; Five Buddha Families, Gyushi).

Vajra – A Sanskrit word meaning 'thunderbolt'. The term originally referred to the thunderbolt weapon or scepter of Indra the sky-god, but over time came to develop the more abstract meaning of 'adamantine' or 'immutable'. In tantric ritual, refers to an actual ritual object, a double-ended usually five-pronged scepter which is coupled with the tantric bell or Drilbu to represent the unbreakable union of Wisdom and Compassion or Wisdom and Means. In the context of tantric Buddhism, the word often appears as a qualifier connoting 'non-dual', 'ultimate' or 'esoteric/tantric'. In some texts it is used as a spiritual code-word or euphemism for the phallus (See Vajrayana).

Vajrasattva (Tib. Dorje Semba) – A male Bodhisattva who is important in confession/ purification practices. He appears as a glowing white youth, bedecked in the ornaments of a king, and is sometimes shown surrounded by the Five Lights. He is visualized above the practitioner's head and nectar or light comes from his hundred-syllable Mantra at his heart and trickles down from his toe into the body of the practitioner. The practitioner confesses various faults and transgressions and is purified by this nectar or light, which saturates their whole being and cleans out all impurities. Vajrasattva visualizations and mantra recitations are a standard feature of Ngöndro (See Bodhisattva; Five Lights; Mantra; Ngöndro; Sambhogakaya).

Vajravarahi (Tib. Dorje Phakmo) – 'The Vajra Sow', an important enlightened tantric goddess or meditational deity. She is depicted as naked and red in color, ornamented in human skulls and bones and in active dancing or standing pose. She is closely connected with Vajrayogini, a similar deity who features prominently in the Mother Tantras, the Six Yogas, and practices like Kusali. She appears coupled with Hayagriva in several sadhana of the Yuthok Nyingthig cycle (See Hayagriva; Kusali; Mother Tantras; Yidam; Yuthok Nyingthig).

Vajrayana – The 'Non-dual' or 'Adamantine' vehicle, the name for esoteric, tantric Buddhism. While tantric expertise and advanced practices of Vajrayana are often associated with non-celibate specialists, Vajrayana is practiced in both monastic and non-monastic contexts. Scholars often class Vajrayana as a separate, third vehicle of Buddhist teachings alongside Hinayana and Mahayana, yet practitioners themselves tend to see Vajrayana as a specific, esoteric expression of Mahayana teachings and the Bodhisattva ideal, one which places strong emphasis on Guru Yoga and Empowerment. Vajrayana relies on an alchemical model where what is impure and poisonous can, through skillful means, be transmuted into the highest medicine. It teaches how, through shrewd and creative re-orientation to sensory experience and afflictive emotions that might normally become sources of suffering and contamination, these seeming obstacles can be transformed into sources of realization (See Bodhichitta; Bodhisattva; Hinayana; Mahayana; Vajra).

Vidyadhara (Tib, Rigzin) – A 'keeper' or 'holder of knowledge', especially secret or esoteric knowledge. Used as a term to refer to realized practitioners of tantra, it is an especially common title for non-celibate ritual specialists or Ngakpa, and sometimes suggest facility in miracle-working or magic. At the same time, given 'Rig(pa)'s other meaning of 'awareness' as understood in the Dzogchen/Ati Yoga context, the title can also imply that its bearer is someone who recognizes (and maintains) natural awareness, namely, an adept in Ati Yoga (See Ati Yoga; Ngakpa; Rigpa).

Vipashyana (Vipassana) – So-called 'Direct Insight' or 'Seeing Through', a form of Buddhist mental cultivation or meditation in which the meditator trains to observe all phenomena and afflictive emotions that arise without grasping. The meditator examines these phenomena impartially to realize their impermanent and dependent nature. Vipashyana, along with Shamata represent the core components of Buddhist contemplative discipline. A primary method for dissolving afflictive emotions, it is partially comparable, but not to be confused with Trekcho. Various modern re-interpretations and re-applications of the Buddha's teachings on Vipashyana are taught around the world today, many of which derive from Burmese traditions (See Shamata, Trekcho).

Yetrol - Rangtrol – Yongtrol (The Three Liberations) – 'Primordial Liberation', 'Self' or 'Innate Liberation' and 'Complete' or 'Total Liberation'. Refers to the different ways in which practitioners of varying capacities should apply the teachings of Trekcho to rest and find freedom in the basic state of natural awareness (See Rigpa; Trekcho).

Yidam – A 'Mind-bound (Being)', a general term for the different meditational deities or enlightened Buddha-forms which are the focus of tantric Sadhanas. Yidam practice typically requires Empowerment (See Empowerment; Sadhana).

Yuthok (Yonten Gonpo): 'The Turquoise Roof (Doctor), The Lord of Good Qualities'. Refers both to the original, legendary systematizer of Tibetan traditional medicine, Yuthok the Elder born in eighth century Tibet, and the twelfth century Tibetan yogi-doctor by the same name, Yuthok the Younger, who continued the older master's legacy. The title 'Turquoise Roof' derives from the heaps of turquoise that were miraculously showered on the roof of Yuthok the Elder's house by Lu or water-spirits in gratitude for Yuthok having provided their father with medical treatment. Yuthok the Elder and Younger were both masters of Ati Yoga, and achieved the greater Rainbow Body upon their deaths (See Ati Yoga; Rainbow Body; Sowa Rigpa).

Yuthok Nyingthig - The 'Heart-essence of Yuthok', the revealed spiritual teachings of Sowa Rigpa or Tibetan Traditional Medicine. A comprehensive cycle of Vajrayana transmissions, it underwent multiple instances of editing over the centuries, as newer devotees of Yuthok experienced visions of him and received and incorporated new prayers and teachings (See Padmasambhava; Vajrayana; Yuthok).

Bibliography

Tibetan sources:

Gnas brtan ldang ma lhun rgyal
(Sri Singha/Padmasambhava/Vimalamitra). 1983.
Rinpoche 'byung ba byed pa sgra thal 'gyur chen po'i rgyud.
In "Rnying ma'i rgyud bcu bdun." Thimpu: Drug Sherig Press, pp. 6-151 (Vol. 2).

G.yu thog yon tan mgon po. 2005.
G.yu thog snying thig (sngags mang dpe tshogs).
Beijing: Mi rigs dpe skrun khang.

G.yu thog snying thig byin rlabs bla sgrub kyi chos skor las ngo sprod 'khor' das rang grol chen mo. 2005. In "G.yu thog snying thig" (sngags mang dpe tshogs). Beijing: Mi rigs dpe skrun khang, pp. 390-397.

Klong chen rab 'byams pa dri med 'od zer (Vajradhara/Garab Dorje). 1991. 'Od gsal rdzogs pa chen po man ngag sde'i gnad kyi bcud phur sangs rgyas kyi 'das rjes gsum. In 'Jam mgon kong sprul blo gros mtha' yas, "Gdams ngag rin po che'i mdzod." Delhi: Shechen Publications, pp. 9-24 (Vol.2).

Mi 'gyur dpal sgron, mkha' 'gro. Ati zab don snying po'i khrid dmigs zin bris su spel ba kun bzang dgongs rgyan (sngags mang zhib 'jug). Zi ling: Mtsho sngon zhing chen nang bstan rig gnas zhib 'jug lte gnas, pp. 52-93.

Ngag dbang blo bzang rgya mtsho, Dalai Lama V. 2009.
Thugs rje chen po 'khor ba dbyings sgrol gyi bskyed rdzogs pa chen po'i khrid yig rig 'dzin zhal lung. In "Rgyal dbang lnga pa ngag dbang blo bzang rgya mtsho'i gsung 'bum" (Gangs can khyad nor). Beijing: Krung go'I bod rig pa dpe skrun khang, pp. 29-104.

Ratna gling pa (Padmasambhava). 1984.
Rdzogs chen klong gsal snying thig gi chos skor (Ratna gling pa'i gter chos dpal yul lugs). Bylakkupe: Pema Norbu Rinpoche publications

Sum ston ye shes gzungs. 2005.
Nyi 'od ces pa'i thog mar lo rgyus dge ba'i lcags kyu. In (G.yu thog, yon tan mgon po/Padmasambhava) "G.yu thog snying thig" (sngags mang dpe tshogs). Beijing: Mi rigs dpe skrun khang, pp. 268-289.

Zhabs dkar tshogs drug rang grol. 2002.
'Od gsal rdzogs pa chen po'i khregs chod lta ba'i glu dbyangs lam ma lus myur du bgrod pa'i rtsal ldan mkha' lding gshog rlabs. In "Rje Zhabs dkar tshogs drug rang grol gyi gsung 'bum." Zi ling: Mtsho sngon mi rigs dpe skrun khang, pp. 581-633.

Zur mkhar mnyam nyid rdo rje. 2005.
Man ngag bye ba ring bsrel (bod kyi gso ba rig pa'I gna' dpe phyogs bsgrigs dpe tshogs, tsho sngon zhing chen bod kyi gso rig zhib 'jug khang). Beijing: Mi rigs dpe skrun khang.

CPSIA information can be obtained
at www.ICGtesting.com
Printed in the USA
LVOW06*2316250817
546451LV00018B/452/P

9 780997 731910